SEX, DRUGS, ROCK and WAR:
The Boomer Generation

Fourteen Boomer Life Stories that Bring a New Perspective to the Conflict Between Generations

Daniel Muller

BookLocker
Trenton, Georgia

Copyright © 2023 Daniel Muller

Print ISBN: 978-1-958889-25-1
Ebook ISBN: 979-8-88531-469-5

All rights reserved. No part of this publication may be reproduced, stored in a retrieval system, or transmitted in any form or by any means, electronic, mechanical, recording or otherwise, without the prior written permission of the author.

Published by BookLocker.com, Inc., Trenton, Georgia.

Printed on acid-free paper.

BookLocker.com, Inc.
2023

First Edition

Library of Congress Cataloguing in Publication Data
Muller, Daniel
SEX, DRUGS, ROCK and WAR: The Boomer Generation by Daniel Muller
Library of Congress Control Number: 2023903024

DISCLAIMER

This book details the author's personal experiences with, and opinions about, the generations, especially the Baby Boomer generation. The author is not a licensed economist or historian.

The author and publisher are providing this book and its contents on an "as is" basis and make no representations or warranties of any kind with respect to this book or its contents. The author and publisher disclaim all such representations and warranties, including for example warranties of merchantability and financial advice for a particular purpose. In addition, the author and publisher do not represent or warrant that the information accessible via this book is accurate, complete or current.

The statements made about products and services have not been evaluated by the U.S. government. Please consult with your own legal, accounting, medical, or other licensed professional regarding the suggestions and recommendations made in this book.

Except as specifically stated in this book, neither the author or publisher, nor any authors, contributors, or other representatives will be liable for damages arising out of or in connection with the use of this book. This is a comprehensive limitation of liability that applies to all damages of any kind, including (without limitation) compensatory; direct, indirect or consequential damages; loss of data, income or profit; loss of or damage to property and claims of third parties.

You understand that this book is not intended as a substitute for consultation with a licensed medical, legal or accounting professional. Before you begin any change of your lifestyle in any way, you will consult a licensed professional to ensure that you are doing what's best for your situation.

This book provides content related to generational and lifestyle topics. As such, use of this book implies your acceptance of this disclaimer.

ABOUT THE BOOK

We have all heard the nicknames for the current generations in the news. Besides the 'Silent Generation' (a.k.a. The Greatest Generation) born before 1946, there are Baby Boomers, Generation X, Generation Y (also known as the Millennials), and Generation Z.

In the past few years, there has been an increasing amount of coverage and discussion about the growing frustration between these generations. Some call it a generational war. Much of the debate has to do with the Boomer generation, with younger generations claiming various failures of this generation to provide a world or country that is sustainable and affordable.

TV shows, podcasts, newspaper and magazine articles, movies, and social media have increasingly begun analysis and discussion about this war. It is a hot topic and, unfortunately, becoming more emotional.

Most of the analysis and coverage has to do with emerging information about each generation, such as wealth accumulation, party affiliation, changing opinions, habits, values and relationships. Facts and surveys abound, discussing all of these aspects of the generations, and more.

But we all innately understand that generalizations and summaries about the generations can be dangerous, and can only tell a part of the story.

What is the answer to this generational conflict that is beginning to stress friendships, acquaintances, and even families? How can we diffuse the emotion and get to positive solutions that will help heal the divide?

I undertook this project in an attempt to understand this growing generational conflict at a more micro level, namely by documenting and sharing the individual life stories of a somewhat random collection of Baby Boomers. Besides their life stories, I asked each individual a series of questions about hot topics today, all in an attempt to understand their opinions, as well as the logic behind the opinions. I attempted to better understand what linkages may exist between their early and mid-life years, and how they think and behave today.

'SEX, DRUGS, ROCK and WAR: The Boomer Generation' is an enjoyable collection of very diverse life stories, as they were told to me by the subjects, combined with an intriguing exploration of the root causes of these generational differences.

DEDICATION

I dedicate this book to my mother Marian and my father Eugene. We lost Dad this past year, and he lived his life without Mom for 13 years as best he could. I miss them both tremendously but know they are in a better place. They both taught me lessons in life that continue to be invaluable.

TABLE OF CONTENTS

FOREWORD xi

INTRODUCTION 1

CHAPTER 1: *Karen, Who Gathered No Moss and Loves Convertibles* 17

CHAPTER 2: *Jesse, The Rebel* 27

CHAPTER 3: *Dr. Lawrence J. Marks, the Marketing Professor Who Championed Distance Learning* 49

CHAPTER 4: *Debbie Mattern Weber, The Postmaster Who Digs Concerts* 75

CHAPTER 5: *Skip, The Entrepreneur Who Served His Country, His Customers, and Our Schools* 93

CHAPTER 6: *Susan Meiburger Marks, The French Fundraiser* 109

CHAPTER 7: *Roy, The Competitor* 125

CHAPTER 8: *Ernie Lallo, The Italian-American Lawyer Who Loved Frozen Yogurt* 141

CHAPTER 9: *Cathy: The Professor from Ireland* 165

CHAPTER 10: *Jeff: The Executive Who 'Changed Collars'* 191

CHAPTER 11: *Jamie Martin: The Boarding School Boomer* 211

CHAPTER 12: *Gregg: The Insurance Agent & Golf Enthusiast* 223

CHAPTER 13: *Jake: The Engineer, IT Geek, and Barbershop Singer* 235

CHAPTER 14: *Jim: The Techie / Scout / Philanthropist* 251

ANALYSIS 267

OTHER QUESTIONS AND CONCLUSIONS 275

SUMMARY 289

EPILOGUE 297

ACKNOWLEDGEMENTS	299
ABOUT THE AUTHOR	301

FOREWORD

It was a warm, humid Sunday afternoon, and I had some time to read a magazine on the nightstand before taking a short nap. As I read the first three pages of the feature article, I felt my pulse quicken, I could tell my face was getting flushed, and that usually meant that my blood pressure was rising. I muttered to myself out loud, which I rarely do - "This cannot be right. It's not possible. This is a reputable magazine! Who in the world wrote this?"

As I read further, and digested the content and the survey methodology, and later checked the credentials of the authors of the article, all looked to be in order and very valid.

What I was reading was an article, one of hundreds on the subject as it turned out, that discussed the opinions and values of younger generations, namely Generation Y / Millennials, and Generation Z. Among other findings, the article stated that these two generations felt *more positive about socialism than capitalism*. Perhaps the average person would not have had such a strong reaction to this, but I suppose I am not average.

I would consider myself a patriot, among other descriptors, and am a core Baby Boomer in terms of age, born in 1957. I love this country, even with all the warts and problems we have.

There was an eight-year period of my career when I travelled internationally a significant portion of my time. I also travelled overseas prior to that period, but less frequently. But during those eight years, I went virtually everywhere in the world, as I held a job with global responsibility. I visited Mexico, Central and South America, Canada, just about every western and central European country, as well as a few in eastern Europe. I spent significant time in China, and made several trips to Australia, Singapore, the Philippines, and India. Each and every time I landed back in the U.S., I took a deep breath of appreciation that I was back home in the 'good old U.S.A.'

I frequently tell students, and others who will listen, that we live in the greatest country in the world. (Not exactly the first person to say this from my generation!) Of late, I have noticed a bit of skepticism from listeners, a few rolling eyes, as if they were thinking "OK Boomer, we have heard this before, but what you are telling us is crap."

Let me say first that in just about every country I have visited, the citizens are usually wonderful people who, like most of us on this planet, want the best for their families, friends, and children / grandchildren especially. They work hard, they are friendly, they are loyal to their countries, and love family and friends. Other countries clearly have positive aspects and lifestyles, but also have some negative characteristics.

With that said, what do I think is so great about the U.S.A? I won't bore you with the details, but in the main, with some exceptions, we have clean water and clean air, usually jobs are available for those who really want to work, our electricity is pretty reliable (few if any brownouts or blackouts), we have freedoms that others in the world envy, and our cost of living, compared to elsewhere, is generally affordable. Housing, believe it or not, per square foot, is affordable versus other countries. Land is available, in suburban and rural areas, for those who want to own land or a home with more acreage. Our educational institutions are highly regarded, and we can vote on a regular basis to elect those to represent us. We have three branches of government that tend to keep each other in check, although some would challenge that currently. Our tax rates are relatively low relative to many other countries. Our standard of living is also the envy of the world. Our dollars go a long way, albeit with inflation of late, less so. Do we have problems? Of course, too many to name here. But relative to what I have seen in other countries, I would never choose to live elsewhere, not that there is anything wrong with the other places I have been. I guess my overall conclusion is that across many dimensions of evaluating quality of life in a country, we rank pretty well in all categories, relative to other countries. Overall, from my perspective, there is not a quality of life any better.

I am a strong believer that our 'system' of capitalism and our constitution enable this country to thrive and to overcome most problems we encounter. I am loyal to a fault, even though I did not enlist in the military nor was I drafted. But I love and respect our veterans and those who did serve, as they sacrificed so much for the rest of us.

So, for me to read that the younger generations thought that socialism is better than capitalism was just shocking to me. I could not understand it, and clearly it convinced me that I somehow had fallen 'out of the loop' in not understanding this sooner.

I began to read more about this, and began, by design, to interact with those in these younger generations more than previously.

Here are some of the comments I heard:

"The Boomer generation left this planet and our country in a mess! Pollution and global warming are terrible, and we cannot afford housing given our wages and the exorbitant cost of housing. You are leaving us to fix the problems you created."

"Boomers have almost all the wealth of this country, and they don't seem to care about our generation's challenges and the fact that we are in debt and poor. The country is $31 trillion in debt, and you voted for and elected the politicians that overspent our budget and got us in this mess. WE have to pay this back, not you, since most of you Boomers will likely die before this is resolved."

"Boomers think that capitalism is just wonderful. Well, it may have been for them, but capitalism today is all about making the wealthy even wealthier, and making the poor even poorer! Socialism would be a much better system in our country, to help spread the wealth."

"Our parents are great, they help us kids out, but the rest of the Boomers as a group just complain that our generation dislikes work, that we don't know how to manage money, and that we must get what we want now, even if we cannot afford it. They don't have a clue about us."

"You created a university system that is completely unaffordable and leaving us in deep debt."

"You created a society that treats minorities, women, LGBTQ, and others as second-class citizens with fewer opportunities than the mainstream."

"Gun violence is out of control. Boomers strongly defend their right to carry a gun, and do not want to have any discussions to make common-sense changes such as background checks or elimination of automatic weapons."

"Good paying jobs are gone, as are company pensions. You enjoy Social Security payments, pensions, and Medicare, but those programs won't be around to help us."

"Boomers grew up in a different world, and how they behave and what they believe today has nothing to do with the situation we are in today. They are just oblivious!"

INTRODUCTION

First of all, let's address the title of this book. Most Boomers recognize a variety of terms to describe the times of their youth.

Clearly, they were known as the first generation to grow up within the sexual revolution, which began in the 1960's. Many attribute this to the invention of the birth control pill, and many youths began to separate sex from procreation and marriage.

The drug culture also accelerated during the late 1960's and 1970's, with marijuana and other more serious drugs such as LSD becoming commonplace in our neighborhoods and universities.

Most of our generation became fans of 'rock and roll' music, a term coined in the 1950's to reference music with a strong beat. Most consider Chuck Berry the father of rock and roll, but it became increasingly popular when The Beatles came to America in the early 1960's.

The Vietnam War became a base of contention for Boomers as they grew up. The Boomer generation at that time seemed to be split between those who supported the war, and those who opposed it. Most men who were high on the 'birthday drawing list' of the draft had to make a choice. They could either proactively enlist in a branch of the armed forces (including the National Guard), be drafted into a branch of the armed forces without having a say as to which branch, or choose to protest the war and refuse to serve. Those in the latter category may have fled to Canada, or found ways to be lowered in the draft pecking order, such as claiming mental or physical disabilities, or enrolling in college and obtaining a deferment, or delay, in required military service.

(Many from younger generations may not know that in the years from 1940 until 1973, during both peacetime and periods of conflict, men were drafted to fill vacancies in the U.S. Armed Forces that could not be filled via volunteers. As the Vietnam war began to wind down, the draft was 'retired' around 1973 when military service became a completely volunteer enterprise.)

Thus, the reason for the book title – 'SEX, DRUGS, ROCK and WAR: The Boomer Generation'.

First, let me clarify again that I am a core Boomer, in that I was born in 1957, right in the middle of the range for Boomers, which are those born between 1946 and 1964, inclusive.

I have never been one to focus upon generational names or differences, but I certainly was aware of the generational nicknames (Baby Boomers, Generation X, Millennials/Generation Y, and Generation Z) and some of the generalizations made about each group.

I learned that the generations discussed today have assigned names, a range of birth years, and estimated accumulated wealth, as a percentage of the entire U.S. population wealth:

GENERATION	BIRTH YEARS	WEALTH %
Silent Generation	Before 1946	13%
Baby Boomers (Boomers for short)	1946-1964	50%
Generation X	1965-1979	30%
Generation Y / Millennials	1980-1994	6%
Generation Z	1995-2015	1%

My research and discussions with those in Generation Y and Z in particular resulted in my discovery that the 'generational war' and 'generation gap' were hot topics. Many from these generations were pointing fingers (maybe not literally, as in public) at Boomers, even making fun of them and their habits, and how out-of-touch they were relative to the younger generations.

After digesting the above comments I heard from Generation Y and Z, I began to understand some of the other claims that I read about in articles and in other media. Besides the complaints I mentioned above, there are follow-on implications for younger generations today. For instance, some claim that they cannot afford to live on their own, that they have to rely upon their parents for housing after high school or college, that they could not get married and start a family given lack of financial resources, and that the government needed to do more to support the younger generations financially. And if socialism was going to be a better way to support the younger generations, then the country should move in that direction.

VALID POINTS?

To an extent, I began to accept some of the claims from younger generations. Was social security going to be there for their generations? It is hard to know, as I am not completely confident that it will be there for the rest of my life and other Boomer lives in its current form. For a Generation Y or Z worker, I could appreciate their resentment of paying into Social Security and Medicare when they had no assurance that they would get any benefit from those investments. However, I do recall feeling the same way when I was in my twenties. I was told by many, when I took on my first full-time job, that I should not count on getting social security when I was retired. (But they were wrong as it turns out)

Do companies provide pensions anymore? I am not aware of many companies that promise pensions for new employees, but most offer a 401K/405c or similar savings plan usually with some employer matching. But the old 'guarantee' of a pension for life after retirement is gone for most in the non-Boomer generations. (By the way, many Boomers lost some or all of their pensions as some pension funds became under-funded and sponsor companies went out of business, so having a 401K where you 'own' the funds, versus being managed by a corporation or other entity, is likely a better approach anyway, in my humble opinion.)

Was housing more expensive than when we grew up? Certainly, but so are pay rates and salaries. Per my analysis, this is about a breakeven, median housing costs have increased at about the same rate as median salaries and pay rates, looking at the period from 1975 thru 2020, with the exception of some very high-priced housing areas, such as California or New York.

Are interest rates higher now than when we grew up? Certainly not, as when we bought our first home in 1982, mortgage rates were over 12%! But with escalating mortgage rates currently, the horizon looks darker than before when mortgage rates were as low as 3-4%.

Is college debt a larger problem now? It would seem so. I recall in 1976, my tuition at a state school (it was all I could afford) in Ohio was about $350 per quarter, with room and board being about $500 per quarter. So, in any one school year, I was paying about $2500 per year. My summer job, on afternoon shift working in a grocery warehouse, paid $3.35 per hour. Working all summer long, all four summers of college, I was able to save about $1200 per year toward my education. Luckily my parents were able to pay the remaining $1300 per year, so I graduated with no college debt, but had no savings to start my new life. College loans were less available at that time, so most students who were not from wealthy families were forced to work their way through school both in the summers as well as during the academic year, taking part-time jobs on or off campus. The 'load' of a full roster of college classes, plus the time required to work part-time or full-time during college, was stressful for many. I recall hearing about suicides on some campuses due to someone getting a poor or failing grade on an important midterm or final.

Back then, being the first in my family to attend college, I was not all that aware of the value of a degree from a top-tier school relative to a degree from a more affordable state school or technical school. To me, it was all about affordability and being able to attend college and get a degree without getting buried in debt. In hindsight, I learned that college reputation does carry *some* weight in hiring and advancement, but that value seems to diminish after the first few years of a career.

I did some research on the affordability of a college education today versus when Boomers were going to college. Each study is different, but in the main, adjusting for inflation, a college education is more expensive by anywhere from 150% to 200% relative to current earnings and the cost of living.

Today, it seems that a higher percentage of students are prioritizing attending the very best school they can, regardless of cost. I was talking to a Millennial about this, and he stated that if you are going to go to all the trouble to attend college, and want to be an engineer as an example, you just have to attend one of the top 10 or 15 engineering schools in the country. (I disagree) He said he had heard stories of business executives telling graduates that 'I didn't even look at your resume or GPA, I just saw that you graduated from XYZ University, and I just made you a job offer based upon that.' Demand is high for the educations from these institutions, and as a result of that demand and other factors, prices may have increased more for these schools. Contributing to the cost escalation is that many universities continue to plow profits into their campuses, new buildings, student services, and new administrative jobs. Tuition, room and board at private schools may be well over $50,000 per year, some are close to $100,000 per year. It is not unheard of for students to graduate in 4 or 5 years with debt of over $100,000 or $200,000.

OTHER BOOMER BAGGAGE

In addition to some of the financial comparisons between current generational problems and the Boomer early years, the term 'Boomer' now can refer less to a specific range of years of birth, and more to anyone who is older and/or out-of-touch with younger generations and their issues. To quote one person from Generation Z - "Boomers are not an age group, they are a mindset of being out-of-touch and ignorant of the current world and country dynamics."

The term 'OK Boomer' has become derogatory, sort of inferring to Boomers that 'OK, you have it made, and are enjoying your lives in retirement or late careers, but what about us and the polluted, costly world you have left us?'

Granted, the Boomer generation (including me) could be considered out of touch by some, given their habits that do not seem to change, in a world where perhaps those habits do not make a lot of sense. After all, according to some of the younger generations, Boomers are the generation that may still use phone books, use cash or checks to pay at checkout lines, may still have landline phones at home, take pride in their 'fine China' dishes and plates (that are rarely if ever used), wear denim for shirts, jackets, shorts and pants, love 24-hour news, use bar soap in the shower instead of body wash, and may still iron their clothes.

On the flip side, there are some nostalgic memories that Boomers have that other generations do not because they were not alive to experience them. Many Boomers remember:

- Walking long distances to school and then walking back home, sometimes in sub-zero temperatures (I am sure we all exaggerate the actual distances and cold)
- Doing their homework alone at home after school, just so they could get out to play in the streets with their friends
- Going to the 'five and dime' store to buy candy (for 5 cents or 10 cents)
- Playing hide and seek after dark
- Collecting and trading sports cards that were included in a pack of bubble gum
- Finding empty soda bottles and returning them to the local grocery store for 5 cents each

- Buying vinyl music albums to play on record players, or buying music cassettes or 8-track tapes to play in their cars
- Collecting photos and news stories from newspapers, and creating personal albums of clippings of their life experiences
- Playing board games and cards with family and friends for hours
- Spending Sundays with family having dinner and socializing
- Passing the time listening to a transistor radio
- Watching their only TV station 'signing off' at midnight

I would venture to say that most Boomers feel as though they contributed to society as best they could throughout their lives, and do resent some of the criticism now being thrown their way. I am sure that some do not begin to understand the resentment that younger generations talk about and express.

In response, some Boomers are using the term 'OK Zoomer' to refer to Generation Z and their 'out-of-touch' attitudes, at least from a Boomer perspective. Some criticize that Zoomers believe that the world owes them something, that they do not have a strong work ethic, that they need instant gratification, that they want things now instead of saving until they can afford them, and that they lack understanding of financials and the value of saving and hard work.

Other Boomers do recognize the challenges today that younger generations face, that were not in place, or not as serious, as when Boomers grew up. Pollution, the national debt, the high cost of living, and very high university expenses are issues that were not usually on the radar for Boomers.

GENERATIONAL FRICTION AND FICTION

I don't perceive that there is exactly _a war_ between generations, but certainly there is a friction between generations that comes out, perhaps not daily, but occasionally in family discussions or friend interactions, as well as in media articles, blogs, social media and TV shows. The generalizations made about the 'other' generations are concerning, if not disturbing. Contrast that to the respect that most Boomers had for their elders during their childhood and adult years, maybe due to their parents absolutely _demanding_ respect from their children, not only for the parents, but for anyone older!

As in any situation where there is growing animosity between groups, there usually is a lack of understanding and appreciation of others, outside of their same-generation peers.

In my research of generational conflict, I began to feel frustrated that most of the generational analyses was focused upon statistics such as '45% of Boomers believe this' or '72% of Generation Z believe this', but where was the real story? Where was the deep dive into the lives of Boomers or Generation X, Y or Z so that we could better understand the specific issues and how these issues have played out in the lives of individuals within their generations? Where was the information and analysis that might help the generations understand one another better, and help narrow the generational divide?

HOW ABOUT REAL-LIFE STORIES?

I began to consider the idea of writing a book about real life biographies of individuals from all generations, as a way for me and others to better understand the issues. I wanted to ask probing questions to shed light on this generational divide. I anticipated that I might better understand how external events and environmental factors affected the values, views and opinions of each generation, hopefully explained via each individual story.

But when I developed an outline for the book, and began to develop questions for individuals, I realized that some questions would not make as much sense for younger generations, especially those questions that asked for their perspective now versus when they were younger, because they are fairly young now, at least in comparison to a Boomer! For instance, I wanted to ask the question – "In looking back over your life, what key lessons have you learned that you could share with other generations?" For a Generation Z person who might be 22 years old and just entering the workforce, I am not entirely sure that their perspective on life lessons would be developed much at all, nor might they want to invest the time to talk to me. I also was curious how an individual's opinions and values *changed as they aged*, as they passed through the phases of life. Those sorts of questions would not make as much sense for Generation X, Y, or Z.

After considering many options, I ultimately decided to focus only on Boomers, with the logic being that for this generation, their entire story could be told from beginning to near-the-end. I concluded that I might be able to understand the key influences on their lives growing up, and to assess how they affected their choices in later life and their opinions now, sitting in their retirement or late working years. I thought it would be insightful to see how they might look back and reflect upon the choices they made, and understand their views of the world today versus in their early years. It would be intriguing to hear how their views had changed (or not) as they aged and as some left the workforce.

Interviewing younger generations, although more of a comprehensive approach, seemed to me to be less of a complete story. Perhaps the choices of some from Generation Z or Y to accumulate high college debt in exchange for the best education, might pay off in later life, but it may be too early to know at their current stage of life. Maybe their sacrifice to live at home with parents until they could save enough to afford to live independently would turn out to be a brilliant choice both financially and from a relationship-with-parents standpoint. It could be that the sacrifices the younger generations seem willing to make to clean up the environment, convert to solar and wind power, eliminate oil and gas, etc., will turn out to be the best investment in the history of the world, but it is just too early to see how that may turn out.

So, I decided to focus this book on the lives of the Boomer generation.

But how would the reader be able to reach any conclusions about the Boomer generation, or other generations, from just fourteen life stories I captured? Clearly, understanding fourteen lives out of the millions of Boomers is not a statistically significant exercise from a mathematical perspective. Broad conclusions about this generation certainly cannot be reached from such a limited number. Furthermore, I believe all would agree that the individuals in any of these generations are not homogeneous, thus even if all in the book believed in one ideal, it would be impossible to conclude that the generation as a whole had the same belief.

However, I did believe that there would be enough commonalities in the stages of their lives, the sorts of challenges they met, descriptions of the times they grew up within, the lifestyle they led as children then adults, and the evolution of their characters and mindset, that the reader could gain a significant understanding of the key issues and contributors to Boomer thinking and behavior.

MY METHODOLOGY

How did I find the individual Boomers I have written about in this book?

My first task was to decide if I was going to randomly choose individual Boomers, or if I should look specifically for certain traits, backgrounds, family situations, professions, etc.

I decided that instead of biasing the selection by looking for something in particular, I would choose randomly, except that I would _exclude_ a part of the Boomer population whom we hear about all-too-often, namely, celebrities, TV stars, movie stars, social media icons, sports stars, and politicians. I was certain that their perspectives, already over-represented in much of what we see or hear, might not represent the views and history of the core Boomer population. So, I concluded that I would seek out those I called 'everyday Boomers', those who quietly lived their lives, those who don't get much attention, and those who did not have high-profile jobs or careers. I have nothing against celebrities, but I do believe that our views of the world get skewed a bit by the exposure they receive in the media.

I began by using traditional methods to find candidates – social media, email, friends, and word-of-mouth.

I used social media, reaching out to friends and family. I used my high school alumni group, asking for interest. I talked to friends directly, asking them if they knew any Boomers who had an interesting life who might want to share their story with me. I emailed a long list of professional contacts I had made during a 35-year career.

I quickly developed a list of about 30 candidates who agreed to participate, which I thought to be an ample population to at least begin my work. As it turned out, over time, some of those candidates decided they did not want to invest the time in answering so many questions, so the list narrowed. But the candidates I did write about turned out to be an all-star team in my view, which I will discuss later, as they satisfied my main criteria for 'everyday Boomers' with interesting lives and stories.

In hindsight, the methodology to find the candidates and their stories did not matter all that much.

I have concluded that every life that I have written about is like a snowflake, (and that is not a jab at any other generation!) very unique in its own way. The stories, although perhaps not worthy of a TV news special or movie, are interesting, touching, and very satisfying to learn about, write about, and understand. Each life story here has its own twists and turns, its own challenges, and its own unique changing environment that impacted the choices they made and how they view the world today. I am convinced that if I had randomly selected a dozen or more *other* people to write about, I would, perhaps, have been just as satisfied with their stories and the lessons I learned.

In every case, I found each story to be very worthy of being told. None were boring or typical of a Boomer life, whatever that might look like. Once I completed writing their life story, I transitioned into the questions I had for them about key issues in the world today, and how they felt about them. In most cases, it was clear to see <u>some</u> linkage between their environment growing up and how they viewed the world today, and what their opinions were about current topics of debate.

I was pleasantly surprised to find that I learned a great deal about history, as well as this generation, at more of a micro level, which was one of my goals. A primary conclusion I reached was 'there is no typical Boomer'. Each story made me consider and question my own opinions and views relative to theirs, and to compare how our lives differed, especially growing up. The diversity in lives and stories was simply amazing.

THE STORY

This book describes the lives of fourteen individual Baby Boomers, <u>as described to me by each of them</u>.

Each chapter is about the life story of one Baby Boomer that I got to know better and interview. I call them 'everyday Boomers' from this very interesting Boomer generation, a generation which mainly grew up in the 1950's, 1960's and 1970's.

WHO ARE THESE BOOMERS IN THE BOOK?

There are four women and ten men. All were born in the U.S. except for one. Politically, this group is very diverse, split evenly between conservatives, liberals, and independents.

Their birthdates range from 1946 to 1957. The birth year of 1957 was a popular one, as 5 of the 14 Boomers were born then.

Six of the fourteen served in the military. Combined, this group lived in about twenty-five states.

Their careers spanned a variety of professions, functions, industries, companies and enterprises. You will read about an engineer, a professor, a fund-raiser, a construction worker, an insurance agent, an information technology manager, a computer specialist, a manufacturing company executive, an entrepreneur, a postmaster, an investor, a lawyer, a waitress, a customer service agent, a 911 call center worker, a newspaper deliverer, a grocery store clerk, a home pet-sitter, a babysitter, and many more.

There are 14 life stories here, but I mentioned that there were more than 19 careers held. How can that be? Well, some held multiple jobs, and focused upon multiple careers during their lives.

Honestly, I would have preferred a better balance between men and women, but for some reason, more of the women I contacted decided not to participate, for a variety of reasons. That is not a commentary of any kind, just a fact.

All were members of very interesting families growing up. The majority of the group referred to themselves as poor or low-to-middle class growing up, with a few exceptions. You can sense the struggle each had during their early years, and how their families became very tight-knit as they cooperated to survive and support one another.

All of this group felt comfortable looking back on their lives and exhibited a certain satisfaction overall with where they are today, and the decisions that they made in life. I sensed zero resentment or misgivings about the past. All are proud not only of themselves and their families, but of our country, albeit most pointed out faults and significant areas of concern. I found it interesting that I would call just about all of them patriots in their own unique way, yet nearly all of them felt that the _country was headed in the wrong direction_. I will cover this in more detail later.

PREVIEW OF THESE STORIES

First of all, I hope that the life stories are of interest and cause readers to reflect on their own lives relative to each story. Second, for Boomer readers, I expect that you will begin to see some patterns in Boomer lives and views relative to your own, given that we all grew up in similar times and experienced similar events. I know some of the stories made me feel nostalgic. Third, for younger generations, I believe you will gain some understanding about this Boomer generation and why they might behave the way that they do, and say the things they do. Last, I hope this book can help reduce some of the generational friction by explaining how the Boomer generation came to be, and to help Boomers realize and understand the differences they have experienced relative to younger generations.

THE QUESTIONS THESE BOOMERS ANSWERED

First of all, the list of questions I asked each Boomer was lengthy. I sent each participant a questionnaire that was thirteen pages long. About half the questions were used to draw out the life stories of each person. The other half were focused upon obtaining their opinions and views about important issues going on in our country and the world today.

Second, each question was optional. For example, I asked about military service, if any. Some did not have any military service thus could not answer that question. I asked about children or grandchildren, if any, and the relationship they had with each. Some had no grandchildren as yet. Some questions were perhaps too sensitive for them to discuss, for a variety of reasons.

Third, I required all candidates to answer these questions in writing. I had several candidates request that I interview them verbally, as they did not want to take the time to write their answers. But I found that having them take the time to read, think about, and write answers to these questions made the candidates think through the questions more thoroughly, and their responses were extremely thoughtful and more detailed.

Once they sent me their written answers, I was able to draft their chapter, then develop additional follow-up questions I had, and I interviewed most of them in person, or on Zoom if we could not meet in person. Once I incorporated their follow-up interview responses into their story, I asked them to review the story for accuracy and content. None of the featured Boomers in the book were aware of who the other Boomers were, with one exception: there is a husband-and-wife duo who each have their own chapter story in the book, and of course they were aware that the other was participating.

I share all the questions I asked in the summary at the end, but here are just a few examples from the list of 'life story' questions:

SEX, DRUGS, ROCK and WAR: The Boomer Generation

1 - If you had to tell a story about your life in 5 minutes, what would that story be? What are you most proud of? What would you do differently if anything in your life?

2 - How well do your friends and family understand your life story and the challenges you have had?

3 - Tell me about your high school experience and rate it on a scale from 1 to 10. If you could, would you want to go back to that time and experience it again?

4 - Please share a bit about your family situation growing up, and your family situation as an adult. Were there any specific family events, issues, traditions, tragedies, etc., that changed you significantly?

Here are some examples of the questions I asked relative to their opinions and views of important issues in the country and world today:

1 - Do you believe that the generations following ours will be, in general, better or worse off financially when they get to our age?

2 - Do you believe those generations will live in a better country and world in the coming decades, versus what our generation experienced as we aged?

3 - How about drinking beer/wine/alcohol today versus growing up? How do you feel about legalizing marijuana and other drugs?

4 - What do you recall about the press (TV and newspapers mainly) when you were a teenager and in your twenties? How does that compare to now?

5 - How do you feel about U.S. immigration, the border wall, and our illegal alien policies?

6 - If you had an audience of receptive non-Boomers in a room, what would you suggest to them that you believe would help them?

7 - How do you feel about the second amendment and gun rights?

8 - Should we reduce our global influence, or expand it?

9 - What are your feelings about green initiatives and the state of our planet? How do you feel about how serious global warming is? Should we be doing more or doing less?

BOOMER COMMONALITIES – A PREVIEW

Within the life stories of the Boomers in this book, I found that in the main, each Boomer had a very individual story, with unique experiences, family lives, views and opinions relative to the others. There were very few experiences or views which were common across all. Surprisingly, I only found a few commonalities. This sampling of the Boomer generation did not appear to be one that adhered to the generalizations made about them!

A _very_ unexpected commonality, however, was that most Boomers specifically mentioned having pianos in their homes growing up, and how they either took piano lessons or recalled the family gathering around the piano and singing songs together. There seemed to be something about how piano music and perhaps the discipline learned in taking piano lessons left a lasting impression on most of the Boomers I interviewed. Or maybe, it was just pure coincidence that most of this group of Boomers had this in common. (In our house, we had an organ, not a piano, but I remembered that all family members learned to play!)

Another consistency was in regards to their views about the planet, global warming, pollution, and green initiatives. _All_ agreed that this was a much more serious issue than before, and that we (all on the planet) need to do more. So much for the Boomer reputation of doubting all the claims about climate change!

There seemed to be common values or beliefs mentioned by most, and by 'most', I would say there was a majority that shared these views, but not enough to call it a completely-shared Boomer view:

1 - Hard work – nearly all mentioned that their parents influenced them to take jobs early in their lives, such as paper routes, babysitting, etc. and that this instilled in them the value of hard work. Some said that when parents forced them to take these jobs, it was required for the family to survive, due to financial challenges. Not one person resented having to work at a young age.

2 - Saving money – this seemed to be a common thread in their stories, stating that the income from these early jobs were used for family needs, or to save for some specific need or future desire, such as a bicycle, a college fund, or their first car. Many discussed the sacrifices they made to save money in lieu of enjoying what they wanted. So, in effect, they were investing in their future selves, versus their then-current selves.

3 - Most talked about the importance of thoroughly learning the skills required to do their job well, and taking pride in doing a very good job. None talked about a priority of getting promotions or having a set career path that they created and pursued.

4 - Helping their children and grandchildren financially – most talked about their habits of financially helping their children, most now grown, and grandchildren. Most shared their plans to continue that practice going forward, although a few indicated that their children were well enough off now and did not need any further assistance. *I did not hear any of them say that their parents helped them financially* after high school or after college, if they attended college. This is a curious and interesting difference between Boomers and their parents, one that I discuss further in the analysis section.

5 - Boomers have a reputation for, over their lifetime, garnering a lot of possessions stocked away in basements or closets. Most of those I interviewed fell in line with this reputation, and most had little concern that they had too much 'stuff'. Strangely, most had minimal concern that once they passed, their children or other heirs would have to deal with all their 'stuff'. One Boomer put it best: "I worked very hard, and saved, to be able to obtain these possessions, and it is just too painful now to give them away, even though I know they are of little value today, and that I will likely not use them again."

ANOTHER INTERESTING CONCLUSION

As I worked through each of the life stories and interviews, I slowly realized that I genuinely *liked* all these people, not only for their stories and their cooperation, but for some of the challenges they faced and overcame. They just seemed to be very good folks who I respected more and more as their story emerged. They all seemed to do the right things, either at that time, or eventually, to overcome a variety of challenges at different times in their lives.

Daniel Muller

I would be happy to share a beer with any of them, or to spend an afternoon together. They are so at ease with themselves and where they are in life, perhaps because they have reached a point in their lives where they do not care about impressing anyone else. They genuinely seemed more concerned about others and the future of younger generations, versus themselves. They are all memorable to me and I plan to stay in contact with them going forward in one way or another.

So, let's get to the most interesting part, the life stories of these Boomers!

CHAPTER 1:
Karen, Who Gathered No Moss and Loves Convertibles

BACKGROUND

We have all heard the saying 'A rolling stone gathers no moss.' Karen is one of those 'rolling stones' who lived a full and adventurous life, holding many jobs and responsibilities in many geographic locations. I will get to the love of convertibles later.

I did not know Karen until I began writing this book. Someone I did not know suggested that I talk to her since 'somebody should write a book about her!'.

I reached out to her, and we traded messages until we finally met face-to-face over the internet.

Over her lifetime, Karen graduated from high school and then beauty school, was a customer service rep for a telecommunications company, married and lived on a military base, divorced, raised a daughter on her own (with help from her mother and sister for a period of time), moved 15 times, lived in three states, and worked for seven different companies. Her career steps included 20 years at a steel mill (out in the mill, not the office!) and 22 years in telecommunications. She also started her own pet sitting business which she runs today! She is 75 years old and lives in Texas.

HER STORY

Karen was born in 1946 in Northeast Ohio, and graduated from high school in 1964. She grew up with two siblings and parents in Ohio. Her mother worked in an attorney's office before staying at home to raise her children. Later in life, after divorcing, she worked at a large bakery until retiring. Her father held multiple jobs after going to business school, including working for a manufacturer, enlisting in the Army, then working in human resources and accounting, where he was recognized as an employee of the year, before opening his own hardware store. Later, he worked as a treasurer for a school system before dying at a young age when Karen was only 28.

When Karen was 15, her parents suddenly split up and stated they were divorcing.

"The divorce was just horrendous. One day, the arguing was very bad, and I called my boyfriend to come get me, and he took me to his house. Later, my grandparents came to tell me that they had gotten her mother and that she was going to live with them, but that they did not know where her father was, so they asked Karen what she would be doing. She chose to just live with her friend's family until things got settled, because the house was empty.

Later, she lived a few months with her father, which did not work out, then her mother agreed to let her live with her.

One day, after the divorce, when Karen and her mother were arguing, her mother said 'Do you think you are too big to be spanked?' Karen said 'Yep!' According to Karen, 'Boy, did I ever get it from her for saying that!' This was when she was a senior in high school!

ON TO A CAREER

After high school graduation, and getting licensed in beauty school, she landed a position with a major telecommunications company in customer service, mainly working on residential orders and collections for two years. Then she met her future husband, introduced through a roommate. He was in the military, and they married and moved to a military reservation in Eatontown, NJ. They soon had a daughter.

Their daughter was over a year old when Karen and her husband divorced. What happened? "I am not sure what went wrong, but my husband said he would rather go to Vietnam than be married to me."

She and her daughter moved back to Ohio then, in 1969, and lived with her mother. She remembers that year because when they moved back, when the moon landing took place, she was watching it on TV, and woke her daughter so she could experience something so important "even though she had no idea what was going on."

She then landed a job at a rubber products company, making rubber gloves as a 'tumbler' and also filled in as a stripper of the rubber machine, but it was a dangerous job. Later, she was able to find a job as a manager of radiology at a local hospital, where she worked with radiologists and patients, scheduling tests, and reading reports to workers on the hospital floor.

Her mother watched Karen's daughter when she worked. Her sister, who had been studying at an Ohio university, moved back with her mother due to financial difficulties, and she helped with babysitting as well. Then her sister graduated and got a job locally.

Later, she heard that a local steel mill was hiring workers in production, and she applied.

She interviewed for the job, and was told during the interview that she was hired, but could not get any training that day because she had not worn 'mill clothes'. They told her the next day to wear gloves and warm clothes (it was February), but to make sure her gloves would allow her to pick-up things and be agile. She was not sure what sort of gloves would work, so she wore white band gloves that first day on the job. 'My supervisor went crazy, and always told others later that I was the one that wore white band gloves into the steel mill on my first day.'

Karen was a loyal employee, working there for 20 years, even though much of that time, she was the only female in her department. Fifteen of those years were in inspection roles. She had to deal with comments from all the men, being the only woman working in inspection jobs all over the plant.

Soon after starting, she was told that a good job in the mill was a 'spark tester', which used equipment to determine the chemistry of the steel being tested. She landed that job and did that job for several years, before wanting to bid on a bar hand-grinding job. She was told that she could not bid on that job to do hand-grinding because she was 'too short and too heavy on top'! She finally did bid on that job, but never held that position as a fulltime job, instead doing it occasionally on overtime, as well as doing a variety of other mill inspection jobs.

As she tackled new jobs, either as a fill-in during vacations, or a new job she took on, what was the most important lesson she had to learn? "The most important thing was that you NEVER asked a question or bothered anyone else while they were on their lunch breaks or other breaks. As long as you didn't do that, they tolerated you and didn't care all that much what you were doing."

Once when she was laid off during a slow period, she went to the union hall and asked for food vouchers, as other workers did during times of layoff. But she was told that 'there were men with families that were not getting food vouchers, why should she get vouchers?' Later, they told her she could get a food voucher as long as she did not come to any more union meetings.

While working in the mill, she was able to buy her first house, under a Department of Agriculture program. She then lived there with her daughter, and drove to work each day. Back then, her credit cards were insured, and her loan was insured, so if she got laid off, her mortgage payment and credit card payments were covered.

Her credit card company also called her, and told her that they became aware that she took the lowest paying job in the mill, and they wanted to help her out, so paid her credit card bill for the first month!

Later, when things slowed down, she applied to work in a salaried position in the traffic department, and began working there, coordinating shipments for shipping departments in mills across Pennsylvania, Ohio and Indiana. Her last three years at the steel mill were in this area.

Karen learned quickly that most of the workers in the mill were related to someone else, and she was not. So, she told others that she was related to the head of the mill. She knew he must have heard that, because after that time, he would wave at her when he walked by.

She drove two different foreign sports cars, and she was one of the first employees to drive a foreign car to the mill. Foreign cars were allowed in the parking lot but not in the plant. At that time, foreign cars were not viewed positively when much of their steel was sold to U.S. automotive companies!

There was a central locker room for women, but because Karen worked so many different jobs, it would take over an hour to go back to her locker room to get equipment or change clothes. When she began work as a mill inspector, she could not leave the area, so she took a locker, without permission, in the men's locker room near one of the rolling mills. Later, they positioned a single locker out in the mill for her to use.

Did she feel resentment from the men? "One time, I walked into the office, and a guy was there, and he said 'You don't belong here! You are taking a job from a man who needs it!' I told him that he couldn't do what I did, either my job, or all the other things she was responsible for at home, raising a daughter more or less alone, etc. I told him that if he didn't have his wife at home to pack his lunch and take care of all the things at home, he couldn't cope."

Another time, a religious man came to work carrying religious pamphlets that his wife had given him to share with the other workers (especially Karen she believes), and some of the content was that a woman should not work outside the home. Out of respect, Karen read the material, but told the man that he should tell his wife that she has to eat just like everyone has to eat, so she needs to work!

Once she was asked by management what they should do differently to improve things, and she told them that they needed to get the guys to work more than two hours per shift!

"Others never understood me working in a steel mill!" As an example, her mother often asked her 'When are you going to get a REAL job?' "Nobody really understood why I worked there. But I enjoyed it, I was mainly outside and not cooped up in an office, and the variety of jobs was fun."

"You know, I keep hearing about this 'Me Too' movement, but I always thought that if something happened when a man offended you, you should try to turn that around if you could and make it work for you. As an example, one night, a plant foreman knocked on my door at 2:00 a.m., apparently after being out drinking. I used that against him until the day I left! He didn't want anyone to know that he had done that."

Eventually, her daughter graduated magna cum laude from college, and moved out of state to work for a major manufacturer. Karen was proud that her daughter was later nominated as employee of the year.

How would Karen compare her parenting style vs. those of her parents?

"There was a vast difference. I realize that some things were just ingrained in my parents' beliefs, but I fought hard for my daughter against what my mother and her husband would tell me was acceptable. I just would not rule over her. I allowed her to make her own decisions, based on what she believed, with some guidance."

About that time, Karen realized that with an empty house, and things degrading at the mill, it was time for a change, and she decided to move to Northern California, as she had a friend there.

After a few months, she relocated to the Houston area, and worked for the police department as a uniformed telecommunications officer. She attended the Police Academy and obtained a state license as a 911 operator. She answered and prioritized all calls coming into the department, both 911 calls and non-emergency. "We were taking up to 40 calls per hour, it was a very busy job, but on special occasions, we were allowed to watch the Rockets in the playoffs, all the while taking calls."

Then she was hired by another telecommunications company as a service rep taking orders for service in an after-hour center, where she earned higher pay and better benefits than with the police department.

She worked in various departments for 22 years. Her last job was working in revenue management, but her employer chose to close that office due to building problems. She had the option to move to another office, but decided to take a package and retire, in December 2015.

Then she went to work as a dog caretaker, and got the idea to start her own dog-sitting business in peoples' homes. "I love what I am doing. And I learned that it is less stressful for the dogs for me NOT to be there when the owners leave or come home, so she leaves just before the owners return, and arrives just after the owners depart for the day."

How does Karen compare living in a small town in the Midwest vs. her home now in Texas?

"I really enjoy living in a part of the country that is very diverse, like in Houston. I always rebelled against my parents' beliefs about other people, religions, races, etc. Living in a small town, everyone knows everyone's business, plus the population was very homogeneous. But when I lived there, it was the late 50's and 60's, and attitudes were much different then. As an example, I was not able to go to college because my parents wouldn't support me attending a Catholic college, even though I had a scholarship." She was also accepted at another private college in Ohio, but her father told her that he wasn't able to support her attending there, as she wanted to major in music, and her parents did not believe there was much of a future in music.

"Also, I dated a Jewish guy from Cleveland. He was not welcome in Mother's home. Once my mother visited me in Houston and we drove to the grocery store. She refused to get out of the car because all the people she saw were Hispanic."

POLLING FOR OPINIONS

What are some of the most important lessons you learned in your life?

I learned from a music teacher, Mr. Marini, that to write music well, you must learn all the rules and know them backwards and forwards. Then, and only then, you will be able to break all the rules. If you take shortcuts and do not have a firm foundation, you will fail. I think that applies to other things in life.

Also, I learned from a high school history teacher, Mr. Marzulli, that learning the little facts ensures you will also know the big picture. I did not get great grades from Mr. Marzulli, but I learned *so much* about history that I still remember.

I also believe that you can never put a man before your job or what you believe. You have to prioritize what you believe and prioritize your work.

Then Karen laughs - "The last lesson, is always drive a convertible! I learned that from Mary Brown, my 5th grade teacher and a friend of my parents."

If a Millennial or Gen X or Gen Z person was sitting next to you on your death bed, and they asked you "What is the meaning of life? What is it all about?" What do you think your answer would be?

Life is to teach you what you must learn so that your next life will be better. I have become friends with some Hare Krishnas, and they believe in reincarnation. I like them a lot, and maybe because of that, their beliefs rubbed off on me. But I worry about believing that!

What else stands out to you about your life?

My parents always called me the dumb one. I keep wondering why they said that, but it may have been because my mother kept telling me that one of my biggest faults was that I thought I could do anything! (Well, I think Karen has proved that she CAN do anything!) It also could be because I can be scattered in talking about things. I can talk about one topic, then switch to another topic sort of randomly. Plus, my siblings were both very smart and both attended college, and I did not.

Do you believe that other people in younger generations appreciate what you have contributed to society through the work you did, and the family you have?

I don't know, but I am not sure I need to be appreciated. I just lived my life one decision at a time.

What does she think about the opinions of others regarding Boomers and her generation?

I think Boomers need to stay independent - I don't always just accept what I hear, if I hear something that doesn't make sense, I say 'wait a minute here!'.

Will we have another Great Depression?

Yes, the government tries to keep buffering the implications of what we are doing, but so many things are falling apart. Crime is getting out of control.

Should marijuana be legalized?

I don't see detrimental things that marijuana causes, unlike alcohol, and it helps people with anxiety and pain vs. so many prescription drugs. I don't use, but if legal, I might.

How does she feel about the border?

I don't like what is going on, there has to be a better way to manage this. Many immigrants are paying the price of the illegals coming across the border who are criminals or gang members.

What about her views about socialism vs. capitalism and how younger generations feel positive about socialism?

We sort of have some socialism, such as social security. I would not have made it at times when laid off without unemployment or sub-pay, but so many now want free things, and we are more dependent upon the government. I keep hearing unemployment is so low, but what about all the people who are not working? They cannot all be counted in unemployment because many are no longer looking for a job.

IN SUMMARY

After talking to Karen at length, and being so impressed with her life and the different jobs that she held compared to others during their lives, it started to dawn on me that if anyone could feel shortchanged in life, she might be near the front of the line.

Think about this....... her parents divorced at a crucial time in her teen years. They left their house, and *neither parent asked her to live with them* during this time. She lived with a strange family for months until she was able to live again with her parents separately. How would that affect most people's self-value?

She was not allowed to attend college because the scholarship she received was at a Catholic college. She was focused on improving her lot by trying to find the best job she could throughout her life. She was a single mother, was divorced two times, worked in a steel mill with nearly all men, was able to buy her own home for her daughter and her to live in, successfully raised a wonderful and successful daughter, moved herself multiple times to find a better life, worked loyally for 42 years at two different companies, and last but not least, lives in a diverse community which she loves, and started her own company at age 70! And at age 76, is still working doing something she loves, calling her own shots.

Add to that, she lost her father at age 28, dealt with what we may today call workplace harassment for close to twenty years, and although she is more or less happy with her family situation, does not have as strong a relationship as she would like to have with her daughter or grandson.

"I seem to upset my daughter sometimes, I don't mean to, but that seems to happen. Sometimes I feel as though she doesn't want others to know that her mom was a blue-collar worker and worked in a steel mill. But she has such a nice life, and I am so proud of her, I don't want to poke my nose into her life and ask her to think differently about me. There is not much I can do about it."

When you begin to appreciate what Karen accomplished in her life, and the challenges she met head on, I think 'dumb' ('my parents used to call me that') is definitely not a word that describes her.

Let me share my assessment.

I believe Karen is very happy with the life she has built for herself, and the memories she has.

I would describe her as 'tough, entrepreneurial, a quick learner, flexible, a hard worker, empathetic, open to different ideas, someone who can get along with a variety of people, street-smart, and most of all, INDEPENDENT!'

Well, Karen, one thing is for sure, nobody will ever say that you want to be dependent on the government or that you don't want to work!

Even though Karen doesn't think she or her generation should be thanked for what she has done with her life, let me say 'thank you' to her for being what so many Boomers are.

Most Boomers are unique individuals who, through their contributions to various employers, and through their contributions to family, have carved out a memorable, if not remarkable, life for themselves, all the while making our country, society, and world a better place for future generations. People like Karen do not make headlines, do not get featured in the media, but they quietly live their lives, pay their taxes, and contribute to others in mostly unseen ways. I am thankful that I got to know Karen and was able to share her story with others. I am also, for the first time, considering a convertible for my next car, after hearing that driving a convertible is one of the most important lessons she has ever learned!

CHAPTER 2:
Jesse, The Rebel

"Work when I have to, quit when I can. I'm one of God's chosen, I'm a motorcycle man."

BACKGROUND

I first met Jesse in high school, but lost touch with him when he dropped out of school my junior year.

He began to show up at our high school reunions a while back, and clearly, he was a different cat. He usually rode in on a motorcycle, and dressed in full biker gear. It seemed that just about everyone at the reunion remembered Jesse, as someone who made an impression with them at some point during their lives.

Through the years, all I knew about Jesse, just from second-hand information, was that he had a tough up-bringing, losing his mother at an early age. I had heard that he had gotten into legal trouble. Other than that, he was a bit of a mystery.

When I posted on our high school alumni site that I was beginning a book about Boomers and that I was looking for volunteers to perhaps be in the book, Jesse reached out to me. Our emails back and forth took a long time to develop, but finally he asked to get my questionnaire. After months, I received four scanned documents, and it turns out that Jesse completed over 30 pages of hand-written information! He clearly spent weeks if not months contemplating how to best answer my questions. I discovered he was a *very* talented writer, which I had heard about back in high school.

After devouring his responses and stories, I asked for a personal meeting for me to interview him so I could fill in a few blanks in his story line. Again, he seemed cautious, asking if he could understand more about how his story might be developed. I sent him a few examples of other chapters, and weeks went by. Finally, he agreed to meet for lunch at a local hangout of his. As I sat there waiting, a bartender asked me if I was Dan, and that Jesse wanted to talk to me on the phone. It turns out his motorcycle had broken down a few miles away, and he asked me if I would pick him up? After finding him and bringing him back to lunch, we had a great discussion, one I will always remember. His story is one of a tough upbringing, rebellion, tragedy, transitions, and pride.

EARLY LIFE

Jesse was born an only child in 1957, and lived in Justus, Ohio. His father was much older than his mother, marrying her when he was 41 and she being in her early 20's, suffering from epilepsy. He lost his mother at Christmas, when he was only two years old, in 1959. His father had a fulltime job working in the steel mill, and decided he could not find a way to raise Jesse himself, so Jesse was placed in a series of foster homes until his father contacted an elderly lady who had actually spent time raising Jesse's father. Jesse moved to live with her in Beckley, West Virginia. His father would come to visit occasionally. After several years, she passed away when he was only 10 years old. After that, Jesse lived with his father again, although he had to be very independent as his father was working. "I had to get myself up for school and later on jobs, because nobody else would have been there to do that. I don't have much sympathy for those who cannot 'get started' in the morning."

Once Jesse hit puberty, his relationship with his father deteriorated. "The war started then because his little boy was becoming a young man enamored with the hippies and later, the Yippies and Abbie Hoffman. Dad was _thoroughly_ disgusted. Our relationship never really recovered. I once wore a hippie shirt with flowers on it, which convinced Dad I was a homosexual."

The first job Jesse recalls having was cleaning out a horse stall for a neighbor and selling seeds from a seed company, which paid workers via merchandise rewards. "Flipping through the catalog, I spied a T-shirt with the Confederate battle flag, and I lost my mind. I am wearing it in my sixth-grade class photo." At age 14, Jesse got a job cleaning and mopping floors after hours at a bar in a nearby town. He would pour a shot of liquor from each bottle into his own bottle, to be enjoyed with other youths who would camp out and smoke cigars. "But that was short-lived."

Jesse always had a love of history during his formative years, and he recalls studying the American Indian philosophies of life, and how 'saving' was not a priority for them. About that same time, he encountered Matthew 6:25-35, which taught him that God would provide the important things of life (food, clothing, etc.) provided you prioritize your relationship with God. So, for

Jesse, jobs and saving money and acquiring things (houses, cars, etc.) were never a priority, a philosophy that he stuck with throughout most of his life. "God will provide."

Growing up, his father did send him to church with some neighbors and friends living near them. "We would go to the steelworkers hall in Massillon, some would rent the hall, and they would try to have their own church service. They didn't have a preacher, so they would take turns preaching as they were called. That is where I learned about religion." So, what did Jesse take away from that religious training? "I was very confused and struggled with the teaching. Here we have, supposedly, the perfect being, God. Yet the Bible indicates that he is so vindictive! It was taught that there is only one way to get to heaven, and that is to accept Christ as your savior, and anything else, you burn in hell for eternity. Why? Eternity is a long-time vs. the short time we are on here the earth. Shouldn't there be other options to earning your way into heaven?"

When he was 16, and got his driver's license, he began working at a restaurant on the late shift, and borrowed his dad's 'souped-up' car to drive to work. In his words, the car was 'too much of a car for a 16-year-old!' On his way home, someone pulled up beside him revving his engine, and before he knew it, he was drag-racing someone on the main street in Massillon. Soon, he saw police lights coming from behind. It crossed his mind that his dad had stated that if Jesse ever got a ticket, he would never drive again, so Jesse decided he was going to try to get away. At a high rate of speed, the car came upon a curve at an intersection, and Jesse lost control of the car, and hit a telephone pole. "All of a sudden, I am laying in the rear seat looking out the rear window, in a lot of pain." He had dislocated his hip, which would have an effect later in life when he enlisted.

"That same night, a friend's sister was hit by a car, and since my accident was reported in the local newspaper, everyone in town assumed I had been the one who hit her."

Also at age 16, Jesse spent a semester in Columbus, and was able to attend a Yippie meeting. "I read their book 'Steal the Book' (which I did!) and reached some seriously warped conclusions. You might say Abbie Hoffman ruined my life. But I will give the Yippies credit, they were trying to correct what was wrong with the country, not destroy it as some of the protesters are trying to do today."

Soon after, Jesse learned that his father was planning to retire, and he realized that this would mean that he would be seeing his father a lot more at home. Given that they did not get along at all during this time, this was one of the causes of Jesse deciding to drop out of high school and enlist. His father suggested that Jesse at least finish his junior year first, but he did not. "I remember that I was getting frustrated at everyone telling me what to do, from my father, my teachers, etc. I don't recall exactly the interchange that day in the high school office, but I recall yelling 'No I am not!' and I threw all my books into the trash can and walked out, and set off to begin my life of high adventure."

EXIT HIGH SCHOOL AND ENTER THE MILITARY

When Jesse enlisted, at age 17, he wanted to go into the 82nd airborne division, but was rejected due his prior hip separation. "I was devastated that I did not get into what I wanted, I sat in the Cleveland recruiting office and cried. I told the recruiter I didn't care where I went, so, with all the travel and educational opportunities the military offers, I went to Oklahoma and was trained to shoot cannons. Being only 17 and being allowed to drink in bars, I slept through most of the Advanced Individual Training."

"One night, my sergeant, his wife, me, and my date (who ended up being the aunt of my children), all went to a concert to see Grand Funk Railroad. We all did acid, and the sergeant's wife and I freaked out so badly that we had to leave the concert. On the way home, I saw a spiral moving in and out, and heard, or felt, the message of 'Be. Just Be.' I have no idea what it meant, but I was overcome with a sense of peace and confidence. Sort of like a message of 'whether you realize it or not, the universe is unfolding as it should'."

Jesse had been on active duty for nine months, when he was arrested for armed robbery. He was found guilty and on his 18th birthday, was sentenced to five years in prison, the minimum sentence in Oklahoma for that offense. "It was the best birthday present I ever received. In many ways, I was so blessed. I had discharged a weapon during the robbery, and admitted to a string of other offenses, yet received the minimum sentence."

While in prison, he got to know a very large black man who was a lifer, who he watched bench press 400 pounds repeatedly. He told Jesse that he had initially dispatched his hippie minions to invite him over to get high with the evilest of intents, but after talking to him a bit, he relented and thought 'I can't hurt this kid.' "In my innocence, I didn't realize that everyone thought he was having sex with me because he wouldn't tolerate people speaking about it in his presence. One guy called me 'a dumpling', and his response was 'he's not a dumplin', he's a man.' 'I thought maybe he was your dumplin', and the lifer repeated 'he's no one's dumplin', he's a man.'"

"Without this guy looking out for me, I might have been raped, and I am sure I would have gotten revenge and killed someone, ending up serving the rest of my life in prison."

After serving 11 months of a five-year sentence, Jesse was granted parole.

Jesse looks back and talks about the miracles that occurred during that time and how he developed a faith in God. "First, my sentence was a miracle, then doing less than 20% of the sentence was a miracle, and having a protector in prison was a miracle. God is good."

Upon returning from the prison and military service, Jesse was struck by the comments of 'Thanks for your service' that arose from the national shame of how Vietnam veterans were treated. "My reply was usually 'I didn't do much'. I was a hybrid of Beetle Bailey and Sad Sack, but overall, the time in the service was a good experience."

BACK TO SCHOOL, ON TO HIS CAREER

He then returned to finish high school, graduating in 1977. "It was one of the proudest days of my life. I had the highest GPA in my academic career, and had worked a fulltime job while finishing. Others told me I could not graduate while working, but I did it."

A few months before graduation, Jesse found a job at a manufacturing company. "I was working about 50 hours per week, plus attending classes, and only sleeping in bed less than an hour per night. I was so tired, I slept through a Led Zeppelin concert!"

While working, during a lunch break outside near the road, Jesse made a large cardboard sign that said 'On Strike', and another which said 'If our demands are not met in 48 hours, we will kill the hostages'. "They had NO sense of humor there. The supervisor told me that I worked like a horse, and if I ever got the kid out of me, I would make a hell of a man. I got fired in April of 1977."

He quickly landed another construction job just after graduation.

Shortly thereafter his father died at age 59. "When he died, I thought to myself, 'well, the war is over.' Dad never talked about his early life or childhood. He was a blue-collar Democrat with conservative views. But he was plagued by drinking. I knew he was in the service, and had injured his back, then worked most of his life in the steel mill. Being an older father when I was born, maybe he just didn't have much patience to listen to me. But I did swear growing up that I was going to be a better father than he was to me. I knew he loved me, but I was disgusted at how he showed, or didn't show it. I am glad that I had visited him at the nursing home a few days before he passed. I will say that Dad's belief in a fair day's wage for a fair day's work gradually became a firmly held belief of my own."

Jesse's father had talked to him earlier that he wanted to leave him the house he owned, or to build him a house on some property that he owned in West Virginia. "I told him I didn't want any of that." So, his father sold his house to someone else but set it up so that Jesse inherited a land contract on the house, and as long as he made rent payments, eventually the house would be his. But Jesse did not want anything that his father wanted to leave him. "What I wouldn't give to have that house now!"

"I did inherit an annuity, and just after Dad's death, I had just enough from the first payment to afford to go to a local dealer to buy a GL1100 motorcycle. After joining a few local motorcycle clubs, I sought out a more substantial 'tribal' group, and shortly thereafter I joined a large, renowned motorcycle club. To me, it was the major leagues of motorcycle gangs."

Jesse recalls that the reason he was accepted was that so many members had gone to jail, that they needed to rebuild and recruit new members. But he realized their rules were not to his liking. "The national president told me, 'You smile too much, that will get you in trouble. Don't talk to the public, they could be agents from the FBI.'" Jesse realized that some women loved bikers, but this club did not want women around the clubhouse until you knew them for at least a year. "What fun was that? So, I had to figure out a way to quit. As it turned out, it was quite simple. I decided to be a man and go talk to someone in the mother club, sort of a board member, and told him that my heart was no longer in it. Too many men get squeamish and run away and hide."

At about this time, he was following the teachings of Abbie Hoffman, a 1970's and 1980's socialist leader who wanted to 'change the country for the better'. Jesse thought that this revolution had patriotic origins, one that did not strive to destroy the country, but rather to improve it.

At age 21, he was laid off from his job, and discovered the benefits of unemployment. He earned $111 per week 'to ride my motorcycle and chase women'. Jesse recalls a personal slogan he developed - "Work when I have to, quit when I can, I'm one of God's chosen, I'm a motorcycle man."

At that time, per advice from Abbie Hoffman, Jesse signed up for as many public assistance programs as possible. "When I signed up, they asked me if I might want to register for classes to become a secretary." Soon Jesse found himself a member of a motorcycle gang studying to be a legal secretary. That led to him eventually earning an associate degree in paralegal studies. "I always enjoyed learning, and being back in the classroom was great. The highlight of that time was that I learned shorthand, and I used it to fulfill our teacher's homework assignment of 'write me a message in shorthand'. My message was 'Would you like to get naked with me?' I got an A but not laid, alas. She did tell me that the thought crossed her mind but it would be inappropriate."

This began a period where he dated various women, and found that he could have a place to stay with his then-current girlfriend. "That first summer set-up my tactical MO for the next several years; work long enough to draw unemployment, find a woman to lay up with during the winter months of unemployment in case it ran out, go back to work, ditch the woman, and repeat."

I digress from the sequence of Jesse's story here, only to quote his _current_ view of government programs... "We need FAR fewer government programs. Forty years ago, I was a hale and hearty young man who was able to get a disgustingly uneven handout compared to my ability to work. You know it hasn't tightened up in the intervening decades!"

At one point, Jesse became a libertarian politically. "Libertarians take a hard look at all taxes and think a lot about them. I learned an interesting viewpoint from this experience. For example, we all think that if we buy a home, we own it, it is ours. But if they can take it away from you if you don't pay property taxes, then do you really own your own home? My goal was always to _not_ own things, both out of the belief that 'God will provide' but also due to the belief that you don't really own anything given our tax system. But here I am married to someone who owns rental properties!" Why has he always shied away from striving to own things such as a home? "I see so many people work so hard and end up with nothing."

FAMILY LIFE

Jesse was married three times in his life, the first being Diane, who he started dating in high school. "Her mother did not like me, and she finally called the sheriff telling him that her daughter ran away from home and was over at my place. The next thing I knew, the sheriff pulls up to me and asks if I knew where Diane was at. She ended up in jail, and I asked if she could get out of jail if I married her. They said yes!" Even after a divorce, Jesse appreciates that Diane was always supportive of him.

In May of 1986, at age 29, Jesse was riding his motorcycle near his hometown and saw a young lady, Judy, out in front of her house. She was the younger sister of a girl he had dated earlier. He came to learn she was only 16, and Jesse was already dating Wendy, someone that he 'could have fallen for'. After getting to know Judy, "Damn, if she didn't upset the apple cart!". In May of 1988, they were married and had their first child. They had two more children over the next five years. "Under my tutelage, she turned into the wife of my dreams. She was the most attentive mother ever, and supported me in all my decisions."

That same year, when Jesse decided to join the motorcycle club, he told Judy about his plans. "She just said 'OK'". As related earlier, he eventually left the motorcycle club after a few years.

After this, Jesse cut his hair and began selling life insurance. Again, Judy said 'OK'. "There was a fraternal organization I joined, and they asked you to sell others into membership, which included a small insurance policy. Then they asked me to go to a class to learn how to sell insurance. Once I got into it, I realized it was not for me either. I did this for about a year. Judy was pregnant and working, and I was trying to transition into becoming a white-collar guy, but that didn't work. So, the union was hiring, and I went to work at a manufacturing company in Orrville, Ohio."

In 1998, Judy's sister, who was married, left her husband for a guy who asked if he could stay with Judy's sister and her husband for a while, and eventually, the husband was out and this guy was in. Later, Judy's sister kicked this guy out of the house, and as it turned out, this guy and Judy were classmates in high school. Since he was homeless, Judy asked Jesse if it would be OK if this man came to live with them for a time. Jesse agreed, but unknown to him, while he was at work, the guy was plying Judy with drugs, and she became hooked. Judy then had a breakdown, and near the end told Jesse; "I am lost and not sure I can find my way back."

"And then she was gone, and I was alone again, this time with three children. It was absolutely the worst time in my life. To this day, I am still not right. I cannot listen to 'Ti Amo' or 'Stand by Me'. I sure miss 'My Rock'. I contemplated suicide to escape the pain, but realized that my kids would be left alone, and the thought of that set me straight. I just had to eat the pain. The only good thing that came out of this was sobriety, as I was concerned that I would lose my kids if I became an alcoholic or hooked on drugs."

"I always meant to get the kids raised and then go all medieval on him, but then I met Sonja, so I guess he gets a pass from TWO husbands and fathers."

Jesse says that during that time, he lost his faith in God, thinking that a just God would never create all the terrible things in his life at that time. "But I came to realize that it was just Karma. Remember all those women I lived with and used? Many of them really cared for me and I hurt them. I figured it was God's way of telling me that I was an ass."

Having three younger children to raise, and having to work, he had to give up everything outside of job and caring for his kids. And his children had to grow up fast. In his words, the eldest, Sky, 'Had to give up everything except school and family.'

"It is a minor miracle that my kids turned out so well, given all my time away from them, having to work. Our relationship is wonderful, compared to the relationship between my dad and me." Jesse fondly calls them 'my little bastards', and takes pride in his parenting. "I spanked each child only once each, and that was when they darted across the street at a young age. They would cry that Daddy had spanked them, and I would cry telling them what my life would be like if they were killed under the wheels of an automobile."

Jesse is adamant that those parents who let nannies and sitters raise their children have it all wrong. "There is nothing as valuable as children who know they are loved and who are guided and raised by parents who are present for them. Some parents decide that both spouses should work, but my view is that they don't have to do this to survive, but they do it for better 'things'. Sure, lots of money is good, but a stable loving relationship between parents and children can't be bought."

Jesse was a blue-collar worker most of his life, with a focus on masonry, working for masonry contractors in union construction projects. "It took a while, though, for me to abandon my freewheeling days. My foreman one day told me 'I just can't count on you'. It's hard to believe how hard that hit me. Unless I was sick, I never missed another day for the next twenty years."

"I dated a lot of strange women while the kids were growing up, from the affluent woman who was 'out slumming', to another whose problems were deeper and broader than I realized, she ended up doing 18 months in prison for stalking me. Another who thought she would make some Christmas money by running guns to Mexico, but who got nailed at the border with three hundred pounds of pot. Oh, and the 18-year-old, when I was 52, who got me over the fascination with younger women!'

Jesse met Sonja in 2011, who grew up in the area. "Sonja's husband Dean was one of my favorite people from the bars. In fact, I had performed their wedding ceremony in 1994. Dean took a long time to die from his cancer and I 're-met' her at his funeral."

Sonja was raised Catholic, and Jesse claims that he knows more about Catholicism than she does. He observes that they are a good match, with Sonja being a bit of a 'control freak' whereas Jesse's temperament is more about taking the path of least resistance. "Maybe her style of looking out for me comes from me not having as much control or concern about things." As much as Jesse avoided gathering assets during life, Sonja owns and manages multiple rental properties. "When we met, it was like we had spent our whole life together in another life. A perfect match. She is very devoted, and I trust her completely. I know she would give her life for me if she had to." They have now been married for ten years.

POLLING FOR OPINIONS

Jesse seems to have made an amazing transition politically. At first, he seemed to be very liberal, some might say extreme. Today, some would see him as a very right-wing conservative.

How does he explain that transition?

Was it Churchill who said 'If you are not a liberal when you are young, you have no heart, and if you are not a conservative when you are old you, you have no brain?'" (It seems that there is a dispute as the origin of this saying, some would suggest a Frenchman in the 1800's was the first to say something such as this)

I also learned that you have to work for what you get, and after a few jobs, I did apply myself to the job at hand.

Jesse seems very wise, logical, and well-read. How did he get to this point?

I think it is one of God's cruel jokes. Finally, through all the life lessons, you have this experience and wisdom, but now you cannot do much with the wisdom due to old age! I do think that I learned a lot by listening to others. I have always believed that you should let people talk, no matter what you think about them. All people deserve to be listened to and heard, because everyone has valid opinions and ideas. 'Listen to others, even if dull and ignorant. They too have their story.' – Desiderata

How did music affect you growing up?

My favorite band was Black Sabbath – the originators of heavy metal. Do you know where the term heavy metal came from? Per their bassist, when they launched their first album, critics said this was not music, it sounded more like heavy metal grinding together! I saw them in concert many times. There was not much of a stage show, as Ozzie was not much of a dancer. I hated disco, though I have mellowed toward it. I believe the Beatles to be the most overrated band in history, although I am surprised how much I generally enjoy covers of their work. I also always liked Motown.

Some say that Boomers did, and do, consume too much alcohol. Did you fit into that reputation?

I drank entirely too much in my life but I did learn that alcoholism is both very real and a very different thing from being a drunk. One of my little quips is 'they had me convinced I was an alcoholic, come to find out I was just a drunk.' At one point I realized I was drinking a half gallon of whiskey a week. Finally, it stopped being fun and I drink only 2-3 drinks in that time span now. I attended enough alcohol counseling and AA meetings to finally enlighten me to my true standing. I asked a counselor once 'What do you suppose is wrong with me, man?' He replied instantly 'You have an anti-social personality disorder."

What was unbeknownst to me at that time was that I was, and am currently, an Omega personality type. It explains a lot about me.

Was there a time in your life that you felt you were treated very unfairly?

Besides my father and the way he was, when I went to prison for a first offense, I was thrown in with hardened criminals with multiple offenses. Before being released, I was approached by some guy asking me if I was interested in an armored car heist where they were going to have to kill a guard! They should not mix first time offenders with multiple offenders, but that is a topic for prison reform.

How might you explain the popularity of socialism in the country today? If it is being pushed, what is the logic for some pushing this on our country and youth?

I have thought a lot about this. I think it is a global push. If socialism spreads into the U.S. and into other parts of the world, you in effect are reducing most of the population to serfdom. Today, the wealth is distributed in a certain way, but under socialism, more wealth moves to those at the top than is the case today. Look at the socialist countries in Europe. They have all these migrants flooding in, just like here. Does anyone care about the quality of life for the existing citizens, the ones who worked so hard to make their countries as successful as they are?

Do you think future generations will be better off or worse off than the Boomer generation?

I think future generations are going to be consigned to a worldwide hellscape. I might just be a cantankerous crazy old man, but I've always been a political junkie and I see very little in current events to dissuade me from this belief. Just one example of what will drive future doom is the simultaneous movements to rid American society of guns, and to dismantle law enforcement. Madness. The whole globalism 'one world government' will bring a return to the Middle Ages with really only two classes, wealthy and poor. The divisions among people that the media pushes, BIPOC (black, indigenous and people of color) vs. white, vaccinated vs unvaccinated, men competing in women's sports……compared to the Greatest Generation when everyone pulled together for the common good and how that turned out. Then look at what we have today. As interesting as it all is, I am glad I'll not be here to witness what they are going to do to our world.

Do you think that another Great Depression is possible?

I absolutely believe it is coming and perhaps imminent. In 2022, I have never seen a more dysfunctional government remarkable at all levels for sheer incompetence. People are appointed to positions of immense power with minimal concern for actual ability but feverish attention to skin color or what's between their legs. In some cases, what they *pretend* is between their legs. It's shameful.

What historical events affected you?

Well, 9-11 was a big deal. I have listened to others who believe that the U.S. government was behind this whole plan. The goal was to force us to go to war in Iraq and to get oil. I watched something where a videographer went into the basement of one of the twin towers, and it showed that the girders were sheared off, not melted as you might expect. It was as if someone had done something to cause the buildings to fall, knowing that the plane attacks were coming.

What about technology today and the internet, social media, etc.?

One thing I think is arguable is that some people don't have anything to say, but the internet enables them to reach out to the entire world, too often to spread nonsense which is then picked up and echoed by others.

What about the 'woke movement' and LBGTQ and the schools getting involved in educating youth about this?

My oldest daughter is very in tune with the homosexual community. Her daughter at 12 years old said she did not like boys, and my daughter concluded she was a lesbian. But this passed. Her daughter has a boyfriend now!

Many say that Boomers have too much 'stuff' and possessions. What about you?

Again, I never strived to own things. But we do have a lot of junk. You never know when you might need it! I do have a 1968 Rambler, a cool little car, but it just sits there. We have 2 licensed trucks, a car and van, and six licensed and insured motorcycles. Like all Americans, we are drowning in 'stuff'. Both the missus and I swear we need to divest, but we can't seem to do so. I guess I will let my kids deal with all this junk when we are gone.

How important is education today versus when you were growing up?

Education is important and never ending. Formal education, however, with its focus on indoctrination is as evil as Satan himself. Put yourself scores, nay, hundreds of thousands of dollars in debt, learning how to hate your country. I would cite myself as an example. I opted for a blue-collar career and the freedom it offered, and ended up happy and loving the country which provided me the opportunities that I passed on.

How about health insurance, is it a good value for you and does it cover what you need?

We have good insurance through the union, but it costs $700 per month for both of us, so it ought to be good. I cannot think of a time the health industry let me down.

What about social security and the upcoming problem of funding given so many beneficiaries, namely Boomers?

I was pleasantly surprised when social security was still available when I qualified three years ago. I paid off and on since I was 17, but never expected I would reach 62 or get any money when I did. I think in order to save social security, we should return it to its original purpose, to serve as a safety net for the aged and infirmed. I think it is an abomination that the wealthy who want for naught draw from it. Most Americans do not begrudge the poor, and don't object to paying into a fund for the indigent.

What do you think of the media today versus when you were young?

The Fourth Estate is a sacred calling. Just as the military protects us from foreign assault, so does the press have an honorable calling to protect us from governmental outrage. Tragically, journalism is basically dead in this country. Every news story and every news show are written or spoken to advance one political viewpoint or another. I love playing with words, and it is so easy to recognize the malfeasance of the charlatans. I don't know what the answer is, but by sacrificing their integrity on the altar of partisan politics, they've endangered the very people they are supposed to be protecting. What happens if a REAL virus is loosened on our country which would kill much more than 1% of the population? I'm certainly not going to heed the warnings of specific broadcasters, as they have proven themselves liars.

What about race and gender equality today versus when you were growing up?

Racism was all but dead in this country until the democrat party realized that it could be used to political advantage, and it's been 'Katie Bar the Door' ever since. They changed the definition of racism to exclude BIPOCs, as only white people can be racist now. The media is right in the middle of it, making up stories of white supremacy in police ranks when some hood reaches for a gun and gets shot, even if the cop was black. So, I would say things were pretty good until the media started to use this as a tool to divide the working class.

Black Lives Matter set back race relations probably as much as the KKK back in the 1920's. We can only imagine how blacks felt about the Klan, but you only need to ask working class white people how they feel about being blamed for all the past misdeeds of past generations, or being vilified by the government or media as vile racists from birth. Not one dares protest out of fear of public crucifixion, but the hardening of hearts and attitudes is there nonetheless. The wounds of the past were nearly healed when some took to the streets burning, because they could, and the pundits excused their thievery as the fault of systemic racism with nary a concern for the victims. The vice-president of the U.S. urged all to contribute to funds for the bail of the rioters!

What about the borders? Should we allow more immigrants in or tighten the security of our borders?

Our ancestors, you know, the white colonizing supremacists, worked to establish a country for their descendants. Americans have it wonderfully cushy here, full employment, accessible medical care, plenty of food. So why should we have all that and the rest of the world, not? Let's open our borders and welcome our international brothers and sisters in. So, what happens to that cushy lifestyle that our forefathers worked to establish? What happens to my union laborer job when my company hires immigrants for less than they paid me? I think U.S. immigration should be significantly restricted, and I support a border wall and whatever security is required to maintain its integrity. There should be a pathway to citizenship for those already here, it would be impossible to locate all of them now. Pretty much the same pathway as legal immigrants. There are thousands pouring across our southern border, while the White House prattles on about the integrity of the Ukraine border. WHAT?

How did you deal with Covid-19?

The 'Yellow Peril' wreaked havoc on friendships. The missus and I agreed to give it one year and see what developed. We have landed in diametrically opposed conclusions. She's absolutely terrified of it, and I am not. I reached my conclusion well before the year was up, in the summer of 'Burn, Loot, and Murder'. Someone recorded a protest rolling by a hospital, from within the hospital. There were people in scrubs, who admittedly could have been kitchen or housekeeping employees, but I assumed them to be front-line workers, battling the equivalent of the bubonic plague. Anyway, the hospital workers were out front of the hospital applauding all the unmasked protesters marching by. Now, it's either a deadly disease or it's not. If the people who deal with it on a daily basis didn't see any danger in thousands of people screaming in each other's faces, then neither do I. But my wife doesn't want to risk socializing as we used to.

In looking back over your life, how do you feel about it and what you accomplished?

It is not like I have a series of monumental accomplishments to relate. Overall, I'd say my greatest success was that I lived life on my terms and now, much nearer to the end than the beginning, I have few regrets and most importantly, I feel I'm happy. My primary feeling is gratitude. As I told my youngest a few years ago, 'I'm ready to die right now. I don't WANT to, you understand, but it's been such a very good life, I don't have any right to expect more of it.' I'll damn sure take all I can get, though. God has been exceptionally good to me. Also, I pretty much ooze positive energy, a knack I've passed on to my kids. Maybe a small thing, but I believe it's still important. I ceaselessly try to brighten people's day whether with a smile, kind word, or compliment. I take pride in my small role as an ambassador of goodwill and the knowledge that after I'm gone, it will live on three-fold.

What is his greatest source of pride?

What I am most proud of is how my kids turned out. They had a hard row to hoe, raised by a single hillbilly biker dad, but they were such great kids that no matter how hard it seemed at the time, in hindsight, I miss it. They were hard but good times.

What will others say about him after he is gone?

I am pretty sure there will be some acknowledgement of my parenting skills and some are sure to mention 'he was one ridin' sonofabitch'. Maybe 'such a nice guy' or 'good man', which really, is all anyone can hope for.

How about the second amendment and guns?

Any thinking person who looks at what our government is doing today should support the second amendment. Any major city run by Democrats is decriminalizing crime and eviscerating law enforcement, leaving the citizenry to protect itself the best it can. All while striving to impose gun control on the people being victimized by their ludicrously inept policies. How's that stupid saying go? 'If you shoot someone for stealing your stuff, you value your stuff more than someone's life.' I love the rejoinder – 'If you steal my stuff, you value my stuff more than you value your life!'

What about green initiatives?

Certainly, I think carbon emissions should be kept as low as possible without throwing thousands out of work or having to burn furniture to stay warm. I don't think China or any of the developing nations take it seriously at all. I don't think any of the reigning activists do either or they would have their conferences on Zoom meetings instead of flying halfway across the world. Hypocrites all of them.

Are taxes too high or too low?

Certainly, we are taxed far too much. I suppose the wealthy who can afford tax accountants can afford to keep proportionately more of their earnings, but good for them. I understand the need to have taxes to fund the military, but beyond that, my time with the Libertarian party kicks in with the simple axiom 'taxation is theft'. Just look at the American Dream, owning your own house, being king of your castle. But just miss a few payments on property tax, and you will find out who the REAL king is!

How about politician pay levels and term limits? Should they be able to accept speaking fees and book fees while in office?

Political service on any level should be a privilege and an honor, not a career of self-enrichment. A pension for a one-term congressman is ridiculous, and another reason why our taxes are so high. Term limits should have been written into the constitution, since the existing politicians will not pass legislation against their own interests. We're just stuck with the same Senate and House leaders until the collapse of the Republic. No politician should be able to profit from anything related to their office. Under my system of no pension for a few months of service, they would be free to make all the money they wanted once they left office. On a scale of 1-10, I would rate them a '1', and only because there are a few who I greatly respect. They are close to being in negative numbers.

How about government programs? Do we need more of them or fewer? What about enforcement for the programs we have?

As I said before, we need far fewer programs. As far as enforcing the rules of these programs to pursue those who are cheating or abusing the programs, I would force all recipients of these programs to work in some fashion. Community service is a joke, but at least it is something. If you can draw a check for doing NOTHING then why would anyone do ANYTHING? If people had to work, they might say 'well, hell, if I have to work, I may as well get a job.' And force the deadbeats on the dole to help screen those applying for benefits.

How serious is the national debt?

What is the national debt? $30 trillion? I don't know what a trillion is, but I do know that you cannot keep writing checks when there is no money in their account, so just let the politicians keep driving up their personal fortunes and driving down our country until the inevitable happens.

Why are our politicians so divided today?

Back in the day, there was a saying about 'the loyal opposition', where each party had its own ideas how to improve the country. There no longer is a loyal opposition. I wondered what happened to the Hippies and Yippies and similar groups. Now it is obvious that they entered politics, education, and academia. We now have politicians bemoaning 'systemic racism', and academia publishing nonsense about Caucasian babies being racists and school boards promoting genderless bathrooms. There is no loyal opposition because the opposition is not loyal, they hate America and seeks only its destruction.

How would you describe yourself politically?

Through my life I've run the gamut from anarchist to libertarian to blue-collar socialist to whatever I am now. Pretty conservative, I guess, although I still cringe when I hear conservatives blasting the relaxation of cannabis laws – it's a plant, dude! Throughout history, there have been rich people and poor people. The difference in the time that we live is that the poor people are fat! All the pissin' and moanin' about poverty and hunger, look at the people going to the food banks. There's never been a better time and place to be alive if you are dirt poor. Sure, I would have liked to have more money when I was raising the kids, but I didn't so I had to settle for the love of my family. Poor me!

How about his relationship with friends today?

I once presented my kids with a wall plaque quoting the film 'Wyatt Earp' – 'Blood is all that matters. All the rest are just strangers.' I've always had a great many of what I call 'small F' friends. I like everybody and if we're friendly to one another, you're my friend. CLOSE friends, the ones who would understand your life story, are very few. A man's struggles should be borne by him.

What about his philosophy of life?

The whole point of my life was to avoid challenges. I know my attitude is pretty much universally frowned upon, but the path of least resistance has always been my preferred route. The challenge of living without 'my rock' and overnight going from the distant father to being the Mom AND Dad was plenty enough challenge for me, thanks.

What are some of the most important lessons you have learned in life?

A few of my dad's axioms I have never forgotten are:

1. The best place to find a helping hand is at the end of your arm.

2. A poor man HAS to keep his word. It's the only thing of value he has.

I would also say that I remember how my freshman English teacher brought in a recording of 'Desiderata', and it changed my life. Not then of course, but I never forgot it and when I was older, I looked it up again and was re-amazed at the timeless truths is contained. I would also encourage our youth to go primitive for a year. To go live in the woods, with no electricity, and learn to grow your own food. Basically, to learn basic survival skills, because we just don't know how bad it might get in this country.

Did Boomers leave this country in better shape than when they were young?

Boomers, in hindsight, didn't position things too well. But who could have anticipated the collapse of journalism or the depths of corruption in politics and the courts?

What about the younger generations and their reported affection for socialism over capitalism?

I am not vehemently anti-socialist as far as workers go. Much of the progress made in the past decades was due to the struggles of the working class to improve or establish some social programs. But what is being discussed today is an entirely different animal. Most labor leaders today recognize that we NEED successful profitable businesses to provide good jobs. What's passing for socialism today is a bunch of spoiled brats who never worked a day in their lives, and don't intend to. They demand that those who did work and profit from that work, be stripped of their wealth, and that they keep getting free stuff. What these fools are advocating today is more like Soviet or Chinese control of everything. Remember where that took the Soviet Union.

If he was on his death bed, and someone from the younger generation was there, what would he tell them about the meaning of life?

Again, I would refer them to 'Desiderata', it covers every situation you're ever going to encounter and while it doesn't give you any answers, it does lend guidance on how to conduct yourself when faced with life's challenges.

SUMMARY

In reviewing Jesse's life, and especially his current thoughts about what is going on in the world today, I find it an amazing story. He is definitely NOT a typical Boomer.

I had to challenge myself to try to imagine what would have happened to my self-image had I lost a mother at age 2, been given to foster care during key years of learning and development, had my caretaker die when I was only 10 years old, then lived with a single parent who was not at home all that much due to working, and one that did not care to listen to what was going on in my life. Then I had to imagine how I would have developed given the lack of direct parental guidance, replaced by readings and popular movements at that time such as Abbie Hoffman. Perhaps Jesse's rebellious spirit in those early years was fueled by a subconscious feeling of 'life has not been fair to me'.

Then life hit him with more tough times *after* a very difficult childhood. How could you expect anyone to emerge as well-adjusted after spending a year in prison with some career criminals, then losing your 'rock', your ideal partner spouse, to drugs? How would any of us cope with having to raise three young children alone without help from a partner? But well-adjusted, at least to me, is what Jesse is, and more.

In preparing for my interview with Jesse, I had virtually memorized his 30 pages of hand-written notes, and the first thing I said to him was 'Dude, you ought to be so proud of how you have done in life given so many things going against you!'

Here is a guy who has learned so many of life's lessons the hard way. He has transmogrified himself over and over throughout his life, as he stumbled upon new philosophies and new life lessons as he went along. Above all, in his words, he listened to everyone he talked to, because 'everyone has something to say and deserves to be heard'. All that listening translated into deep thought, and that deep thought has resulted in a man who strikes me as wise beyond his 65 years!

I cannot find any fault in his logic, given his assumptions, what he has observed, and what he has read. In writing his story, I found myself nodding in agreement at his observations most times, and cringing a bit because we have all become so accustomed to reading and hearing politically correct language. His thoughts and notes were refreshing to say the least, given what comes out of our TV shows and media today, and what comes out of most discussions, out of fear of being labelled in some way due to speaking the real truth.

I am so fortunate that at this later stage of life, I got to know Jesse a bit better, and can appreciate his story, his life, and the personality that is him. Had I not undertaken writing this book, I would have missed out on a real treat for me, and missed out on the opportunity to re-think how I see the world. I hope in some small way, I have become his 'small F friend'. I hope you can appreciate him too.

CHAPTER 3:
Dr. Lawrence J. Marks, the Marketing Professor Who Championed Distance Learning

BACKGROUND

I first met Dr. Lawrence J. Marks during the latter part of my career. I was involved with a university faculty / student / business group advising about the information technology curriculum and direction. Somehow, I discovered that Larry, as head of the Marketing department, was seeking experienced business leaders for interviews. It turned out that during these interviews, he recorded the sessions, and then shared them with students over future years. The questions were all related to marketing.

I found the questions excellent, and I thought that what he was doing was innovative and very productive. The genius of his approach was that he was injecting very current, real-world situations and cases into his class content, mixing the theory of marketing with the real-world application of marketing principles. And by recording the sessions, they could be re-used repeatedly. I still occasionally run into someone who says something like 'I remember listening to you in Professor Marks class!'

I believe that his life story is interesting, as he had extensive experience in the 'trifecta' of the military, business, and academia. What he has to say about the university environment during his time there is insightful and enlightening.

EARLY YEARS

Larry was born in 1947 in Pittsburgh, Pennsylvania, at the very beginning of the Boomer generation. Larry describes his parents' status as lower white-collar, with his father working as a draftsman and his mother as a secretary. Both were Depression-Era children, and money was always a concern in the family. However, education for the children was a priority, although Larry does not recall why his parents were so adamant about college, even though neither of them held a degree. He and his younger brother were able to attend college paid partially by his parents' savings.

Daniel Muller

"In our youth, one day my dad walked my brother and me to the local jail cell, just to show us what happened to us if we would get into trouble. So, I was never really a trouble-maker and don't recall ever getting into any serious problems."

"My father was a World War II Marine, and I grew up with stories about the war which gave me a strong sense of patriotism. My parents were active with the Cub Scouts, my mom was a Den Leader and my dad became a Scout Master. Under my dad's tutelage, our Cub Scout group marched in the local Memorial Day parade with toy rifles and did various drills during the parade. Most, but not all, parents liked this."

At the time he was growing up, the perceived threat of a nuclear war was quite high. Larry remembers feeling anxious about this, and recalls doing 'duck and cover' drills in school, where students were instructed to duck under their desks and to take cover, apparently in a drill to help prepare in the event that a nuclear warhead was on its way. "Everyone remembers participating in fire drills in school, these were similar."

"My Dad was quite a do-it-yourselfer, and I spent a good deal of time helping him with various projects, early on as a 'go-fer' and later as a participant. I was never as proficient as he was with projects, but did become comfortable using home shop tools. These skills proved helpful later in college when I made use of them in the theatre and many times since as a homeowner."

His parents stressed the importance of chores, including washing/drying dishes, weeding the garden, mowing the lawn, and assisting with things like cleaning out the gutters. Later, Larry took over a paper route in the neighborhood and enjoyed earning his own money. "I took pride in providing good service to my customers AND in my tenacity when it came to collecting for the service."

His father was a disciplinarian, especially when he was young. He knew the right way to do things and wanted them done correctly. As was typical in that time period, corporal punishment was accepted. So, the occasional use of a belt to bring home a point was not unheard of. "But NOT in an abusive way."

However, one incident did affect their relationship significantly. "As a mouthy young teen, I was unhappy with my father about something and used an expression which did not have much significance to me at the time. I said, "Darn you...." to him. He walked up to me and gave me an open-hand slap to the face. I was stunned and asked what that was all about. He told me to look up the word "darn," that it meant "damn," and that I was most certainly not to "damn" him. On the one hand, he was correct. On the other hand, as a young teen, I felt this was unfair in the extreme. This incident resulted in a cooling in our relationship which lasted well beyond its time, into adulthood."

Per Larry, his mother also could be hard to please, and he did grow up feeling that nothing he did would be good enough, as his efforts would often be criticized.

"My parents differed quite a bit from one another in terms of personalities and interests. So, when I was growing up, there could be a good deal of arguing and tension in the house. To this day, I do not like getting into loud arguments."

Since his parents experienced the Great Depression, how did their attitudes and behaviors surrounding money and habits affect him?

"My wife has provided some insight into this. She notes that I am fiscally conservative and do not like to throw anything away, which she attributes to my parents' Depression Era upbringing. Certainly, my dad had a strong belief in re-using things rather than throwing them away. As a do-it-yourselfer, if an appliance was not working, we would try to repair it. If we were taking nails out of boards, we would straighten them out for reuse later. He had cabinets with containers of nuts, bolts, screws (that occasionally I needed to sort) from old projects. While not to the same extreme, I DO like to save things for some unknown future use rather than throw them away."

His parents were both strong supporters of the Democratic Party, feeling that the party's social programs provided much needed support for people like his family. In his younger voting years, Larry leaned Republican, but later came to support the Democrats for pretty much the same reasons as his parents.

In different ways, both of his parents contributed to the community as members and leaders of various organizations. "My Dad raised funds via "walks" for the Democratic Party and cures for illnesses. My focus has been more on my work, and my community support has been more financial than an investment of time."

HIGH SCHOOL YEARS

In high school, Larry describes himself as 'a bit of a geeky and cheeky kid, and not much of an athlete.'

His best memories involve the group of guys that he connected with, and his high school girlfriend, who was a part of the group. "I did eventually get involved in track (cross country and "flat track") but was only average as a runner."

His worst memories of that time are of physical altercations of one kind or another. One time, someone had plugged up a water fountain nozzle so that when it came on, it sprayed into the person's face. "I unplugged it, and as I walked away, two students, slammed me up against a locker and let me know to not mess around with their pranks. Another time, I had begun to share my lunchtime candy with another student in my class. Eventually this sharing became a bit much so I told him I was stopping. After class, as I was walking away, he tapped me on the shoulder and sucker-punched me in the face, chipping a tooth."

"I would not be interested in going back to high school to relive those days. While there were certainly good times, I do not look back and think 'boy, those were the glory days.'"

If he had to relive that time period and do something different, Larry indicates that he would take academics a bit more seriously and develop better study habits. "Of course, it is mildly amusing that the only high school class I ever failed was French, and I ended up marrying a woman who loves French! Life is funny."

Larry graduated from high school in 1965.

ON TO COLLEGE

His personality and his family background resulted in Larry being quite independent and leaving home as soon as it was practical. "While I did get accepted into the University of Pittsburgh, a very good school, I chose a less prestigious college to get away from home. It all worked out fine, but I often say that I left home when I was 17, even though it was still my permanent residence and where I spent my summers until I graduated and went into the Army."

Given his father's career in drafting, Larry thought architecture might be a career for him, but was not accepted into any architecture schools, but he did get accepted into an engineering degree program.

"As is true for many students making the transition from high school to college, I was not prepared for the homework and independent work needed to succeed. In my first semester, I joined the Pershing Rifles, as this organization aligned nicely with my thoughts about the military and patriotism, but my first semester grades were not up to the organization's requirements, and I was dropped from the organization. These results got me thinking about whether engineering/architecture was a good fit for me. A trip to the Career Counseling office brought up several areas of interest including teaching and business. I was not interested in the idea of teaching, and noted that business did not require a second language, so I switched to a business major and learned to apply myself to academic work a bit better."

While in college, Larry wanted to work in one of the steel mills in the summers in Pittsburgh, but had no connections there. He did land a summer job with a downtown department store handling stock in the women's fashion shoe department. He was able to return to that job over several summers during his college years.

In the 1960's many universities had ROTC (Reserve Officers Training Corps) as a required course for the first two years of a male student's curriculum.

[https://www.beaconjournal.com/story/lifestyle/around-town/2019/01/21/a-salute-to-rotc/6243374007/]

"In 1967 I entered my junior year and needed to decide whether to continue with ROTC or to take my chances with the draft. Given my background, and my assumption that I could be drafted, I opted to continue with the Army ROTC program. My thinking was that this choice would give me some options that being drafted would not offer, plus ROTC students received a $100 a month stipend."

About this time, Larry became involved in the University's theatre area. Many of the theatre students were anti-war, and he had the amusing situation of marching back from ROTC drills with his theatre friends protesting the war on the way, and then joining the group for theatre activities later in the day. "Our viewpoints about military service and the Vietnam war differed. At the time, I subscribed to the "domino theory" of Communism, wanting to help save Vietnam and other countries from being consumed by Communism. Given my background, I felt that serving would be the right thing to do."

His connection with the theatre group was a happy one, working on stagecraft (set building, lighting, sound, acting, stage managing) and enjoying the social interactions with the theatre students.

"The experience I had with the theatre helped me to get engaged with groups later in life in Huntsville, Alabama, and after the Army back in Ohio. It may have played a part in developing my teaching 'stage presence.'"

In the summer of 1968 between his junior and senior year, he attended training at Indiantown Gap Military Reservation in Pennsylvania. He graduated from college as a Distinguished Military Student/Graduate and was offered a position in the Regular Army, which he declined.

In 1969 he graduated with a Bachelor of Science degree in Industrial Management. But before beginning his tour of duty, that summer he completed a cross-country camping trip with a theatre friend from college, visiting a variety of cities including Indianapolis, St. Louis, New Orleans, Dallas, Phoenix, and San Francisco, plus ended up in Los Angeles for several weeks. "My friend had this great convertible, and we loaded up all our stuff from campus to return home after graduation, with the intent to start our trip the next day. We stopped in Pittsburgh to have a bite, as it was late, and we went into a Jewish deli. When we came out, the car was gone, with all our stuff gone too! Luckily my brother knew some people who figured out who had stolen the car, and somehow my parents funded the buying of the car back from the thieves. The car was damaged and was on blocks, but we managed to get it repaired and ready for our trip."

During his trip, he ran out of money, as the job that he and his travel partner had anticipated getting did not pan out. He had to call his parents for help to continue the trip. Finally in LA, he landed a job to start generating some income. "I got a position with a restaurant. This restaurant concept was a luxury hamburger chain, in Beverly Hills. In the time I was there, I quickly worked from making the sandwiches (bun man) to making the burgers (grill man) which I felt was quite an honor."

In August, he returned home to begin his service as a 2nd Lieutenant, and was assigned the position of Ammunition Supply Officer.

His training began at Aberdeen Proving Grounds in Maryland, then moved to Ammunition Supply School at Redstone Arsenal in Huntsville, Alabama. He was then assigned to a company on the base that was being deactivated, so there was little to do. "That did not appeal to me, so I asked around and was able to get a position teaching ammunition storage in the program which I had just completed."

ON TO VIETNAM

In August of 1970, during the Vietnam war, he was assigned to the 661st Ordnance Corps stationed in Chu Lai, Vietnam, which was the headquarters for the Americal Division. He was brought into the company along with a new captain, first sergeant, and transportation officer to replace the existing cadre who had not been able to manage the company well. "By chance, I had actually trained the new captain while he was at the Ammunition Supply School at Redstone Arsenal."

Many of the men in the 661st had previous problems with their military service, and some had come from detention in Long Binh military stockade. So, the company had discipline problems. "On the first night our new leadership group had settled in, someone "fragged" the First Sergeant's sleeping area." (Fragging describes a situation when a soldier threw a fragmentation hand grenade into someone's sleeping area in attempt to kill them either because the person was seen as being incompetent or seen a being a threat to the status quo. It might be done out in the field or at the home base or barracks.) "In this case, our new First Sergeant was unharmed, but that was quite a welcome to the company."

With that incident, the base commander gave the company troops one day of 'amnesty' to turn in any illegal ordnance, weapons, etc. that they had in their possession. A 55-gallon drum was set up on the basketball court. The next day, the drum was overflowing with ammunition, explosive, hand grenades, and weapons, and the rumor was that some of the troops had buried illicit goods in the sand around the compound.

"To establish order, the captain requested that I stroll the barracks in the evenings to show we were 'present.' We then were allowed to remove up to 10 men who were deemed the biggest problems. Inasmuch as we were new to the situation, we did interviews among the more reliable people, drew up a list and were able to have those identified as ringleaders removed, but not without some threats to our personal safety."

"The captain was a disciplinarian, which was what the initial situation called for. Based on various misbehaviors, it was not uncommon for him to issue Article 15 punishments."

(An Article 15 is considered non-judicial punishment, meaning that it is not considered a judicial proceeding. Non-judicial punishment is a military justice option available to commanders. It permits commanders to resolve allegations of minor misconduct against a soldier without resorting to higher forms of discipline, such as a court-martial.)

"However, in an odd twist of military judgment, the company was told that it had issued too many Article 15's. That set up a situation which encouraged undesirable behavior."

After a few months, the company was assigned to a new storage facility that was being left by the Marines. This entailed several very long days and nights of moving tons of ammunition from one storage site to another and a change of company location.

"Not long after our move, the captain's barracks was fragged. He was unharmed, but the tin roof was filled with holes. The individual responsible for the incident had let others know of his plan, then executed the plan, and then told others what he had done. One person let us know who the culprit was. However, as no one had seen the person in the act, no action was taken, and the person who reported the details was transferred out for his own safety. This approach to the situation was certainly frustrating."

"I was fortunate in that Chu Lai was a fairly safe environment. There was the occasional rocket launched on the base and some nights when we were put on high alert, but I rarely felt in personal danger. I did take on the attitude held by many in Vietnam that 'if your time was up there was little that you could do about it' and so there was no point in worrying about it."

Other than working daily at a supply point with many thousands of tons of ammunition stored, the most dangerous part of his job was helping in the demolition of 'bad' ammunition. Over time, some ammunition lots were determined to have problems, and it was accumulated and stored. "So, under the supervision of an explosive ordnance disposal warrant officer, we would load up one or more 5-ton trucks, go into the hills outside of the base, use a bull dozer to dig a hole, load the ammo into the hole, and blow it up. I would ride with the ammunition in the back of the truck and certainly knew that if one rocket were shot into the load there would be little left of the ammo, the truck, or me.

The typical tour in Vietnam was for a year, but it was possible to get out a bit early if you had been accepted into a graduate school. It was always his plan to continue his education with a Master's degree, so he applied to a program, got accepted, and departed Chu Lai after 11 months in September 1971.

In reflecting back on his military stint, Larry feels fortunate about his assignment there. "I was fortunate that my job was a hot, rainy, sandy office job, more or less. So, I did not have traumatic experiences. When I went into the military, I did feel that I was acting 'for God and country'. Hearing about the My Lai massacre certainly made me wonder what we were doing there, but, I do not think at the time it changed my mind. We were there to do good. It was only later, in the face of 'new to me' facts and reality, that I changed my perspective."

Do others who did not serve in the military appreciate the sacrifices of those who served? "To show appreciation, we should be sure that things like the G.I. Bill are in place, and we should improve the V.A. Hospital system to be very high quality and should include programs for mental illness, drug problems, PTSD, etc. We should fully fund job training programs for those who need it. Those actions would show appreciation and thanks."

ON TO A CAREER

"In addition to having the support of the G.I. Bill, I was lucky enough to have a graduate assistantship in my Master's program. Although I had a focus on Management, I was assigned to the Marketing Department. My assistantship duties included grading papers for an instructor and occasionally filling in for him in the classroom. I ended up developing a good friendship with the chair of the department, and along with another graduate assistant, worked on a significant marketing research project for the city. This work clearly became a foundation for my eventual career."

After earning his master's degree, his vision for his early career was that he would work in industrial management, perhaps starting on a manufacturing shop floor somewhere and working his way up the corporate ladder. "But, in fact, I never stepped onto a manufacturing plant floor. When I graduated with my Masters in June of 1973, the US was in a recession and manufacturing jobs were few." After typing up and sending out 100 application letters (this was before home computers and email) he found a position selling business computers. "It was not what I thought I would be doing, but it was a job, and I had an understanding of customer satisfaction from my time as a graduate assistant in the marketing department."

"While I had the attitude that we should deliver what we promised when we made the sale, I discovered that my attitude was a bit naïve. On one occasion during a cold call on a business I would find out that the business was suing ours because we had not delivered what they were promised. When I made a sale of a complex system and found that the programming was not right, I stayed with the customer and re-worked the programming to deliver what was promised. This was not the intended role for salespeople, and management was not pleased that I was not out getting new business. After over three years, where I had a fair amount of success in sales, we decided that we were not a good fit for one another."

Larry had stayed in touch with the chair of the marketing department from his graduate work, and the chair suggested that he should apply to a Ph.D. program in Marketing. "I had not thought about that as a career path and did not pursue the idea very far at that time. Instead, I applied for position as a sales forecaster with an appliance company. As my Master's thesis project, I had written an elaborate program to predict economic cycles, and this foundation along with my experience with computer sales appealed to the appliance company management. I was brought on board to do sales forecasting in their marketing research department. After working with sales forecasting, I was offered the opportunity to work on industry research reports, then to do focus group research for new microwave panel ideas. So, once again, I found myself in the marketing area. I found the marketing research work interesting but soon tired of the repetitive nature of sales forecasting."

After about a year with the appliance company, the chair of the marketing department called and asked if he would consider a one-year full-time teaching appointment in the department, for better pay, and he accepted.

"I enjoyed my year of teaching marketing, and was pretty good at it. I felt as though I was having a positive impact on the students in the classes. At the end of the year, the department chair once again suggested that I consider a Ph.D. in marketing, and with this experience under my belt it seemed like a good idea." So, Larry was accepted into a Ph.D. program with an assistantship.

"Once in the Ph.D. program, I discovered a few things. First, I was no longer one of the smartest people in the room, and second, I would need to decide on an area within marketing as a focus. Strategy? International? Logistics? Consumer Behavior? In my undergraduate program I had an affinity for psychology, and my research with the marketing department and the appliance company had focused upon consumers and their behavior. This became my area of focus."

As a graduate student, Larry worked with several different faculty members in differing roles, as a research assistant and a teaching assistant, including eventually working with the professor who taught Principles of Marketing.

"As I wrapped up my 4th year in the program, I had the good fortune of being invited to work with two faculty members on a research paper that eventually got published in a top-rated journal. I was still working on my dissertation, so I stayed on for one additional semester as a part-time instructor of marketing. I applied for full-time faculty positions and had several offers, deciding on a rather prestigious private school in California."

Moving from a large, public, land-grant institution to a private school proved to be a bit of a shock. Larry related well to the students at the public university but had a disconnect with those at the private school. "My style of teaching, which had received good ratings previously, did not work well. In one class evaluation, a student criticized my choice of ties (of all things). So, I had a bit of a challenge. I was still working on completing my dissertation, my teaching style needed improvement, and apparently so did my wardrobe."

Larry was able to improve his teaching evaluations, complete his dissertation, and connect with another young faculty member on another research project which resulted in a second top-rated journal publication. However, this level of productivity did not meet the university's standards, and he was told that he might want to look around for another position as the likelihood of him getting promoted and tenured was very low.

Sometimes when people get this sort of news, they disconnect from their work, but that was not Larry's nature. "I sustained my teaching and research and continued to provide appropriate service to the department. I was quite pleased that the chair let me know that he recognized and appreciated my continuing efforts in my last time there."

During his time at his Ph.D. program, Larry met a lovely woman who was working on a Master's degree in French and then in Public Administration. "She had spent a year studying in France, was a member of the "county club set" in Washington, D.C. and, oddly, seemed a bit interested in me."

One of Larry's classes was jointly taught as a graduate/undergraduate class. Several undergraduate women in the class made it a personal challenge to get the Ph.D. students to go out for drinks. "We resisted that for quite a while, but when we had a make-up class held in a room above a bar (I don't know if that would be permitted today), there was not a way to avoid the invitation. It was a fun event and the Ph.D. students, myself included, and the undergraduate women became "drinking buddies."

The women were all in a sorority, and they were having their Spring Formal. They invited the Ph.D. students to join them. Larry was not inclined to do that, but one of the other Ph.D. students said he would go. "I agreed to go and was set up with one of the sorority sisters who had graduated the previous year and wanted to come back for the event. Amusingly, the other Ph.D. student did NOT go, BUT ended up marrying the undergraduate woman who invited him. Of course, my blind date was Susan, and we began dating the following year when she returned to school to earn her Master's degree."

After a few challenges, they married in 1984 and soon moved to Ohio. "She was 8 ½ months pregnant with our first child as we made the move from California to our new home at a university in Ohio. Our daughter was one of the first births at the newly established Kaiser Permanente in the area, in 1986."

After settling into their new environment, Larry found out that the improvements he had made in research and teaching worked out well. His class evaluations were quite good, he had two top-level publications to his credit, and other research under way. "As a result, I received a promotion to Associate Professor and tenure early after three years."

The next year, Larry and his wife had a second child, a son. Larry describes his parenting style:

"In my younger years, I was not a warm fuzzy fellow. I had strong opinions about what was right and wrong and wanted others, including my kids, to do what I considered to be right. I have mellowed quite a bit, but did not develop deep emotional connections with my kids when they were young, which I regret. Fortunately for my kids, my wife's view of child-rearing was different from what I considered appropriate given my upbringing. Early on she let me know that corporal punishment would not be used in our household. Today, my children and I have good adult relationships."

On the professional front, focused upon teaching, Larry enjoyed the opportunity to work with undergraduate students, students in the M.B.A and Executive M.B.A., and Ph.D. students. The feedback from each type of student reinforced the feeling that he was making a contribution to their success.

Two years after he was promoted/tenured, he became the chair of the department. The shift to a combined faculty/administrative role was not an easy one for him.

"Previously I had not needed to deal very much or very directly with bureaucracy. A chairperson's life is pretty much bound up in rules, policies, and directives from the university, the college dean, the department handbook, and so on. The chair also needs to deal with student issues, faculty issues, secretarial staff issues and to both represent the department's interest to the college dean while also representing the college's position to the department. Whew! Nothing in my prior experiences prepared me for these interactions."

Early in Larry's second term as department chair (which was a four-year term), a faculty member in another department suggested that he might be a good candidate for the open position of Associate Dean of the College. He ran for the position and got the appointment in 1996.

"The relatively new Dean and I had a very good working relationship. For one thing, in moving up in academia, the Dean had never been the chair of a department. So, with my experience I was able to give him that perspective. A major undertaking in my first two years involved assisting in putting together the 10-year report for reaffirmation of accreditation."

Larry was able to continue teaching during his 10-year term, primarily in the Ph.D. program. It was also during this time that he got involved in the College's International Business Experience (IBE). The IBE was developed by a faculty member who thought that since the Executive MBA program included an international trip, that it may be something of interest to regular MBA students. He developed the class as a two-week trip in May to university facilities in Geneva, Switzerland and then to Paris, France. When the faculty member wanted to move on to other responsibilities, he thought of Larry because he knew that his wife Susan had a strong interest in international travel in general and in France in particular. Larry says that if it had not been for his wife's strong support and encouragement, he might not have accepted this challenge.

"I accepted the opportunity and followed his basic approach to the trip, running it for 14 years. In each trip, I needed to arrange for hotels, train travel and visits to businesses, and cultural sites. In Switzerland, visits included the International Red Cross, the United Nations, the World Trade Organization, the International Labor Organization (ILO), the World Intellectual Property Organization, the Swiss Exchange, the Geneva Financial Center Foundation, the U.S. Embassy, the European Union Parliament, plus many larger corporations."

"Setting up all of the visits, the travel plans and keeping track of the students was an education in itself. I do not want to be a travel agent in any future career! Meeting with these businesses and organizations and going to the various cultural sites was not only interesting for the students but educational for me. I was able to bring those experiences back to campus. As a side benefit of these trips, my wife, and occasionally children, were able to come to Europe after the class and we were able to enjoy some personal travel. Back at the College, the dean had a strong interest in the accreditation agency (AACSB) and in working with an incubator program in the city. He needed to spend a good deal of time away from the college and, over time, Larry became the 'inside dean' dealing with budget and faculty affairs, along with the physical building.

"This meant that I needed to deal with some difficult internal situations, including telling a faculty member that a family member had died in an accident, and during a budget problem letting several staff members know that we would need to eliminate their positions. Nothing in my past experiences or Ph.D. program prepared me for these types of interactions."

DISTANCE LEARNING

An executive who had spent time as a business instructor in the College was kind enough to donate funds, along with his company, to help Larry and his team build one of two 'electronic classrooms.'

"Our team traveled around to see what 'distance learning classrooms' looked like at the time. We then oversaw the creation of two classrooms from which we offered courses from our program at an off-site college. Developing the room and teaching in this environment was an excellent learning experience for me." Since that time, Larry has continued to be a leader in applying leading technology to improve the online classroom experience for students.

In addition, the chair of the Marketing Department was interested in finding a new way to teach the Principles of Marketing class to both in-person students and to students on the web. He asked him to investigate potential approaches. "I liked an approach being used by Dr. Bruce Robertson at San Francisco State University and, with his permission, adapted it for use at our university. The adapted approach was to deliver the class in-person and to video the instructor (me) and record the computer screen (PowerPoint lecture slides, web sites, videos). Then after the in-person class, I edited those files together, rendered them, and made them available the same day to web-based students. The intent was to have students on the web see the class as though they had been in it."

This approach turned out to be very well accepted by the students and very efficient for the department. At times in the past, as many as 10 instructors, often adjunct professors, were teaching smaller sections of the class, all in-person. Using the new method, Larry was able to teach 200+ students in-person, in a large lecture room, and virtually an unlimited number of web-based students. "At its peak, I was able to successfully teach a combined class of 950 students."

That expertise proved quite useful as the COVID Pandemic crisis hit in 2020. On short notice, Larry was able to switch his lectures from a format where the in-person lecture was recorded, to doing the recording from his home office. The end product was very similar to what web-based students in prior semesters had been receiving!

Wouldn't this concept be extremely attractive to administration as a productivity boost (fewer paid professors to teach more students = higher profits or wages)? "The general reaction was positive by students and the department, but it was not a university-wide initiative, and I did not try to sell this approach across the rest of the university. The classroom solutions the University developed to deal with the Covid pandemic worked fairly well for students who were not allowed to be on campus. My approach of recording in-person lectures and making them available for students on the web works well in lecture-style courses, but probably would not work well in courses where high interactions were required."

So, in looking back over a university career as instructor, department chair, associate dean, and pioneer for online learning, how would you summarize your contributions, and is there anything you would do differently?

"As I reflect on my time as Associate Dean, I realize that I was, and continue to be, a task-oriented, hard-working individual, but I had a degree of emotional intelligence that could be better. My dean quickly realized that he should not ask for my opinion on a topic in a meeting with others unless he actually wanted to know it. In other meetings, my colleagues would say that I asked the hard questions that others wanted to, but were too politically savvy to give voice to."

In Larry's words, while others always knew what his thoughts and opinions on a topic were, this 'refreshingly blunt' approach to bureaucracy was not always well accepted and, as he now considers, may not have always benefited the College.

"After 10 years of administration, I decided that I had made as much contribution to that area as I was able to and decided to return to my faculty position. The Dean waited another year before following my example. As of December 2021, I have taught Principles of Marketing to over 19,000 students and based on feedback, have had a positive impact on their understanding of, and appreciation for the field."

Larry has no plans to retire soon, being 74 years old, and still enjoys the classroom experience. "As long as my faculties are solid and my student ratings are good, I plan to continue teaching."

After such a long career in various roles in education, in looking back, how important was Susan's support role?

"Susan has always been supportive of my career whether it was completing my dissertation, earning promotion and tenure, or engaging in administrative work. She has put up with my spending long hours at work, often including weekends, along with my bad moods due to the frustrations of administrative life, and with my often putting the work before the family. Fortunately, Susan was focused on the family even when she was working. She has been the family event planner, travel agent and trip planner. She dealt with the day-to-day household matters, and has been a great mother, supportive of the children, resulting in a wonderful relationship with them today."

In addition to working with students in traditional classes, Larry has also been involved in various Junior Achievement and Upward Bound programs.

POLLING FOR OPINIONS

So, in looking back over his life, what are the most important lessons he has learned that he might share with others?

I tell my students and my children 'don't lie, don't cheat, don't steal' in school, in your personal life, or in business. Said another way, be ethical! Too many people in politics and in business seem to have missed the message. Second, treat others with respect, and keep your promises. Third, be flexible. You never know where the future will take you and so you should be ready to adapt and adjust." But do his students today appreciate that their career paths will likely not match their expectations? "I believe there are segments of students who clearly understand this, while other majors do see more of a structured career path for themselves. I suppose my son has demonstrated flexibility in his career, when he changed companies in order to gain a particular experience, and encountered career challenges in doing so, but has pursued success.

(Just to exemplify this third lesson, consider the variety of responsibilities Larry held – he was an engineering major, then a business major. He was in the Army, in graduate school, sold computers, did forecasting and then marketing research, taught classes, earned a Ph.D. degree, was a department chair, associate dean, and then back to faculty.)

Besides those three lessons, how would you describe, for other generations, the meaning of life?

Doing the best that you can for your family, your community, your organization, and your country. Clearly, this will play out in different ways for different people depending on their abilities, opportunities, and interests, but that is what it is all about.

In observing the values of his children, core Millennials, how would he describe any differences between his views and theirs?

Our children's values are different in interesting ways. My daughter is a lawyer with a strong interest in helping the immigrant community. She works to get them immigration status and documented, to help them with social service issues involving their children, and with any problems they have with the law. She recently opened her own law practice to serve these clients. My son works in the financial arena and is interested in being financially successful as early in life as possible. They are both very hard workers with a good sense of ethics. My daughter's interest in social issues likely reflects my wife's views more than mine. It is not that I am dismissive of these, but it is not my focus. My son's interest in doing well financially (likely better than I have done) may be closer to my values. I have spent a good deal of my life focused on work.

<u>Compared to the relationship he had with his parents, how would he describe the relationships with his children?</u>

Although I have never been the warm and fuzzy parent, I feel that my relationship with both children is much better than what I had with my parents. Of course, in their adolescent years we butted heads quite a bit. But, as they moved into adulthood, we have developed solid, respectful relationships. They are, however, closer with my wife than they are with me.

<u>Do Larry and his wife help their children financially even as adults?</u>

We have occasionally helped our children financially. We have paid for them to be on family vacations (to the beach, on a cruise, to travel home for a visit), provided the occasional generous gift, and in some instances provided significant loans and are happy to do this. Although we are beyond the time when helping them to move residences is necessary, we certainly did that quite a bit. Our kids are intelligent and trustworthy, and we support them.

<u>What is he most proud of from the years raising his children?</u>

Both kids made excellent decisions in high school to get involved in special programs that allowed them to work with the community, to travel, and to broaden their horizons. They were comfortable and confident enough to travel abroad. Our daughter volunteered to work with an aid group in Arusha, Tanzania, and on other occasions travelled to Puerto Rico, Mexico, Australia and New Zealand. Both kids spent a college semester abroad in Geneva, Switzerland and had internships there. My son spent a summer traveling Europe with two friends, where he acted as the planner and director of the adventure.

<u>Does he believe that the generations following his will be better off, or worse off, financially when they get to his age?</u>

Any question dealing with forecasting the future is tough. I think that our kids will do quite well for themselves financially, but I do not know about the generations to come.

Will they live in a better country and world in the coming decades versus what he has experienced?

I have concerns about the whether the current divisiveness in our society will heal or continue. The rising nationalism in Russia and China do not bode well for the coming decades. The issues surrounding the environment may become more complicated and dire. Some experts feel that the U.S. may have peaked as an economic and political powerhouse and may be on a bit of a downward slope. So, I do have concerns for the future.

What will happen to your possessions after death?

We plan to leave our estate to our children.

What is your philosophy about dedication to your employer?

I am less concerned about my dedication to my employer than I am to my "client," whether that is a company buying a computer or a student's education.

Like many Boomers, was Larry thrifty in his early adult years?

My attitude was somewhat different in terms of spending. I never went into debt, but I also did not save much. As a bachelor, I spent what I had, but did not make use of credit cards to get in over my head. When I got married, my wife and I began saving money for retirement and our children's education. I was not thinking about a Great Depression but rather about having funds for future events.

How did the music of the 60's and 70's affect him?

My parents were not into music as I grew up. However, I enjoyed rock and roll and the Beatles and enjoyed dancing to the music. I liked the transition to Disco and had fun on the dance floor with that genre. Today I listen to pop music, but still prefer classic rock.

Boomers have a reputation for partaking of alcohol, what about him?

I enjoyed and continue to enjoy drinking beer/wine/alcohol. I drank a significant amount of beer in the Army, and in the years in which I was earning my Masters and Ph.D. These days that consumption has dropped off. A glass or two of wine in the evening or a couple of beers on the weekend are not unheard of. Some of my friends and I may have used marijuana, but we were not into any other drugs. Those experiences were fine and did not lead to any problems.

What about legalizing marijuana?

From my perspective, either decriminalizing or legalizing marijuana for both medical and recreational purposes is fine. I am sure that this will create some problems for some people, but much like Prohibition was not a good solution for alcohol and did not stop its use, the criminalization of marijuana has not been a workable solution. I am less sure about legalizing "other drugs." I am not sure which ones might be considered and what issues/problems they might bring.

How has the loss of loved ones changed you?

Two of my close college theatre friends passed before they were forty. That made me think about how lucky I had been to go to Vietnam, get back without any physical or psychological issues, and still be going strong. I think a feeling of gratitude for my situation describes my thinking, although I am not too sure how it affected my daily life. Both of my parents have passed. I think that the greatest impact that had on me was to reflect on the fact that I never fully moved beyond the angry teen attitude in my relationship with them.

How would Larry describe himself politically?

In my early years I was more conservative, influenced by my World War II Marine Dad's views. The Cuban missile crisis just proved we needed to be strong against Communism. I was in the military when the Kent State shooting happened and I do not remember being too concerned, at the time, about the situation, but my attitude has changed over the years. My attitudes were then influenced by the Nixon impeachment, Watergate, and the "fall" of Vietnam as I moved to more liberal thinking.

What is Larry's view of the press today?

I mostly trusted the press when I was growing up. I mostly trust the traditional media today. However, the networks' pandering to conspiracy theories, non-factual news, and unscientific views of the world are worrisome and not something that I recall from the past. Some networks have attempted to stay true to journalistic ideals, but I recognize that they work from imperfect information and so may not be able to present information that is entirely accurate.

What about 9/11? How did that change his thinking or attitudes?

Clearly it was a deep tragedy. I did not have a good awareness of the possibility of terrorism on our soil before 9/11. I was aware of terrorism at the Munich Olympics, Entebbe, the U.S. Embassy bombings in Kenya, etc., but did not connect them with the possibility of terrorism in the U.S. Being more aware of the issues in the Middle East and beyond has not made me smarter about what the cure might be for these complicated international issues.

Regardless of your race or gender, is there anything you would offer in terms of your thoughts about minority / women's / men's rights and equality? How would you compare our gender and race equality status now vs. your years growing up?

My attitude about these things is liberal. Some of my theatre friends were gay, but that did not keep us from being friends. There was most certainly strong prejudice against that community when I was young than there is today. When a director had a black student kiss a white one on stage it was a major controversy. This is no longer a big issue. So, I support the idea of equality for minorities, women, and the LGBTQ communities, but we have a very long way to go before there is true equality.

How does Larry view our U.S. immigration policy and how we manage our borders?

This is clearly a complex and divisive issue. Our current policies are not working well. While we need to be aware of criminal elements who want to take advantage of opportunities in the U.S., we need to recognize that the vast majority of immigrants on our Southern border are looking for honest work and better living conditions than they can possibly get in their home countries. We need a better immigration policy for those who are here and for those who want to come here.

Surveys show that non-Boomers are much more positive about socialism than Boomers. In fact, one study showed that Millennials and Gen Z think slightly more positively about socialism than capitalism. Why do you think that may be? How do you feel about socialism vs capitalism?

Many Millennials and Gen Z's feel that the success which Boomers had may not be available to them. They feel burdened with student debt and are not too sure that hard work will pay off. Capitalism has certainly treated different segments of society quite differently and there is the significant have and have-not split. If you feel that capitalism isn't working, then socialism (in the sense of government providing more and better social programs) looks good. These folks may not have the mental connection between repressive communism and socialism which many Boomers have. Personally, I think that a mixed economic system (which is actually what we do have in the U.S.) makes sense. The question is the balance between the public good and an individual's rights.

What about how our society deals with crime and felons?

Convicted felons who would want to go "straight" likely have little real chance to do so. They cannot vote, will find it hard to get legitimate work, and generally will find limited support systems. We should outlaw the death penalty. It is not effective in preventing capital offense crimes, and, more importantly, it is clear that innocent people have been put to death. With judicial judgment, repeat offenders should be subject to different penalties. But judges should have the ability to take circumstances into consideration.

How do you feel about the second amendment and gun rights?

There may not be too many guns in America, but there are most certainly too many guns in the wrong hands. In the U.S. gun-related killings are about 70% of all homicides. Compare this to 4% in England and Wales, 22% in Australia, and 39% in Canada. (https://www.bbc.com/news/world-us-canada-41488081).

I support background checks, control over non-retail sales of guns (at gun shows, for example), elimination of assault rifles, extended size magazines, and bump stocks."

How do you feel about the US role as being 'watchman of the world' and the significant capital being spent for global aid?

In general, I am in favor of our foreign aid. However, as is true of domestic programs, I feel there is likely significant waste, fraud, corruption, and misuse of dollars. Of course, there are domestic problems that need to be solved. But I do not think that we can only focus on domestic issues for both humanitarian and practical/political reasons. We need to do both. And, it goes without saying that Russia and China will be happy to use foreign aid to develop influence in any area which the U.S. chooses to ignore.

What are your feelings about green initiatives and the state of our planet?

Green initiatives are good. "Green-washing" by businesses is bad. The state of our planet is quite bad, with global warming being a serious threat to the world food supply, increasing ocean levels, causing severe weather, and more. The U.S. should be doing more and leading the way.

Do you feel that we are taxed too much or too little? Do you believe that the rich need to pay more or fewer taxes? Do you believe that the poor need to pay more or less taxes?

The rich pay too little taxes. The poor pay too much. The tax system is broken. In Congress, money talks a bit too much.

What about the political system and our politicians?

We want and need politicians with good skills. While people may have a sense of doing the right thing for the state or country, they still need to be compensated appropriately. However, when their pensions and benefits go far beyond what other members of society (and their constituents) can expect, there is a problem. Most politicians are much wealthier than their constituents. PACs, Super PACs, lobbyists and influencers who do not actually represent the constituents have too much power.

Why are politicians so divided? Has it really changed, or has it been like this for a long time?

Politicians have been divided for a very long time as they rightly or wrongly reflect the perspectives of their constituencies. Think about politics at the time of the Civil War, differing opinions about WW II (initially), the McCarthy era, Vietnam, Civil Rights, etc. I am not a scholar of how Congress works, but there has been disagreement in that body since its creation and there was actual violence on the floor prior to the Civil war.

The press talks a lot about the growing disparity in income – is that a big problem in your opinion?

Yes. The American Dream is becoming a nightmare for too many people. The disparity of income is growing. Just look at the wealth of the top 20 people in the country versus all else. Inflation is wiping out any advances in income growth, so younger generations likely are having a more difficult time than we were growing up. Having said that, my university students are not extremely vocal about this, my opinions are more based upon what I am reading generally.

<u>Do you think the country is headed in the wrong or right direction?</u>

"Given the divisiveness of recent years, our country is heading in the wrong direction. People ignoring science, news programs promoting false stories, politicians not being able to negotiate in good faith, all worry me. On the other hand, if I think about the state of the country when I was growing up, we had anti-war protests, the civil rights war, the killings of John and Robert Kennedy and Martin Luther King, Jr., the SDS, the riots in Watts, Chicago, Birmingham, Chicago. So it may be that the changes I see as problematic today are indeed just the current manifestation of our ever-changing culture.

SUMMARY

Larry's story is certainly different, diverse, and interesting. In my one-on-one interview with Larry, it was very enjoyable, more of a pleasant discussion than an interview. Larry repeatedly stated that he is blessed, and is a delight to talk to. He is Jewish, and is a Vietnam veteran, yet does not recall any harassment or discrimination of note due to either.

He shared insights into the university world in a way that let us know how things operate and how decisions are made, without being critical of anyone or any institution. In my view, he has dedicated his life to service of his 'customers' more-so than his employers. He continues to create value in society through his teaching, even though he is in his 70's. He has never been a trouble-maker (in his words), and has been, just in my view, a role model for many, both within his generation as well as younger generations. Larry and I share a passion for excellent customer satisfaction, which we both believe is the key to success in any enterprise.

Larry is reflective and thoughtful, and tends to see his weaknesses more than his strengths (unlike some people we all know), and is very well-spoken. He is very proud of his two children, even though they have taken very different career paths driven by very different goals. Larry went into much detail about both and their careers, and both would likely be the focus of a future book for some author, but I lack space in this chapter to detail those two careers!

Even though he is critical of himself as 'lacking any insight', I found Larry to be extremely insightful, and about as sharp mentally as any Boomer I have met. Unlike many in his generation, Larry continues to work (not that he has to financially), and to add value to society. I want to thank and recognize Larry for his life's work and what he has done, in his own way, to make this world a better place.

CHAPTER 4:
Debbie Mattern Weber, The Postmaster Who Digs Concerts

BACKGROUND

I first met Debbie in kindergarten or first grade at our local elementary school. I recall that her house was right across the street from the elementary school, that she had several sisters, and that her dad was called Red (family had red hair, so I assumed that is where the nickname came from) and her mother worked in the school cafeteria.

Throughout our school years, I got to know Debbie as primarily a very smart young lady, but our paths seemed to run in parallel with our tracks never crossing much, if at all. In high school, we were rarely in the same classes.

I lost track of Debbie after high school, but ran into her again at a class reunion 30+ years later. In a brief chat, I found out that she was the postmaster at a city to the south of us.

Once I reached out to former classmates about this book, Debbie responded that she may be interested in participating, but it took a bit of coaxing to get her to commit. What I learned about her, once we spent the time discussing her life, was surprising to me, inspirational, and interesting. I had no idea that my classmate back in school was going through so much, with so many challenges. I know you will be inspired reading her story.

EARLY LIFE

Debbie was born in Brewster, Ohio in 1957 in the heart of the 'Boomer years'.

She grew up the youngest in a family of five, with two sisters and her parents.

When she was about 4 years old, her father got injured at his job. He became disabled, but got little compensation from the accident. He accepted a small monthly income in a settlement, not nearly enough to provide for the family. This changed her childhood significantly. For several years, he was unable to work, and that left her mother to join the workforce to support the family.

"We became comfortable with less and made do with what we had. Even though not many in Brewster had means, we were very poor because of my father's disability. I think close neighbors knew, and kept secret, that my dad drank a lot. He was 6'3" and athletic. He could not use one of his legs properly and kind of dragged it due to the accident. In my opinion, this life-changing event was the cause of his over-indulgence with beer and liquor. I also think it contributes to the fact that my sisters and I rarely drink or overindulge."

Debbie recalls that her mother was a very hard-working woman. "She took on many jobs after my father got hurt, but always stayed caring and loving. My father, on the other hand, was great when we were young. I guess when I realized the drinking was abnormal and saw how he treated my mom after all those years of her doing everything for him, I got frustrated with his actions. My dad was a racist, like many people of that generation. Opposite that, he was hard-working, and honest in his dealings with others. My parents worked hard to provide, and showed what tenacity meant."

Debbie recalls that her parents lived through the Great Depression and it showed in their frugality during her childhood. "I can only imagine what the Depression was like!" Could another Great Depression happen again? "I think it could!"

Her grandparents lived in Sugarcreek and Zanesville, and Debbie recalls that her maternal grandparents were not all that active in their lives, since they passed when she was young. However, she visited the other grandparents often, and when she did, she remembers eating cookies and having tea.

"I was a decent student and enjoyed learning. I made mistakes in high school, but memories of that experience are all good. I didn't switch into taking college prep classes until the middle of my sophomore year, and the delay in doing so was simply because I thought my family could never afford college for me."

FAMILY LIFE

When Debbie was 15 years old, she got pregnant, and her son was born when she was just 16. In her junior year of high school, she had to drop out to get a job to support her son. "I kept saying to myself, this cannot be happening to me! It was a scary time. But I remember later in life, I read that back in

1973, 510,000 15-year-olds got pregnant in the U.S. that year! When I read that, I did not feel that badly, that I was not the stupidest girl in the world."

She got married, but the marriage only lasted a year and a half. Alone with her son at age 17, she was living in Massillon earning $1.00 an hour as a waitress, and paying $100 per month in rent. "I did the best that I could."

Debbie had to walk to the laundromat, which was about 8 blocks away, and had to haul fabric diapers, as they did not have disposable diapers at that time. "I don't know how I made ends meet, my mom and dad couldn't help financially, but my sister did a lot. Otherwise, I don't recall much about that."

"I learned responsibility very quickly. My son Bryan went to a preschool, and I did not drive, so I caught the bus to the preschool, then caught the bus again to go to my job, once it turned around on the street. Then after my shift was over, I did the same routine to pick-up my son and take him home. On Sundays, the bus didn't run so I walked."

Then she moved back to Brewster in an apartment downtown, and got a job in a factory in Strasburg, earning $3.25 per hour. She recalls that her parents did help out with babysitting occasionally once she moved to Brewster, closer to them.

Later, she was married for the second time, and in 1981 had her second child, and another followed a few years later. They were married for 23 years. In the later years, Debbie was focused upon earning enough money to save to send her two youngest children to college, as her eldest son was already out of high school and working. She typically was working her fulltime job at the post office, and an evening job at a restaurant during the week, with a third job in retail on weekends. Her husband also worked as a wastewater superintendent.

"All that time, I was very focused on making money and saving, working a lot of hours, and I assumed that my husband was managing the money in our joint account and putting any extra into an account for college for the kids. Unfortunately, that was not happening as I expected, and in the end, he met someone else. It was a big mess; I rented a place from a friend until things got worked through. We got divorced, and I then purchased a home of my own."

Meanwhile, since she and her ex-husband had a mortgage on the prior house, she signed a deed to remove her name from the mortgage, but apparently the claim was never filed. "When the bank foreclosed on the house, the bank came after me! It was a very rough time, and I struggled a lot. I was always a hard worker, and wanted to do things the right way, but this experience was very difficult to handle. Due to that experience, I'm not sure I could live with someone else. I am used to doing what I want, whenever I want, while handling my affairs myself."

Where are her children now?

"My eldest, Bryan, is a head chef at a country club in the area. Earlier, he started a restaurant, but got cancer. He went through multiple surgeries, and got hooked on painkillers at age 38. Then he went through another bout of cancer. He ended up being an addict for a time, and every phone call I got, I expected bad news. My sister and I did provide money to help him with his first restaurant, and later, a food truck. It was a very rough go, but now he has been clean for seven years, and well-known in the Stark County restaurant scene. He has a son Dylan, now 27, and Dylan has a daughter Penelope, who is almost 3 years old, my first great-granddaughter!

"My daughter Melinda lives in Delaware Ohio, she is married with one daughter, and teaches at a preschool now, earlier she did social work. She is doing very well. Her daughter comes to visit each summer and stays with me, we have a great time. My youngest son Nicholas lives near Washington DC, and works for the National Institute of Health, he is involved in bioinformatics. He has travelled internationally for his job, and he and his wife have three kids and two foster kids that they may adopt soon. I am not as close to him mainly due to the distance we are apart, but I do visit them occasionally."

Her father passed away in 1994 at age 78, and her mother passed in 2012 at age 96.

HER CAREER

One of her first jobs she remembers was babysitting during high school. This was followed by a series of different jobs throughout her life.

Debbie relates that she found out early in her working career that she cared a lot about customer service, and that she was happiest when she was interacting with customers. "Maybe the waitress jobs taught me that more than anything else. My factory job was boring working alone, so I would sing to myself. The more I was around people, the happier I was in my job. For example, as a postmaster, working the window occasionally was much more enjoyable than the administrative part of the job. Middle management and administrative work can be tough."

She relates that she did end up later finishing school. Some of her other jobs, to earn money for her family, were being responsible for water/sewer billing, reading water meters, and driving a school bus. These in particular allowed her to be home in the evenings with her children.

"At one point, I started studying for the postal exam, and I decided I was going to ace the test. It was a much harder test back then, and I ended up getting a 100% after taking it several times. My first postal job was a city mail carrier in Wooster. I did that for a year, when the supervisor asked if I was interested in management one day. I said yes, but once I learn all there is to learn about post office duties. He said to be here at 4:00 a.m. tomorrow! I then became an acting supervisor for six months, then I saw that they had openings for postmasters in the area. I took correspondence courses, and applied for three different postmaster jobs. My first one was in Winesburg. It turned out that my family had lived in Winesburg just before I was born. Talk about going back home!"

Debbie relates that she was an acting postmaster in other locations while she was assigned to the Winesburg area. She worked in Strasburg, Navarre, Malvern, Magnolia, and Louisville among other places. "It seemed that sometimes, when they would ask me to go to another location, things were a bit of a mess there. It was nice to follow a postmaster who had kept things in order."

"Then I transferred to the capital district in Maryland and was the postmaster there for three years. It was away from the hustle of D.C., but very cool to be so close to everything. It turned out it was too expensive to live there, while making the same wages as I was making in lower cost-of-living areas. I eventually moved back to Ohio."

She relates that many of her co-workers said that she was the best postmaster with which they worked. "I always tried to do things for them, such as recognize them for service anniversaries. They said some other postmasters never did that for them."

One time, while at Winesburg, she was asked if she wanted to take on the additional service of processing passports. "I said sure, why not? It became one of the best places to get passports in the area due to our focus on service. Word got around, and the number of people driving there for passports grew. Treating people right makes all the difference."

Debbie retired as the postmaster in Bolivar, Ohio. "I made some great connections there, and really enjoyed the time."

How did she think about her role in being a postmaster in multiple locations? "My goal was to help employees understand their jobs and to relate to them their worth and importance. I saw many dedicated employees, but overall, I think the mindset of loyalty to an employer has waned. I learned how unfairly we were mandated to do more with less over my career, and feel badly for the current state of employment in my field. I think those that work hard can be taken advantage of, myself included, so I had to show my employees their worth in the interim."

HER PASSION FOR MUSIC

Debbie smiles when she talks about how she spent so much of her pre-teen and teen years memorizing lyrics and music while spinning records with her 'bestie' Jayne. "I saw my first big-time concert in 1972, The Rolling Stones at the Rubber Bowl in Akron. I made it up front and was hooked! Even prior to that we felt like "groupies" for neighborhood garage bands. We talked adults into driving us to The Elms golf course where they had an area to feature live bands. There were Grange dances where a band would play. Over the decades I have continued that musical addiction. I could never play, or sing, so I guess I was mesmerized by people who could."

"I have seen so many big-name bands, from Led Zeppelin to Kiss to Billy Joel and the Eagles. I've seen ZZ Top, Tool, BB King, orchestras, Zydeco bands, blues and jazz bands, local, new, old, famous, unknown. It's my favorite hobby of all my hobbies. I'm so thankful that I kind of had the ability to connect to music. I remember the performance of "The Age of Aquarius" in maybe 5th or 6th grade. Of course, I learned all the words, and I loved the singing and the music. I recall a guy named Jim who attended our school, who was years older, soloing in some performance and I thought he'd be a rock star! If I had saved the money I have spent on concert tickets, I would be a lot wealthier! Music has been a big part of my life."

Debbie guesses that she has been to over 400 concerts to see major acts, but that now she has tinnitus from all those concerts, which creates problems with sleeping. "I just got a pair of bone-conducting headphones, which helps, I put them on at night, and play background sounds, such as waterfall sounds."

UPON REFLECTION

Debbie remembers starting out in life facing a few obstacles, but that now she is satisfied with how her life ended up. She is very proud of her three great adult children, that she worked 45 years to better her lot in life, and that she retired in 2021 after 31 years with the Postal Service. "I was Postmaster for most of that time. I can honestly say that during all the time I spent managing employees, 99.9% of them think of me fondly!"

POLLING FOR OPINIONS

If forced to list only three of the most important lessons in life you have learned, what would they be?

Nothing is handed to us; we must work hard to get the results we want.

Life is made up of choices. We can't control all the twists and turns that lead to those choices, so we have to make the best of the things we choose and learn from our mistakes.

Life is short and time is a thief, so take advantage of opportunities to make the best of it.

If a Millennial or Gen X or Gen Z person was sitting next to you on your death bed, and they asked you "What is the meaning of life? What is it all about?" What do you think your answer would be?

I can't begin to imagine I know enough about the meaning of life to advise anyone on that, but I would say you should, as my dad used to say, take the bull by the horns and make the best of it. Don't give up and expect someone else to take care of you. Your destiny isn't pre-determined; it's consequential. You hear people say, 'Don't you think that the choices you make determine your destination?' I don't believe that God has this grand plan, we have choices we all make. If you don't learn from the choices that you make and your experiences, why go through life? Things are not going to fall into your lap.

Is there anything you would do differently in parenting in looking back?

I wish I could have found a way for my kids to spend more time outside. When we were kids, we were outside so much more than now.

Do you believe that the generations following ours will be, in general, better off or worse financially when they get to our age?

I think the work ethic of younger generations is different from Boomers. When I first worked at the post office, my bosses said "Do this route, part of this other route, and be back to run Express Mail and stay for collections." I didn't question it. A few years later, as a supervisor, I would instruct younger employees in a similar fashion and almost always got push-back, such as "Can't you find someone else?", or "I can't do that".

It shows me that they want things but may not be willing to work as hard to get them. Some think you don't have to do more to *be* more. But your determination and energy will do a lot more for you than just showing up. That is why I think I became successful because of the extra effort. You have to be willing to go above and beyond expectations. Maybe I am old school!

Do you believe those generations will live in a better country and world in the coming decades, versus what our generation experienced as we aged?

I am pessimistic – I think that the future holds worse experiences in the coming decades. Many younger people are dedicated to fairness and inclusion, and I can only hope they are successful in their efforts to change the world. They are so focused on this because of social media, all these issues are in their face, they see the injustices and feel like they have to fix this, whereas our generation was not that aware or close to the injustices, therefore we focused more on our jobs and just surviving.

Did you worry too much or too little about your parents as they aged?

I worried too little and, sadly, perhaps missed some opportunities to spend more time with my parents when they were alive. My dad was at home when he passed, and so was my mom, but she was in and out of a nursing home several times. My sister still worked, but she also had to do the most to take care of them when they were at home. My dad was a big guy, and my mom was short; it was a challenge for her to take care of him.

What are you planning to have happen with any funds or possessions after you pass?

I feel like my children are better off financially than I am. If there is anything left, funds will be divided between the three of them, but that is not my goal with the money I've invested and saved. My goal is to use it to make my own life better, and if I can share that while I'm alive, all the better.

How would you characterize your contributions to your employer / customers / society during your career?

I feel like I was a valuable asset to my employer and to the communities I served. I tried to be active and involved, not only where I was posted, but also in business associations and work-related organizations in those locations. I learned a lot as president of a postmaster's district organization. I was essential in planning community events and bettering the towns. I am proud that I perhaps set an example of good leadership to employees resulting in promotions for many as they developed and gained experience. I'm proud that I was able to help and that I was acknowledged by these employees as a champion to their success.

Boomers have, and had, a reputation for drinking beer/wine/alcohol. Did you drink growing up? Did you have any drug experiences?

I experimented with drugs for a short time. They were so available. I'm not sure they are that accessible now, but I'm in the wrong demographic to know. I smoked marijuana at times, and my doctor recently said that I would be a good candidate for marijuana due to back pain. I don't use it a lot, but it does help when I need it. I believe marijuana should be federally legal, and applaud the current policy of forgiving marijuana-related non-violent offenses. To me, if someone smokes weed, but it doesn't negatively affect their life in terms of financials or job retention, it is OK. I never drank much, only with friends on special occasions. Some will say 'If every Boomer smoked marijuana, maybe we would all be happy!' I'm not sure if that is true, but…. Having said that, if you are smoking weed but cannot make your car payment or house payment, that is a problem!

How are your friendships now?

I have several groups of long-time friends from different social interactions, and some life-long friends. I am appreciative of the time we are able to spend together. One group of friends from work meet almost monthly. Another group is a card club of people from over the past 40 years. I have a hard time meeting new friends, but maybe I have not expended much energy to do so because of time limitations. I do some mystery shopping and volunteer to deliver Mobile Meals. I also have three dogs – two goldendoodles, and an Aussie mix, that I spoil that takes time. I would like to meet more people. I do feel sad that some friendships are slipping away. One friend has developed Alzheimer's, another is raising a child, and some have various other happenings. I'm also thankful to have recently rekindled some friendships that had languished.

In what ways have you changed as a result of losing someone close?

When my mother passed away in 2012, I was on the verge of moving away from the place I'd spent my life near to her. I lost her but gained so much because of her! She was 96 and sharp as a tack, so I was blessed. What I regret is that when she was alive and I was working all the time, I missed opportunities to spend time with her. Now that I DO have time, sadly she's gone. She was my biggest fan, always smiling, and I wish I'd asked more stories of when she was growing up and written down what she did say about that and about relatives.

Consider for a moment all of the history of the time you were growing up. Anything stand out as having impacted you?

I recall not having a television when I was very young. We had a huge radio with the tubes and such. We listened to music and broadcasts. I recall 'Big Bad John' by Jimmy Dean, 'King of the Road' by Roger Miller, everything Dean Martin sang, with my dad singing along. When we did get a TV, of course it was black and white. We watched the Wizard of Oz (still my favorite movie) at my grandmother's house because their TV was color and it was magical! At home we watched many TV shows and my favorite part was my parents laughing. My dad's laugh was hearty and often, my mom's was a giggle that built up until it was unstoppable and often ended up with her in tears.

What do you recall about the press growing up vs. now?

Currently, it's almost impossible for me to keep up with all the media sources; Facebook, Twitter, Instagram, TikTok, news outlets with differing points of view. I want to be informed but feel overwhelmed at times. I don't think it was like this as a teen or young adult. I think it's unfortunate that broadcast media can be manipulated and corrupted.

What about 9/11? How did that affect how you think about our country and about terrorism?

I feel it's very unfortunate that the events on 9/11 seemed to bring division and hate into the forefront. Don't misunderstand my point; Americans came together, but found out in a clearer way how hated the United States is by some radical factions. I don't understand why.

What about minority / women's rights and equality? How would you compare our state now vs. your years growing up?

I applaud how far we've come since I was younger, but I feel we have a long way to go. I cannot believe that some don't believe that there is systemic racism. Minorities still do not have the same opportunities as us.

How do you feel about U.S. immigration, the border wall, and our illegal alien policies?

I am of the opinion that the United States is a melting pot. I think everyone deserves a better life if they are willing to work for it, and it seems like that may be a small part of a solution to our labor shortage. There are so many jobs that are not being filled. Somebody has to do the jobs that others will not do. But I disagree with the border as it is, there needs to be some coordination with cities that can accept them and support them, versus busing them to places that cannot handle them well.

How do you feel about the US role as being 'watchman of the world'?

I don't necessarily like it. However, especially after 9/11 and related events that followed, when we were reminded how other nations feel about the U.S., I can't imagine letting some of our "strongman" status wane. Foreign interference in our elections and the current war between Russia and Ukraine are other examples of why we should be willing to help and to police other nations.

What are your feelings about 'green initiatives' and the state of our planet?

Global warming and climate change are very real and extremely serious. Countries who can least afford to mitigate the effects of climate change are the ones suffering the worst effects. The U.S. is one of the largest contributors to the problem, so to me it only seems fair that we, along with other polluters, take responsibility for leading. I don't believe some countries are doing everything they could, and this is a global problem. The earth as we know it is changing. Whether there will be solutions or simply adaptation, a strong U.S. response is necessary. But who makes some of these decisions such as giving Indonesia $20B to help them clean up their pollution? I'm not sure that is a good example of leading.

Do you feel that we are taxed too much or too little? Do you believe that the rich need to pay more or fewer taxes? Do you believe that the poor need to pay more or less taxes?

This is such a travesty. How can billionaires pay a lower tax rate than me?

How do you feel about the compensation of our political representatives at the state or national level, including benefits and pension?

Our elected officials are much wealthier than a huge percentage of their constituents. I think term limits are needed. The politicians do not represent average Americans very well, in my opinion, and this needs to be addressed.

Should we have more or fewer governmental programs to help the underprivileged?

We have to do more for the underprivileged. The wealthy and/or scammers who take advantage of government programs should be made to pay back their ill-gotten gains.

What about the growing national debt?

It is so outrageous at this point that I can't even get upset about it anymore. Will someone ever really pay back that debt? Or will our politicians just keep kicking the can down the road?

Why are politicians so divided? Has it really changed, or has it been like this for a long time?

In my opinion, it is due to the rudeness brought to the fore in recent years. You can disagree and work toward solutions without name-calling and insults. This seems to be the only country where, regardless of which party is in power, the objective of the opposing party is to thwart forward progress for the next four years by stopping or battling anything their rivals propose.

Do you consider yourself to be a conservative or liberal or somewhere in between?

I vote Democratic but don't feel I am a "bleeding heart" liberal. I feel strongly about helping others and inclusion.

What about the growing disparity in income?

I think it is a problem. It is almost obscene that the "1%" control most of our world's wealth and do so little to make changes that would benefit so many. I don't know the answer, but first and foremost I think they should be taxed at a higher rate than they are.

Do you believe the US should be more focused upon our country mainly, or more focused globally, in terms of how our tax dollars are used?

More certainly needs to be done about our country's poor and homeless. However, we only have ONE world, so we all must contribute to make it work.

Do you think the country is headed in the wrong or right direction?

To me, it seems clear that the changes in recent years are due to folks being open with their absolute worst behavior. Why name-calling and racism are tolerated and covered as "normal" is beyond my understanding. There are a lot of politicians and pundits that do not deserve the media attention they are receiving. That in itself is a big part of the problem. Don't amplify this abhorrent behavior! I don't believe anyone is above the law, and those higher up should be just as accountable as those without power. I recently asked a conservative why they liked a certain politician, and of course policy came into the conversation. I stated I can accept that, but what about behavior? What if those comments were aimed at your child, or someone you cared about? What if the lies had consequences for you directly? There was no satisfactory answer.

Slanderous comments and name-calling are just not OK, but somehow that is how politicians and citizens behave today. There is no reason for nastiness. I won't vote for someone who is nasty even if I agree with the policies they are going to push.

Do you have more 'stuff' now than when you were younger?

Over the course of my adulthood, I accumulated much more stuff than when I was younger. Luckily, to date, I have removed and consolidated much of it. I no longer feel the need to decorate for each and every holiday. When I do, it is a much more scaled-down version of what used to be Christmas in every room and hundreds of Santa's displayed! I used to enjoy craft shows and antique stores. Now I try to avoid them unless it's for a gift or something specific. I'd much rather have "experiences" than more "stuff!"

Many Boomers believe that education is very important for the younger generations. Is advanced education more or less important than it was when you were growing up?

That is a tough question. I still strongly believe education is important, but considering the state of the current job market, I think a re-tool is necessary. How many graduates are not working in their college major? Higher education absolutely needs to cost less, and more opportunities need to be presented to those who do not choose college, as in tech and vocational schools.

Tell me about your health care coverage and your thoughts about the benefits you get.

I am very fortunate to be able to keep my employer's health coverage into retirement. I also have Medicare and the premiums for both are acceptable. The coverage should be good, not excellent, but I thankfully haven't had to test it since retiring. I had back surgery in the past and was happy with the employee plan. I still don't understand the lack of coverage for physical therapy, chiropractic, and dental. Those services are necessary but costly. I know from talking to others that it could be worse! I am glad that there is still a "government" option for those unable to get insured through their work.

Relative to other concerns you have, where does your health and your family's health rank?

Most important! Preventive care should always be available.

How do you feel about social security and the projection that the surplus will run out in 2035?

It is not an entitlement; it has been *earned*. Policymakers need to keep their mitts off and take their reductions from elsewhere. Something does have to change, but wouldn't it be OK to tax the current workers more? Once it is taken out of your check, you don't miss it as much. I don't know where the money will come from, but I agree something has to change. Why not take the $20B that we are giving to Indonesia for pollution and bolster the SS fund? For those who are retired, this inflation is going to eat up our income.

SUMMARY

Debbie's story is, in a way, similar to other stories in this book in that she grew up in a relatively poor family and worked hard to overcome that to become successful. What is different is that she had to not only deal with that, but also had to deal with becoming a single mother at age 17!

The picture of Debbie working at a job paying $1.00 per hour, catching a bus to take her son to daycare, catching a bus to work, catching the bus to go back home, walking on weekends when the bus did not run, walking to the laundromat, etc., is one that I am sure we will all recall about her story. Perhaps the experience of seeing her father get injured at his job, and becoming disabled making a small monthly income, helped Debbie in ways she did not realize, in that perhaps she learned how to make do with less, learned how to make her dollars stretch.

I am also struck by Debbie's modesty. She commented that she was a 'decent' student. No, I can tell you that she was one of the brightest students I can remember in school! She talks about how, as a postmaster, one of her most important responsibilities was to ensure that her employees knew their roles and were recognized for the job that they did. This is another indication of her modesty, even though she was very successful. I never heard her say 'I did this', or 'I made that post office a success', it was always her view that the team accomplished things together. It sounds as if her employees enjoyed working for her or with her, and of course that says a lot about her leadership style and how she respected others.

I liked her responses to the question – 'What are the most important lessons you have learned in life?' Her responses are just as you would expect given what she had to overcome, that you have to work for what you get, and you have to make the best of the situation you are in. These clearly are lessons that she learned through the struggles she went through. I never once heard her say 'At that point in my life, I just about gave up', or 'I had so many tough breaks in life'. When she answered the question about her most memorable events in life, instead of thinking about the negative things, she talked about the experience of not having a TV at one time. Instead of describing that as a negative, she talked about how her family listened to a radio instead. She remembers the specific songs that were most impactful for her at that time. Maybe that experience listening to the radio with her family developed her love of music, a love that lights up her face when she talks about going to concerts.

Her positive outlook now, as she looks back over her life, likely mirrors her outlook throughout her life. She seems like a very positive person, when others might not have that positive outlook given some of the challenges that she went through.

Her response to one of my questions says everything about Debbie and her ability to overcome some tough challenges in life. When I asked my question 'what is life all about?', I was floored by her simple, six-word response: "Your destiny isn't pre-determined; it's consequential." Wow. Not only very smart, but maybe she has a career in late life as a philosopher! Thank you, Debbie, for sharing your story!

SEX, DRUGS, ROCK and WAR: The Boomer Generation

CHAPTER 5:
Skip, The Entrepreneur Who Served His Country, His Customers, and Our Schools

BACKGROUND

I've known Skip for years, but just casually, as a fellow golfer at a local club. What I learned about his life, through the discussions for this book, helped me get to know Skip much better, and I truly appreciate the life he has lived.

It is not often that you run across an individual who runs his own business, but has also <u>*created and* *grown his own business from scratch*</u>. He did not inherit a business, or acquire a business, but concepted and developed a business, step by step, to serve a growing need in the community and in the economy, which I will describe later. He also served in Vietnam, and served over 22 years on two different school boards. His story is both captivating and educational.

EARLY LIFE

Skip is a mainstream Boomer in terms of birthdate, born in 1949.

He calls himself 'very fortunate' to grow up with great parents who set a good example via hard work all their life. They had careers in hospital administration and banking.

"I had two younger brothers. We grew up in at a tightly-knit community with life revolving around a lake, which provided a variety of lake activities, such as swimming, fishing, boating, etc., and the community also had sports fields and a clubhouse for residents. I got my first job there mowing grass, lots of it, when I was in 6th grade. I worked that job on through high school. There were four of us in that community who became good friends, and we all grew up together. It was not a wealthy community, but the neighbors were sort of like family to help each other when they needed something."

What about his parents and their beliefs? Were they liberals or conservatives?

"My parents were very conservative. Dad was a Banker for over 40 years, mom was in administration at a hospital. Today's world would have caused them stress, it's so different than their generation and not for the good! I wouldn't say I think differently than them, I just have to think in a way that will work with today's younger generations. Some days what I see is just overwhelming."

Skip attended Northwest schools, a smaller district in Northeast Ohio, throughout his educational years. This enabled Skip to keep many of his student friends all twelve years. "Some of my classmates now work here at my business today."

In his senior year, his principal called Skip into his office, and suggested that he apply for a job at a telecommunications company as a residential service technician, a job he performed a total of 16 years. He was hired while still in high school.

Skip had 86 students in his graduation class. "It was almost like a Mayberry community, town, and school." The Northwest school district included the towns of Clinton and Canal Fulton. "Clinton never passed a school levy in its history, and eventually shrunk like many small towns in the Midwest."

How was life growing up with his parents? "When Dad said something and 'gave you the look', there was no debate, no arguing, no talking back, you knew he meant business, so we stayed in line. Of course, as a teenager, you tried to do things, but we never got away with anything. There were no 'timeouts' for bad behavior, like some today think is the right way to discipline kids." In talking to Skip, you get the sense that he strongly believes that is a proper parenting style, and likely one he continued with his children.

How about when he or his siblings wanted something and asked their parents if they could have it?

"As kids, if we wanted something, we had to save money from chores to be able to afford what we wanted. But Mom and Dad always had a nice Christmas for us."

ON TO THE MILITARY

Skip graduated in 1968, and just one year later, received his draft notice, as the Vietnam War was in full swing. His draft number, based upon his month/day birthdate, was number 86 out of 365, which meant he had to be drafted for service. He chose to enlist in the Air Force. He went through basic training in Texas, then was stationed in Illinois, then Wichita, Kansas for about a year. Then he was sent to Ubon, Thailand, at an Air Force base, which was about 100 miles from many of the aircraft missions in North Vietnam.

"I was mulling around the idea of just going into the Army, but I had the feeling I could get better training in the Air Force. I visited the recruiter for the Air Force and of course he filled me with all the training "bull" I was looking for. But that career track didn't exactly happen as I had hoped, they needed me in a whole different job classification."

Skip served in the ground crew, working on and supporting airplane generators, bomb loaders, and other military jobs. At that base, there were F4 Fighters, A1A Sky Raiders, and C-130 Gunships. He served for just over four years, and returned to civilian life in early 1973.

Skip is a fan of the draft. "The military takes kids, and exposes them to the real world, where you have to do chores, have to maintain your own finances, you have to be on time for everything. You have to grow up fast, and you develop a respect for your country. Kids today, in the main, don't have a solid way to develop that structure and discipline. The military made men out of boys."

When Skip returned from military service, wearing a uniform, protesters were there at the airports, and he was pelted with vegetables. "These were kids my own age, and they were protesting against me and others, and they had no idea of the sacrifice we made for them and how we invested a lot of time from our lives to serve."

The military advised him and others to not wear their uniform when returning due to the sentiment at the time. "That was fine, but if you had to hitch-hike home, like I did, you could get picked up if you had a uniform on. Without one, it was tough to get a ride."

ON TO A CAREER

"When I got out of the service, I went back to my old job. It was a great job but I wasn't satisfied with just being a technician. With the GI bill, and with my employer also helping with tuition and books, I enrolled at the local state college at nights in 1973."

Shortly after enrolling, Skip met Cindy on a blind date, setup by a good friend. They dated for several years before marrying in 1979. They have been married for 43 years, and have two children. "She just hangs around with me to see what might happen next!"

"Cindy is still gorgeous, but back then, she looked like Farrah Fawcett. I used to take her to some of the school board meetings, and boy, did we get the looks from older, conservative guys looking at me bringing his tall, blonde woman to the meetings!"

Skip eventually graduated in 1977 with an associate degree in business management. During this time, he was also invited by some close friends (Roland Lindsay and Glen and Don Swigert) to join the local Rotary Club.

It was at a Thursday dinner of the Rotary Club, where he sat next to the president of the local Exchange Bank, where a discussion was held that may have changed Skip's life.

During the dinner, Skip was talking about his interest in cars and Corvettes in particular. He was asked if he might be interested in working with the bank to fix and sell their repossessed vehicles. "And then it began."

"In a few months, I was out doing the repossessions with my pickup truck and flatbed trailer winching them on and hauling the vehicles away. I also started auctioning off those vehicles standing on a ladder!"

An acquaintance told Skip that if he wanted to do the repossessions well, he needed to get a wrecker truck, plus he should acquire more space to do the auctions. He bought an acre of land and had a friend, Roland Lindsay, build the auction building for him, costing about $35,000. He also acquired a wrecker truck which allowed him to load a vehicle easily.

I had no idea how repossessions and the subsequent auctions worked, but Skip explained it to me. "A small percentage of car loans result in a repossession. There are many delinquent payments to a bank, but most of those are resolved and do not result in a repossession. But after several months of delinquent payments, usually two or three months, the bank will inform the client that other actions may have to be taken if payment is not made immediately." At such times, the bank might send a notice to Skip's company to go ahead and repossess a vehicle.

Are you backed up or supported by police when you go to re-possess a vehicle? "No, we just have a written statement from the bank that I am to re-possess. I get the address and the vehicle ID. I can show that to the owner if they ask to see it, but there is no warrant or court order of any kind. In the main, the bank really owns, and has a right, to the vehicle, and they make the call when it needs to be repossessed."

What if the owner sees you out looking at their car and hooking it up to tow it, can't you get in trouble?

"The ideal situation is that the owner never sees anyone taking the car." But many times, the owner will see what is going on and confront him or his employees. In those situations, discussions take place, and they usually allow the owner to remove any possessions from the car. Sometimes, if the owner promises to go pay the bank immediately, they will give the owner a few days. But if no payment is made, they return to re-possess.

The bank pays a flat fee for each repossession and for each auction. There is also a buyer fee that is charged at the auction which Skip's company gets. "We never take a percentage of the value of the vehicle; we are just a service company and get a fixed amount per each vehicle we handle."

What happens if the bank is lenient and allows the client to skip payments for more than 2-3 months? What happens then?

"Usually, the owners begin to disappear and move the car to some unknown location. So, it is in the interest of the banks to be prompt to resolve issues quickly. Divorces are a key reason for delinquent payments too."

As time went on, Skip also started providing the same service for First National Bank of Massillon, and this evolved into him also doing the car auctions for them. These auto auctions started on a half-acre grass area. The auction for the first few years totaled about 30 cars per month. "But in 1983, I landed the work from Bank One Ravenna, and overnight my volume quadrupled. That same year, we were outgrowing the small lot we had, and I decided to build the first auction building on Locust Street in Canal Fulton. There were challenges, as at that location, there were no services such as water or sewer. We ran a hose from the house next door and brought in port-a-johns. Even with the obstacles, it was doing well."

Then came October 5, 1984. "I was going out that Friday night to assist on a motorcycle repossession. A young staff member wanted to take my place, which was helpful because I had an auction the next morning. This decision has weighed heavily on me ever since. He was killed during the recovery by the debtor."

"This turned into a crisis for my staff, as several left the company creating issues for the business. I was fortunate that my employer then gave me some leave time to rebuild and keep moving forward."

In December of 1984, the telecommunications company offered a buyout program with transitionary medical coverage and a pension. "After talking with management, given the growth of Skipco, Cindy and I decided to take the buyout."

The buyout was for cash and other incentives to leave. "We were so busy with Skipco, it was crazy, so the timing of the buyout was good."

In the summer of 1985, Skip opened a satellite office in Cleveland, which expanded his service area considerably. He rented a garage facility and added 6 more employees. "Volume was good and we were outgrowing that facility rapidly."

In 1990, he bought another satellite office in Columbus, expanding his service area to the south and into central Ohio. That same year, he also expanded his Canal Fulton facility with offices and lot space.

"In 1993 we were awarded the U.S. Marshal's contract for the Northern district of Ohio. This was quite a feat to get the Marshals contract out of Cleveland and move it down to Skipco (the name of his company) in 'Little Canal Fulton'."

As I learned from Skip, the Marshal's contract covered anything seized by the DEA, FBI, border patrol, etc. Skip's company picked up the assets and stored them until the cases were resolved. If there was a vehicle involved, they maintained the vehicle and stored it, but the assets could be anything, such as pinball machines. "There are fees per day for the storage, plus hauling fees to take the assets to their storage locations."

Then in 1994, they expanded into the Youngstown, Ohio area, opening an office in the Lake Milton area.

Fifteen years later they moved to Vienna just north of Youngstown.

In 1996 the Mansfield Office was opened, which provided Skipco access to more western Ohio counties. Then in 2002, they purchased a 17,000 square foot building in Obetz, Ohio for their Columbus office.

"2003 brought us a successful bid on the Southern Ohio district of the Marshals contract. With this came a nice facility we were able to purchase, and began the recovery part of the business in Dayton and Cincinnati. Also, in 2003 we split Skipco into two different corporations:

(1) Skipco Auto Auctions, and (2) Source One Adjusters of Ohio Inc.

This gave us several advantages in the marketplace with selling both Skipco auction services and repossession recovery services. Through all this time, business was good, but stressful given all the growth. Space became an issue with the Auction building as well as for vehicle storage and maintenance services."

"Our own fleet had grown to over forty vehicles. In 2004 we started on extensive grading and purchasing more land attached to the Locust Street facility. In 2005, we held a grand opening of the current 12,000 square foot Auction Building and the 5,000 square foot Detail Shop. This same year, my son Keith graduated from college and began to manage Skipco Auto Auction."

In 2019, Skipco was awarded the Marshals Contract to cover 4 states, Ohio, Kentucky, West Virginia, and Western Pennsylvania.

Today, Skipco employs 114 people, and Source One Adjusters Employs 52. They now have a large maintenance building, with an office building of 2400 square feet, and land of close to 30 acres.

Skip speaks frequently about how good customer service was the key to his success.

"I always focused on doing the job right and satisfying the customer, and as a result, the business grew. The mistake I made was that I did not have the right accounting focus so that I knew our costs. But if I had not been focused on doing the job right, we would have been just like anyone else out there. Our customer service set us apart! If I had to do it over, I would have had a stronger focus on costs and accounting right from the beginning."

One night at one of his rotary meetings, he asked a superintendent about the schools and taxation, wanting to know how the whole process worked. He was told "I could tell you Skip, but you wouldn't understand it."

"That sort of got me upset, as if I was too stupid to understand something. So, a few months later, there was an opening on the school board, and I was only 29 and unmarried, so I decided to run for the board seat. That November, I ran and won!"

Once on the board, the same superintendent then went out of his way to explain all about the tax structure and school district funding. "I ended up serving 24 years on the Northwest Board of Education, 18 years as the president, plus 22 years on the Stark County Joint Vocational school district board, 15 years as President. I put a lot of time working to better the schools. I am a big believer in vocational education. Too many parents push their kids into college, and many have no business in college given what they want to do or their capabilities. Luckily, we have gotten other community schools to participate in our county vocational school, and we are getting some traction."

But how would a student know if they are cut out for college or not? "The beauty of a vocational education is that a student can learn a skill, get a job, and find out if they enjoy that field or work environment. Then later, they might decide that if they were to invest the time to get a degree, they might be able to progress in that trade or industry. So, it might be a stepping stone to college later, or it might be a pipeline to a solid job with a good career."

Currently, Skip is still involved in his business but has help of his wife, son and daughter, and has others to rely upon. He also has retired from the school boards. What was life like while growing his business?

"You have to remember, while starting and growing the business, it was just me, there was nobody else to rely upon. And I was on two school boards, many years serving as president. I was going crazy, I had no spare time, and didn't have time to think about much else. But all through that time, I had help and advice from close friends who provided counsel and sometimes direct help. Today, I still go to work in my business, but focus mainly on projects. I have more time now in the evenings or to go to lunch with the guys. But what is different now is that of those close advisors and friends, many have died."

"Because you have to devote your life to a business like mine, it's hard for others, even close friends and families, to understand the process of growing a business. Obviously, my wife was in it from the beginning doing accounting, and my son and daughter were here also and still are. My son is really running the business now as I've stepped back to doing projects or whatever. My daughter is an attorney and handles contracts, human resources, etc. Now that they all are involved day-to-day, they learned all about the many hurdles we face."

POLLING FOR OPINIONS

What are the most important life lessons you have learned?

First, always keep your eyes wide open, and do not assume anything. Second, if you take on a task, give 110% to its completion. Last, be honest and straightforward.

I found his answer very interesting, as I find those answers very much aligned to the values of my main employer, who stressed, among other things, that 'if something is worthy of doing, see it through to completion', and that 'ethics should be the cornerstone of operating in business.' Might those be keys to success for any business? I suspect that they may be!

Do you believe that you had a superior educational experience that enabled you to succeed in business?

The education I received at Northwest was a good school with a solid community backing. It was a good basic education. My education at Stark State was solid training for management tasks that I would take on. It was the right education for me, as I really was willing to invest my time in training I needed, whereas I likely would not have had the patience for a four-year degree program with all the responsibilities I had.

What about your Vietnam experience and how you were treated upon returning? How did that affect you, and how do you think that may have changed our country?

If there are problems with the next generations, I don't blame them, some of this began with Boomers who protested the war and treated veterans the way they did. While some of us were serving our country, others our age protested and took drugs and had little responsibility.

What about the divisiveness in our politics, and our political leadership?

This world worries me. It just seems to have so many splinter groups that have no idea about the big picture. Our government leadership is terrible. From their financial management to handling world issues.... it is just mind boggling. How could any country trust America with the decisions they have seen us make lately? Coming from the Vietnam debacle to the absolute disaster of Afghanistan. What the hell are we thinking?

Will future generations be better off financially than your generation?

I think future generations will be better off due to the foundation we will have left them with. I am proud of my kids, Keith manages a strong business, and Courtney is an attorney, they both did well in their education and both have strong work ethics.

What about the 'independent press' and how it seems more political and biased than news-reporting, where bad news and political news sells ads?

Our media has gotten so politicized you cannot believe a damn thing they say or do. I never was a person that delved into the headlines. I just wasn't that interested. I do get angry on what we see on TV. Every time you turn on the TV you see an ad or show that tries to legitimize views that are just not everyday American views. This left-wing crap is a real issue and will someday raise its ugly head and it won't be pretty. But you have to have confidence that eventually people will wake up and change things for the better. I have faith, but I do worry.

Do you remember your parents or older relatives talking about the Great Depression? How did their comments affect you and how you thought about the world and your life?

We were fortunate that the depression era didn't really sink into us. I heard from my parents and grandparents about it and how tough it was, but there was little effect on us that we could see. I have a stock certificate hanging above my desk that my grandfather bought in 1920, for a car company named 'Templar Car Co' that went broke during the depression. I do not feel that another depression will happen, but there will be ups and downs like we have seen in the not-so-distant past.

Looking back, what are you most proud of about yourself?

I have always had a strong work ethic and built my business on customer satisfaction and strong service, and that has paid off.

Tell me about music in the 60's and 70's. What do you remember?

I never let music affect my life. My favorites to this day were The Moody Blues, Emerson Lake and Palmer, and Neil Diamond. I can't stand Rap or most of today's so-called music.

What about the criticism of Boomers that we drink too much?

I never have been much of a drinker, even in the service I just passed on that. Today I have some CC&7's especially at the club when my golf partner is around, go figure! I have never tried any drugs or marijuana. I am not opposed to someone smoking a joint, but I absolutely believe that it leads to other things, painkillers, heroine, etc. Legalizing marijuana is a stupid mistake.

How happy are you with your friendships at this point in your life?

All through my life, I maintained a core group of friends, not through business, but these were the friends that I grew up with at my lake community, and friends I had made early through common interests. As I ran my company, and served on school boards, I didn't have much time for friends or for making new friends. But lately, some of my good friends have died. Now, my son Keith and I do things together, but now my job is still my focus. I still have an interest in cars (Corvettes especially), and I am never bored. My kids are in town, both are members at our golf club, so we see each other there."

Just as a testament to how busy Skip has been, he told me that he has been a member at his golf club for 21 years, and has never been in the swimming pool!

Boomers experienced a flurry of events in the 60's and 70's that some would say shaped how the Boomer generation developed and behaved. Which events affected you most?

I do not feel events should affect one's life. If you cannot control or affect an event, you should not let them affect your daily life. March on!

Some of our younger generations are critical of Boomers that they let their opinions about tattoos influence them as to hiring. How about you?

I am not going to put a person with a lot of tattoos on my customer service counter! Do they think I'm crazy? Customers don't want to see that.

What about your attitude about guns?

Why do we need automatic weapons? This makes no sense. But Americans do have a right to bear arms.

I also believe guns should only be sold by licensed dealers and tracked."

Is there anything you would offer in terms of your thoughts about minority / women's / men's rights and equality?

I'm all for equality but it also must be earned. Forcing this issue causes the issues. I find it hard to believe in today's America anyone who puts forth effort cannot strive ahead.

How do you feel about U.S. immigration, the border wall, and our illegal alien policies?

Absolutely ridiculous. How can any country not protect their borders? How about crime, drugs, diseases? Who is going to pay for all this? A solid immigration policy must be established and followed. We will have a 9-11 again from all this stupidity.

If you had an audience of receptive non-Boomers in a room, what would you suggest to them that you believe would help them?

I would just list the problems that I see and let them decide what should change.

1 - Too much money given out through welfare. Why work?

2 - An education system that does not teach respect or a work ethic.

3 - Respect yourself! Tattoos, dress appropriately, cleanliness.

4 - Way too much use of the internet and phones.

5 - Too little respect for authority.

6 - Too little respect for others' property.

Did Boomers do a good job of positioning the next generations for success?

Boomers started the mess. Think about the music, Woodstock, demonstrations, treatment of our military on return from Vietnam, etc. These are parents that raised the children that raised the children that we see now that disgust us. It all follows a path.

Surveys show that non-Boomers are much more positive about socialism than Boomers. In fact, one study showed that Millennials and Gen Z think slightly more positively about socialism than capitalism. Why do you think that may be?

History has shown us more than once that when the populous get 'Fat, Dumb, and Happy' they get off on these ideas till reality hits them dead in the face. One of the big causes of all this is academia. What the left-wing professors cram down our kids' throats is disgusting.

Are we too hard or too easy on convicted felons?

I believe in 'Do the crime, do the time'. Our criminal justice system is totally broken. Criminals face no punishments and today you see over and over the escalation of crime for that reason. Defund the Police? You have got to be kidding! We will not get our justice system fixed till we have strong Police and a justice system that is effective.

How do you feel about the US role as being 'watchman of the world'? Should we reduce our global influence, or expand it? We spend billions on foreign aid. How do you feel about your tax dollars being used for non-US aid, versus it being spent here?

America has always been a very giving, caring country and I'm proud of that. I do believe we have lost our way on this subject and need an overhaul on what and who we give it to. Giving just money has backfired on us too many times.

What are your feelings about green initiatives and the state of our planet?

There is no doubt we need to change our ways regarding climate change. The hard part will be to get the industrialized nations on the same page. For example, just look at India, their pollution is unbelievable.

What about our taxation? (Just for reference, the Tax Policy Center reported that in 2020, 61% of Americans paid 0 federal income taxes. In 2021, that number is expected to be 57%, then fall to 42% in 2022 due to expiring child tax credits. In 2019 it was 44%, and in 1986, it was only 18%.)

I have no issue with paying fair taxes. But watching our government just throwing our tax dollars away makes me ill! We all work hard for our money, so should others. Our welfare state is the issue.

How do you feel about the compensation of our political representatives at the state or national level, including benefits and pension? Do you believe we should have term limits?

I'm familiar with several of our state and national representatives. Their lives are totally encompassed in their work. They earn what they are paid. I am not in favor of term limits. There are cases that weigh to the side of term limits but for the most part, it is not a good idea. It takes time and experience to learn the job, it's not easy at all. Yes, representatives are wealthier than most of us, but they are the success stories of working Americans. Would you want your neighbor to go to Washington for just one term with his "pet peeve"?

Should we have more or fewer governmental programs to help the underprivileged?

Disabled Americans need assistance, no doubt, but all the lazy asses that won't work or make "bullshit" claims need rooted out.

What about the growing national debt?

The national debt will bury our kids. We must live within our means. This debt, if not altered, will force us into socialism.

Do you believe the US should be more focused upon our country mainly, or more focused globally, in terms of how our tax dollars are used?

We need to fix our own issues first, but giving money not earned is a mistake.

Tell me about your health care coverage and your thoughts about the benefits you get vs. what it costs.

I have been fortunate to always have health care coverage and thankful for it. We here provide health care for our employees and feel that's a must. But the cost has been stifling. That is not a good thing.

Relative to other concerns you have, where does your health and your family's health rank?

Without good health you have nothing. We all are very blessed with good health.

SUMMARY

Skip is someone who seems to have always had a vision for what he wanted to do, but at the same time, stayed flexible to learn and consider a variety of opportunities throughout his life. He seems to have made tremendous sacrifices for the benefit of his business, and also invested his own time in making his community a better place.

If this isn't a classic 'The American Dream' story, I am not sure what is!

We should also thank those like Skip who served our country, invested his funds as well as his personal time and energy, and built a successful enterprise which employed many in the community. Building his business was a priority throughout his life, yet there were so many benefits to the community via his success (employment, services, opportunities, etc.).

Skip is one of those Boomers who would never ask his country to help him. Just the opposite, he created so much societal value in terms of jobs and customer benefits, that he has helped his community and country to be a better place, all throughout his life!

CHAPTER 6:
Susan Meiburger Marks, The French Fundraiser

BACKGROUND

I first met Susan after being referred by her husband Larry, who is also featured in this book. After hearing a bit about her life, I had dozens of questions to find out more about her journey. When I interviewed her, my reaction was that here was a Boomer woman who had an extremely interesting life story, with a number of twists and turns. In asking her questions, I found her to be very open, introspective, thoughtful, and interested in my questions, as if she was learning more about herself as she considered each response.

As you will learn, Susan is a person who feels as though she has made the world a better place in her own way, is extremely proud of her family and how she cared for her family members, loves the French language and culture, and who seems to have an ideal lifestyle today, full of rich friendships, learning, time for reading, and time with the love of her life, Larry.

I think you will enjoy hearing about her journey.

EARLY LIFE

Susan was born in 1957 in Missouri. She describes her childhood as one of being extremely lucky growing up, starting with her parents. Her father was very much a self-made man. He grew up poor during the Depression, and his father, who was an alcoholic, deserted the family when her dad was 12. "This created a drive in him and an appreciation for education as a path to success. He put himself through undergraduate school at St. Louis University, and then Georgetown Law School at night so he could work during the day."

Her mother meanwhile, just after high school, had won a full scholarship to Maryville College in St. Louis (Maryville University now) and was a commuter student. This was in spite of the fact that her father said college would be a waste of time, because she'd 'just end up raising a family'. "He refused to pay for college for my mom and her sister, who also won a scholarship to Maryville. But he paid for college for my two uncles. But it was another era, obviously, and my mom once told me that she considered her family to be her job. But being home with 7 children while my dad worked long hours was difficult and I know she somewhat resented it."

Since her parents valued education so highly, Susan and her six siblings attended private Catholic schools until college, except for her brother Richard who went to public high school. They lived in Bethesda, just outside Washington, DC. Susan describes their family as tight-knit, and with six siblings, it was a bit chaotic, but they had a lot of fun. "My dad worked long hours and he also traveled a lot. My parents were very involved in our church and school and they eventually joined Congressional Country Club where we spent our summers swimming and, my brothers, golfing. It was quite a privileged upbringing."

Besides education, her parents believed in hard work and the Catholic Church.

Her parents guided Susan and her siblings into working for spending money, and Susan started taking on odd jobs at age 12. "My parents thought it was important and, I don't know about my siblings, but I enjoyed working. It gave me a sense of accomplishment, contribution and independence, which of course, aside from the money, was the point from my parents' perspective. I babysat, had a paper route, was a server at a local ice cream shop, and worked at several restaurants and department stores."

I find it refreshing that even though her parents had become well-off, they still wanted their children to begin working at an early age. When I asked Susan why she thought this was so important to them, she thought that since her parents both grew up poor and during the depression, that they saw the value in personal development and responsibility through working at an early age. "My father's family at times did not have enough food during the Depression, as his father left the family at an early age, so their only salvation was working to earn enough money to survive. He was so used to working since childhood, that he had such an appreciation for what work did for him and others. I also remember him sharing his views about tipping, that you did not want to save money for yourself by going light on tipping, that people in service jobs relied upon those tips to live, and that they worked very hard for their money, and that you should be a generous tipper. When people came to the door selling something, he always was gracious and listened intently to their story and tried to help them. My mother also told stories of her working in her upbringing."

One of her first jobs was babysitting for a family of four girls down the street. Her older brother cut their grass and got $1 per hour, while Susan got 50 cents per hour for babysitting. "My mom pointed out the inequity of this, saying that I was responsible for the wellbeing and safety of their children! She insisted I call this family and tell them from now on I would not babysit for less than $1.00/hour. They acquiesced. An early lesson in insisting on equal rights!"

Susan was always close with her mother. However, especially when she was a teen, she recalls that she didn't get along with her father. "He had such a strong personality and I was always introverted and shy. He was very opinionated and I think he just overwhelmed me. We grew much closer when I became an adult."

Susan had two younger identical twin brothers, Jim and John, who were diagnosed with schizophrenia. John was diagnosed at 18, and Jim somewhat later, around 21. Susan was about 20 years old when John was diagnosed. "My parents took care of them emotionally and financially. They made sure they saw the best psychiatrists and bought them each a condo, held in trust, so they would always have a place to live. They were each able to work for a time thanks to medication and therapy. But they eventually both lost their jobs because of a psychotic break. Both are now deceased."

Susan tells how terribly sad it was to watch this happen to her brothers and to see how it affected her parents, as they understandably were devastated. "Jim and John were only two years younger than me and we were pretty close. This was the first time I became anxious about life and realized that very bad things can happen. When I saw my father cry about my brothers after he dropped them off at the hospital, it hit me very hard. Today, I consider myself an anxious person, maybe a result of that experience. We never felt neglected, just felt terribly for my parents and brothers. My parents tried EVERYTHING to make them well, and paid a lot out-of-pocket given the lack of health care coverage for mental health issues at that time."

One of her first serious boyfriends was Asian-American, and she sensed that her parents did not approve, though they didn't stop her from seeing him. "It simply never occurred to me that you couldn't marry someone with a different background than you. My parents were disappointed that I married someone outside my faith, but they were gracious about it always. I would not care one bit if my children married someone of a different race or faith or if they were gay."

Susan graduated from Stone Ridge High School in 1975. Stone Ridge was a small, girls-only, expensive school run by nuns of the Sacred Heart order, considered an elite college-prep school. There were only 35 in her class. "There were few people of color and just a couple of Jewish girls in my class. Everyone else was Catholic." Susan recalls her mother cautioning her that she would meet a lot of rich people in her school who would have things that she wouldn't and that this might be difficult for her.

"In any event, I never felt that I was any different or lacked anything materially. This is a credit to my parents, the school and my classmates. I am still in touch with many of them today and make it a point to travel to DC a couple times a year to visit. They are great friends who have supported me in everything. Stone Ridge was a great education – small classes and wonderful teachers. They really taught you how to think and how to write. Academically, for me, college was less challenging."

Stone Ridge had a program called "Social Action." Every Wednesday during the school day, all students would go out in the community and volunteer with an organization for a couple of hours. Susan does not remember all the places she volunteered, but she does remember volunteering one year at a hospital and another year at a local orphanage. "I particularly loved the orphanage. It was a well-run organization and the kids were amazing."

Another program called Intersession took place every January. For two weeks, instead of going to school, students had a volunteer internship at a workplace. "I remember my sophomore year, I worked at a Congressional office on Capitol Hill. This was really fun and interesting. I learned a lot and felt like such a grownup. I remember seeing famous politicians in the hallways, on elevators and on the subway tram that runs between the two houses of Congress."

"The only negative at my high school was that there were a few bullies who bothered me from time to time. Of course, this was before bullying was recognized. It was bothersome but not horrible."

Susan talks about how close she still is with some of her friends from Stone Ridge, and how they are now into a routine to attend class reunions, a tradition that began with her 20-year reunion. What from that high school experience cemented the relationships with some of her classmates? Susan explains that her classes were small, the nuns were strict, and there was a lot of shared experiences from those years. "We all received a wonderful education, we all had to study hard in study groups, and those times created bonds that seem to have lasted a lifetime."

ON TO COLLEGE

Susan describes her college years as unsettled. She began at Dickinson College in Carlisle, Pennsylvania, a small liberal-arts college. "I absolutely hated it, though I made good friends there. It was so small and felt very confining. There wasn't much to do there aside from studying of course. The first year I came home almost every weekend."

After a year and a half, she decided to transfer to the University of Maryland and came back home and started commuting. "However, I couldn't seem to settle in and wasn't doing very well in the large classes, so I dropped out and took a job as a server in a restaurant. I knew I would go back to college, as not finishing was out of the question, but I just couldn't figure out where I wanted to go and what I wanted to do. I was rather stuck."

Susan's mother had a friend whose daughter had just returned from a year at the American College in Paris (now the American University in Paris). "I was always good at languages and Mom thought this would be a great place for me, so in the fall of 1977, off I went. I almost changed my mind and didn't go but my mom talked me into it. She gave me confidence, whereas my dad didn't want me to go. He changed his mind after I came home at Christmas and was so happy."

When I asked Susan some of the things she is most proud of in life, she named her year in Paris as one of them. "I was scared to death but I am so glad I went, as it changed my life."

Susan indicates that even though she didn't know anyone there upon arrival, everything just clicked for her. Her first semester she rented a room in an apartment owned by Mme. Van der Heyden. "I can't believe I still remember her name. She sounds German but she was French. Anyway, she was a grandmother and was very kind to me, helping me get settled and introducing me to her family. I had a good grasp of French thanks to Stone Ridge and a year and a half at Dickinson. I've always been an introvert but in Paris I had to just go up to people and introduce myself, as that's how I made friends.

Since this was an American school, there were many Americans there but also many international students. I loved it."

The second semester she rented an apartment with another girl she had met. "She and I traveled and partied a lot to the detriment of my studies."

I found it curious how happy Susan became when she went to Paris and lived independently, as others may have been overwhelmed or feeling estranged in a foreign place. "I guess that the independence was key, I needed to get away. I was a little lost at that time in my life. In Paris, everything was new! I could be who I wanted to be, the city was beautiful, it was easy and inexpensive to get around, and I felt safe. Being alone made me become more outgoing, I had to approach people and engage just to get through the basics of living, even though I always considered myself a shy person."

After the year in Paris, Susan enrolled at Penn State University's main campus. One of her friends at Dickinson had transferred there and they roomed together. "I ended up majoring in French and graduated in 1980. Except for spending money, my parents paid for college for me, and all of my siblings." While there, she was introduced to a guy named Larry in a bar. Later, she went to a sorority dance and attended with Larry. "Although I was possibly interested in a remote relationship after I graduated and moved away, Larry was not, as he was still pursuing his PhD."

ON TO A CAREER

After graduating, Susan moved back to DC and had various jobs until deciding to go to graduate school back at Penn State. "My first real job out of college was working in the HR department at the US Customs agency because my dad knew the Director of US Customs from Congressional. I didn't last long there though, it was boring!"

About a year later, after enrolling at Penn State, she switched majors from French to Public Administration, and graduated with an MPA degree.

Susan's career was mainly working in higher education development for over 30 years, raising money for scholarships and other needs at three different universities. "The money I raised, particularly for scholarships, will benefit generations of students who don't have the means to attend college. Education is life-changing and I hope I contributed to expanding access to it."

While at Penn State, she renewed her relationship with Larry, who would become her husband. "My husband and I are very different people and I'm sure many people were surprised when we fell in love and got married. I never met anyone who could make me laugh so hard, he was and still is a lot of fun. I love that we are able to travel. I love that Larry is so open to new experiences and that he's an extrovert. I love his intelligence and his loyalty."

FAMILY LIFE

Susan married Larry at age 27 in 1984. "We had Carolyn in 1986 and Stephen in 1990. From the very beginning, I loved being a mom and I still do. I loved every single phase of parenting – babyhood, toddlerhood, kindergarten, elementary school, adolescence, and into adulthood. It's the best thing I ever did." Susan recalls that everyone told her the hard parts about being a parent, about the many physical and emotional demands, but that they did not tell her enough about what a joy it was. "Really the hardest part is when one of your children is unhappy and you can't fix it. It doesn't matter if they're 2 or 22, it's hard." Susan indicates that since her husband is Jewish and she was Catholic (lapsed), it was difficult at Christmas-time. "We raised our kids Jewish in a small town and I know that was hard for them."

How did Susan balance a career and also being a mom? "When our daughter was born, I became a fulltime mom, but after 8-9 months, we needed two incomes to buy a house, and we found Judy, who was not only a fulltime mom but a childcare professional with a master's degree in childhood education, and I felt no guilt in leaving Carolyn with Judy during the day. When Stephen was born four years later, we realized that it would be best for me to become a fulltime mom. My mother did not like that decision at all, she wanted me to continue with my career, probably because she never had a choice to work or not. However, when Stephen became four years old, I went back to work part-time doing some fund-raising work for the girl scouts and other organizations. Once Stephen was old enough to go into first grade, I began working fulltime again, mainly at the university-level. I appreciated those occasions when my employer allowed me the flexibility to take the time I needed when family issues arose."

Would she do anything differently in raising her children if she had to do it over again? "I would have stayed home longer. When I was a fulltime mom, I always wanted to be with our kids, did not want to go out, did not want to travel, etc. I'll never forget how delighted our daughter was when she got off the kindergarten school bus and ran up to the front door eager to tell me about her morning. I'll never forget how happy our son was when we would play with his action figures or go on outings to watch construction workers."

In talking to Susan, you quickly get the sense that her family means so much to her, in fact, she describes her family as one of her life's proudest accomplishments. "Without a doubt, I am most proud of my family. I married a wonderful guy, my husband Larry, and we built a good life together, not a life without problems but we persevered. We've traveled and had some fun. Our kids are fantastic. I believe that raising children is part luck but I also hope that I helped to create a nurturing, loving environment where they felt encouraged and protected. I hope they know I always had their back, and still do, and I always believed in them, as they believed in me. Above all I wanted them to be kind and caring and they are. They have already far exceeded my hopes and dreams for them."

In 2013, since her brothers needed additional assistance, they moved to Ohio to be closer to Susan.

In 2016, due partially to her brothers needing more help after her mother died, she retired from development, and with her family's encouragement, enrolled in the master's program in French at Kent State. "My husband and kids were my biggest cheerleaders in going back to school."

Jim passed away in 2017 and in 2018, John died.

"John had a lot of insight into his illness, and knew enough to discuss medications and effects with others. Jim on the other hand was not functional, and had physical side effects from the medications and ended up in a wheelchair, and eventually had to have a tracheotomy. John would stop in and check on Jim while he was able, but Susan visited both of them daily throughout this period, and helped line up doctors for them after their move. Eventually John got his own apartment only 20 minutes away and did well for a while."

"I am proud of taking care of my brothers after my parents died. They needed a lot of help and I did my best to give it to them. You simply have to be there for your family. Before you get the family you choose, you have the family you are given. Jim and John were part of the family I was given and I owed it to them and to my parents to be there for them. It was so difficult watching my brothers struggle with the suffering, pain and problems, especially Jim. In looking back, though, I would have better established boundaries so that their care was not so all-consuming. I would have accepted the fact that Jim was never going to get better no matter what I did, he was too ill."

A SIDE NOTE ABOUT CAREGIVING

I find her comment about 'having the family you are given' as so interesting, since these days, many families seem to fall apart after some challenging situations, but Susan had the loyalty and commitment to be there for her brothers.

We discussed her caregiving and my own experience as well, and we both felt at a loss in terms of our lack of being prepared for what we were getting into, as well as the personal time investment in the care of others. We both saw how medicine today could extend the lives of so many, yet the quality of life was not good for many of them. "We are the generation where people are living longer due to advances in medicine, but sometimes you have to ask at what cost for the patient and family."

This issue of spending time, sometimes years, as a caregiver for aging parents or siblings, seems to be a commonality for some within the Boomer generation today. Most admit to being unprepared for the duties and responsibility required, the sacrifices of time, and the emotional challenges, as they at times had to put their own lives on hold, and spend much less time on things important to them, including immediate family. It is common to hear Boomers say things such as 'I feel I have aged five years in the last year' when talking about time spent as a caregiver.

I admire the commitment Susan had to her family, and her feeling proud of the sacrifices she made for them.

If nothing else, younger generations might think about what may be in store for them in the future, and be better prepared than many Boomers were. If nothing else, we all need to think about how we might minimize the impact to our families as our own health declines in later life.

CURRENT LIFESTYLE

After earning her degree in French in 2019, Susan now spends a lot of time reading fiction and also about World War II, and spends more time with friends. She also watches movies with Larry, and also walks, runs errands, gardens, and plans travel for her and Larry. Her son lives in New York City while her daughter lives in Cincinnati, and they enjoy visits with them. She leverages her background in French by occasionally teaching classes in French history, as she is an adjunct professor, and is especially well-read about the history of France in World War II. She enjoys visiting France, Italy and other locations occasionally as well, and very much enjoys speaking French. "I just love the French language and culture." She also is a proponent of international travel as a way to learn about other cultures and people. "I know it is expensive, but I think if people travelled more, it would be a better world."

"At this point in my life, I can look back and hope I am leaving the world a better place through my children and through my work at colleges and universities."

POLLING FOR OPINIONS

Besides family, what are you most proud of in your life?

I am proud of choosing to stay home after our son was born, and I am also proud of leaving my job in development in 2016, which was a difficult decision but the right one.

If forced to list only three of the most important lessons in life you have learned, which might benefit others, what would they be?

Successful relationships are the key to happiness.

Kindness matters.

Don't be afraid of failure; embrace it when it happens because you will learn a lot about yourself.

Tell me about how your religious beliefs have changed throughout life.

I was raised in the Catholic church, but I have become a lapsed Catholic. It's something I can't completely give up, but I used to be quite religious as a child. Even away at college, I used to go to Mass on Sundays from time to time. I am ambivalent about many of the tenets the Church holds. My mom developed a skepticism about the Catholic Church as well toward the end of her life. She once walked out of Mass because the priest's homily was all about how evil abortion was. I also am wary that all the chapters in the Bible were written by men.

I have been fortunate enough to be able to travel outside of the country, and that has created a sense of more tolerance for other beliefs and religions. Also, during the feminist movement, I became more aware of how most religions were male-dominated, and I began to question some of the tenets of many of them. I have become wary of others who try to impose their beliefs on others.

I would call myself a spiritual person now, and not a religious person.

If someone from another generation asked you the meaning of life, what would you say?

It's about being kind and helping other people whenever possible, and finding out who you are at your core and living it; that's a journey.

Tell me about your relationship with your children.

I would rate my relationship with my children a 10. I think they feel they can tell me anything and I will always love them unconditionally.

How would you compare the values of yourself to your children?

In some ways my children and I have similar values. They both went to college and did well. They are not religious but believe in caring for other people, being open-minded and tolerant. They love to travel and appreciate other cultures. My children care more about the environment than I did growing up, although I've become more concerned about climate change, landfills, etc. as I've become more aware. They opened my eyes about this, as well as acceptance of the gay culture. I was never homo-phobic, I just never gave it much thought. When I was growing up, gay people had to hide who they were (and to some extent they still do) and I didn't know any gay people until Larry and I moved to Los Angeles.

Were your parents stricter than you were as a parent?

My parents were much stricter than I was. I consciously chose to be a more laidback parent. I knew I would never spank my kids, as my parents had done, and I very much wanted my children to not be afraid of or intimidated by me.

I was also very aware that stress could be a contributing factor in mental illness and in the back of my mind I had a nagging fear that what had happened to my brothers might happen to my kids, since mental illness can be hereditary. This was very much an underlying worry, not something that overwhelmed my thinking. It was definitely a factor, however, in my parenting style. My mother's sister, my Aunt Mary, had schizophrenia and eventually committed suicide. I could think of nothing more disastrous than something like that happening to my kids.

Do you still help your children financially even if they are adults?

We occasionally help our children financially. My parents helped us from time to time. For example, when they sold their house, they gave each of my siblings and I a part of the proceeds. Earlier in our married life, they would give us a small amount every now and then.

Do you think you worry too much about your children?

I worried about my children's' mental health even into adulthood. The worry was along the lines of if they would have the fortitude to overcome the setbacks and difficulties that life would inevitably throw their way? Would they become depressed? Would they develop a severe mental illness?

I didn't get the sense that my parents worried about us, at least until Jim and John got sick. Then their needs were all-consuming, and they didn't express much worry about anything else.

Did you ever fear some sort of physical punishment (e.g., spanking) from your parents if you misbehaved?

I was occasionally spanked by my parents but it was mostly my brothers who were. They were always up to mischief, so I don't think their fear of spanking ever stopped them. I don't think our daughter was ever afraid of being spanked, but our son was, somewhat. But I don't think it was a major fear, as I think we only spanked one or two times that I can remember. I remember completely losing my temper over something and spanking him, but not hard.

Spanking is not good and I don't think our children will ever spank. I know my dad spanked because that's what his parents did.

Do you think that society does or does not value enough a parent who stays home with children?

Society definitely does not value this enough.

Do you believe that the generations following ours will be, in general, better off or worse financially when they get to our age?

I think it will be about the same. There will be continued economic disparity; those with access to education and training, graduate school and therefore good jobs will do well and those without will do poorly.

Do you believe those generations will live in a better country and world in the coming decades, versus what our generation experienced as we aged?

I think the U.S. will continue to decline in influence and economic power. This is because we aren't truly a democracy, as gerrymandering, lobbyists and dark money have taken voting power away from ordinary people.

Do you worry, or did you worry, too much or too little about your parents?

I worried about the effect of my brothers' illness on them. I worried a lot about my mom after my father died.

What are you planning to have happen with any funds or possessions after you die?

It's very important to me that we leave funds to our children. In addition, it's important to me that I am leaving a small bequest to Maryville University to a scholarship fund that my brother John started which helps disadvantaged students.

Did you drink growing up?

I didn't drink until I went to Paris. I smoked for about 5 years but quit before I got married. I tried marijuana a couple of times and didn't like it.

What about your friendships today?

Friends are very important. When I was working and had small children, I didn't have time for friends. Any time I wasn't working, I wanted to be with my kids. As I got older, I have realized the importance of friendships and have made sure to keep in touch with girlfriends.

Which historical events influenced you the most?

I remember clearly when Roe v. Wade was announced. I was at school (Stone Ridge) and we had an all-school assembly to discuss it. Well, 'discuss it' meant really that the high school principal told us how terrible it was and that if we agreed with Roe v. Wade we were going against the Church. My parents were very pro-life at the time so I was pro-life. This changed when I was about 20 and I became pro-choice. I started to know people who had abortions and they were just ordinary people who were in a terrible place. My mom became pro-choice eventually. I'm not sure about my dad.

What also affected me a lot was the rise of feminism. In the 70's, many more women were choosing careers and there was the idea that you could "have it all." I flirted with the idea of law school, but ultimately decided it wasn't for me, nor was I interested in business. My mom saw all the opportunities I had and both my parents wanted me to have a career. I embraced this idea but when I had children, I saw the advantages of staying home. I also realized you couldn't have it all, at least not all at once.

Of course, the internet has completely changed life. It's mostly a good thing, but I'm glad my kids didn't have the internet readily accessible when they were very young. Same with a cell phone. Kids have way too much screen time now and there's too much online bullying.

How do you feel about U.S. immigration, the border wall, and our illegal alien policies?

We need to fix the immigration system so that more people qualify for asylum and don't have to wait 10 years to gain legal entry into the U.S.

How do you feel about the second amendment and gun rights?

Guns are much too accessible in the U.S. I support peoples' right to bear arms, but not semi-automatic and automatic weapons. People should have to have training to own a firearm. It's stupid and scary how easy it is to get a gun.

Do you consider yourself to be a conservative or liberal or somewhere in between?

I consider myself a moderate who leans left. I used to be more conservative, probably due to my parents' influence and the fact that I led a sheltered life. Over time, due mainly to travel, I learned that other people and cultures are fine also, and I became more tolerant of others.

The press talks a lot about the growing disparity in income – is that a big problem in your opinion?

It's a huge problem, probably the biggest (along with growing religious fundamentalism) in my lifetime. Aside from the sadness and wasted potential of people living in poverty, this breeds resentment and bitterness which only leads to more problems.

Are you more worried about the environment now vs. when you were in your teens or in the middle of life?

Definitely. There's more awareness. Nobody was even very concerned about littering when I was a kid.

Do you believe the US should be more focused upon our country mainly, or more focused globally, in terms of how our tax dollars are used?

We need to be focused globally because global problems become/are national problems.

Do you think the country is headed in the wrong or right direction?

I think there is currently a lot of back-lash from the democrat leadership years. Some of this is just plain racism. The rise of our next president shocked me. There is a meanness in people that was probably always under the surface but is now acceptable to be shared out loud and put on full display.

SUMMARY

I hope you enjoyed hearing about Susan's story. Here is someone who others might say grew up in a very privileged environment, yet due to the values of her parents, and her own experiences, she has become someone very tolerant of others, and someone who is still learning and questioning her beliefs.

I was particularly impressed with the decisions she made to retire to enable her to take care of her brothers, and her experience in caregiving. Susan has created a life which today is rich with friends, family, experiences, travel, reading, and hobbies. In talking to her, you get the sense that she is very happy in her current life as well as the memories she has created.

It was so enjoyable writing about a person who made a lot of good decisions in her life, worked hard, was loyal to family, and tried to make the world a better place. Thank you, Susan, for being an exemplary Boomer!

CHAPTER 7:
Roy, The Competitor

BACKGROUND

I first met Roy at my first professional job, as we both worked within the Information Technology department. After a year or so of gaining experience, I was placed on a project team with Roy and two others, and we were to replace a manufacturing plant system with a new mini-computer system that was fairly untested and new technology. The project seemed to go on forever, but Roy was the more experienced of all the 'junior' team members, and I learned a lot from him. He struck me as extremely organized and logical. His desk, at end of day, was completely clean, while mine had all sorts of paperwork and in-progress programs and testing material.

Over the years, we became friends, mainly due to common interests, plus he and his wife had two children who were about the same age as our two children. Eventually, we both joined the same golf club where our children got to know one another either via swimming, tennis, or golf.

Both Roy and I spent our entire careers at the same company, something very rare today. He retired about a year before I did. This followed about 30 years of both of us talking about, and dreaming about, retirement, a favorite topic for sure.

As you will read in his story, Roy was a very good basketball player, from a basketball family. One year, while we were in our 30's, Roy asked me to play on his league team. I was not much of a basketball player, and was honored he would even ask me. I did not contribute much to the team, but in watching Roy play in multiple games, I came to respect his hustle, and how competitive he was. It was almost as if he had a chip on his shoulder towards the other team. Unlike me, he never feared driving under the basket against much taller and more physical players, and would somehow usually score a basket inside against those taller opponents.

Later in our careers, we worked in the same IT area again, and it was fun having Roy as a teammate. I relied on his advice a lot, after having been away in other functional areas.

Once retired, we got into the habit of meeting for a beer once every few months, and trying new craft beers and having a bite to eat. We also socialize as couples.

Roy's story is a classic Boomer one, with some interesting twists and turns. The one word that describes Roy, above others I can think of, is 'competitive'.

EARLY LIFE

Roy was born in 1956, and had three older siblings, two brothers and a sister. His father was a teacher and renowned basketball coach, and his mother was a stay-at-home mom. Roy recalls that great parents and sports were an important part of his early years.

"What immediately comes to mind is how blessed I was to have the childhood I did. I grew up with a father who was a very successful high school basketball coach at one of the best basketball schools and facilities in the local area. This was in an era where sports like basketball was a big deal and of great interest, unlike today. It gave me opportunities that most kids didn't have. I was able to go to practices with my dad, to attend most of the games and sit behind the bench, ride the bus to away games, go into the locker room at halftime (obviously not just anyone can do that), and to be around players older than me. This gave me a great sense of pride and made me feel special, especially amongst my friends and even some adults who were fans. This established, in my opinion, the primary foundation for who I am today."

Roy recalls that he cut a few of his neighbor's lawns as a grade schooler making $2 each cut. "I enjoyed cutting so it seemed to be a no brainer."

Roy's two older brothers and Roy grew up playing a variety of sports. His older sister was very athletic but unfortunately, at that time, organized girls sports were very limited. "Given my father's success as a coach, I was very proud to be my father's son. He instilled in me a sense of pride and competitiveness that lives with and guides me today. Our family name, back in the day, meant something. I felt special, but not entitled."

Roy talks about the 'burden' that he felt that came along with his father's success. "My siblings and I did not then, and do not now, want to do anything that would in any way shape or form tarnish the reputation my dad built, and the legacy he left behind. It's a feeling or sense that requires us to live to a higher level of standard than most, although that feeling is really self-imposed, rather than ever being stated as an expectation by my parents. I wouldn't have it any other way though."

Since his dad was a basketball coach, Roy indicates that this was a major part of his family's life for a long time. "Not much time was spent paying attention to current affairs, politics, religion, and other basics of life. Granted basketball was not a yearlong activity, we just didn't pay that much attention to other things, at least that I recall. At that time, I was more interested in hanging out with a few friends just trying to enjoy the moment."

When Roy was a junior in high school, a tragedy hit the family which has had a lasting effect on Roy ever since. Roy's older brother was 26, and died in a car accident in Virginia on a Saturday night around 10:30 p.m., the night before Mother's Day.

"I was at home that Saturday evening and around that time of day, I had a very uneasy unexplainable feeling about me. I decided to go for a walk in the neighborhood and at one point, I stopped in the middle of the street, looked up at the moon, and had a brief shiver (for lack of better description). I continued on with my walk and stopped at my best friend's house. His mother answered the doorbell, and she was like my 2nd Mom. She noticed I wasn't right and asked me "are you ok?". My response was "I don't know" and I left to return home without seeing my friend. Around 2 a.m. Sunday morning, the Virginia police called my parent's house to tell them my brother had been in an auto accident and was killed. My mother let out a scream I will never forget, nor do I want to hear again. My Dad tried to call my brother's apartment phone many times hoping he would answer and that this was a case of mistaken identity. There was no answer, and reality set in. It was awful! No parent should lose a child, especially in a way such as this."

A week later while in Virginia, when his parents were cleaning out his brother's apartment, they received a copy of the death certificate, and the recorded time of death was just about the same time Roy went for his walk the night he was killed. "It made sense to me then that what I experienced, prompting my walk, was some form of a premonition and I determined that a part of me died that evening, too. This was the first experience I can remember where something way beyond my control happened to me and that made me realize there is something much larger than us."

"My brother was a very good high school basketball player. Even though we were 9 years apart, I was close to him as I always looked up to him. I recall the following school year (my senior year in high school) I prayed to myself in the locker room before each of my basketball games, asking that he be with me and be proud of me."

In high school, and throughout his college years, Roy worked in the summer for the local school district, doing a variety of jobs, but mostly cutting grass at each of the school buildings. "I loved the job, sitting on a tractor all day long. It was lonely, especially at the grade schools where there was no activity. But I was able to make enough money to pay my share of the following year's college tuition. I took a great deal of pride with how the grass looked after each cut and that pride carried over into future work."

In high school, Roy played basketball and therefore was known by most of the student body and staff. "I have many great memories, many of which were associated with basketball. I am a fairly private person, like my dad was, even though his profession put him in the spotlight. I preferred a small inner circle of friends back then, and that is true to this day. If I could do it over again, I would try to be more social than I was."

ON TO COLLEGE

Roy attended and graduated from Bowling Green State University, following in the footsteps of two older siblings. As he found a proficiency in math in high school, he decided to be a math major with a computer science minor.

"I was 18 or 19 years old, not really thinking of the future. Therefore, most of my classes were in those fields. Any electives I chose tended to be something simple and easy. Knowing then what I now know, I would have taken more courses outside my major and minor, such as finance, economics, and business to give me a broader and more diverse background to better prepare me for life."

Roy indicates that his college experience was a great one, where he met a small number of friends who became part of his inner circle, and they continue to be in that inner circle today. "While I was not good enough to play for the BGSU basketball team, I spent many hours in the gym playing pick-up basketball games as well as intramurals. A memory I'll never forget was being on an "on campus" intramural basketball team my sophomore year coming in first place in the tournament out of roughly 300+ teams. After becoming the 'on campus' champs in the post-season tournament, we beat the 'off-campus' champs, who were slightly older, and then the fraternity champs to win the overall title."

ON TO A CAREER

In 1978, Roy accepted a job with a global manufacturing company in the area of his home town. "I've always taken pride in my work. I feel part of that comes from being competitive and having a sense of accomplishment." He held a series of information technology jobs during his career with the same employer, culminating with him being responsible for the company's data center, a significant responsibility.

"During my 35 years, I was able to contribute, in a small way for sure, to the company's success. I broadened and enhanced my skillset in areas such as budgeting, finance, leadership, interpersonal skills, communication, etc. that I still benefit from today. Leadership to me seemed to be a natural skillset that I attribute to my upbringing watching my father in action. This, combined with my basketball playing days, enabled me to develop the ability to easily deal with pressure and stressful situations. I recall a few of my coworkers telling me that I brought a calming presence to stressful situations which I took great satisfaction in hearing."

FAMILY LIFE

Roy met his wife Katie at his place of employment, and they subsequently married and had two children. Those children are now married and raising their own families. "It's a blessing to see how well our children have grown into adulthood. I hope my wife and I, at least in some small way, have influenced and had a positive impact on their young lives much like our parents had with us. Katie shares many of the same values and beliefs as I do. We are a good team in that we complement each other very well. While she worked professionally in the IT world for 35 years, she volunteers her time at several organizations, one of which is Habitat for Humanity. She learned many of the construction trades in that role, to the point that she can fix issues and maintain many aspects of home ownership which is one thing that never appealed to me due to lack of skills and interest. Conversely, I enjoy outdoor work such as grass-cutting which Katie doesn't have much interest in. She continues to impress me with her ability to focus in on the task at hand, regardless of how difficult or how much time it takes. There's never a challenge she's not willing to take on."

In 2010, not too many years from retirement, Roy was diagnosed and treated for melanoma, and today remains cancer-free. "That was sort of a reminder to me that there is no guarantee of how long you will be around."

Roy lost both of his parents at different times, both while he was employed. But his father's passing seems to have affected Roy significantly. "He spent the last few days of his life in a compassionate care center heavily sedated. He was not fed any food or water, basically there to die a natural death. My two older living siblings and I spent much of that time there to be with him. During those days, my dad was not awake and did not move, until one point out of the blue he raised one arm up in such a way that it looked like he was reaching out for something. I never did talk to any of the staff to understand what might have caused that. Instead, I chose to see it that he was reaching out to his savior and that his spirit left his body at that time. He passed a very short time later. That experience, combined with my experience when my brother was killed, have made me realize there is a higher power and my level of interest in religion and faith have increased since."

Shortly after his father's passing, Roy decided to retire, realizing that life on this earth is too short. "I wanted to be able to enjoy the smaller things in life and adjust my values and priorities accordingly."

ON TO RETIREMENT

Roy retired in 2012, and feels blessed with how his life has played out.

"As I age, I realize that the changes in how I view and value things, is a natural progression of life. There may be a few things I'd do differently if given the chance to go back in time, but none of those are significant in nature. I'm happy being who I was and am."

Roy and his wife Katie enjoy visiting their children and their families, and travel a fair amount in order to spend time with them.

Roy indicates that like the relationship he had with his parents, the relationship he has with his two children is excellent. "They more or less have the same values that my wife and I have. And we love and get along wonderfully with the five grandchildren."

POLLING FOR OPINIONS

If forced to list the most important lessons in life you have learned, which might benefit others, what would they be?

In no particular order:

1. Do the best you can and give it your all
2. Treat people as you would want to be treated (kindness, honesty, etc.)
3. Given these two, you'll build credibility and should be trusted and respected by others. Therefore, continue to uphold and honor that reputation, especially knowing to compromise that can have a damaging impact on others (loved ones).
4. Understand, appreciate, and respect your past but continue to look forward.

If a Millennial or Gen X or Gen Z person was sitting next to you on your death bed, and they asked you "What is the meaning of life? What is it all about?" What do you think your answer would be?

A couple of things come to mind, in no particular order. These might be more "lessons in life" than "meaning". However, doing these should make one's life fulfilling and meaningful:

Be kind and respectful of others. Be confident in and true to yourself. Perform good deeds for others when opportunities present themselves. This could be something as simple as giving a smile to another or holding a door open.

Be patient with, and less judgmental, of others. Continue to challenge yourself and grow as a human being. One can always do more than what one might think. Minimize the number of regrets you might have. In other words, take advantage of opportunities even though they might seem difficult at the time.

Were your parents stricter than you were as a parent?

Given that I never gave any reason for my parents to perform any disciplinary action combined with me being the youngest of 4 children, there was not much of this needed. I felt I was stricter in raising my children, especially with my oldest being a male. In hindsight, I expected more perfection than I should have.

Do you help your children financially as adults? Do you help them also with your time?

Yes. It's a combination of spending time and providing monetary gifts. My children and grandchildren live out of state so Katie and I don't see them as often as we would like. When we do though, we try to help however we can, whether that's with errands, watching the grandchildren, and any other daily activities. We receive a great deal of satisfaction when we're able to help in that way and it provides us a chance to spend quality time with our family. Both Katie's and my parents did some of the same for us when we were raising our family and we greatly appreciated the extra support. We want to do the same for our children and grandchildren.

Tell me about the pride you obviously have in your children?

My children never got into any serious trouble growing up, and always seemed to be selective in what friends they had. They made it through those teenage years well, which admittedly was a concern of mine at the time, as those years can be very influential to them. Both my children are now adults raising their own families. I give them a great deal of credit in that they were willing to move away from Ohio where they grew up to pursue their own life and opportunities, whether that be a professional career or otherwise. They have become very self-sufficient and independent.

How do you feel about the family structure of today versus when you grew up?

I feel the lack of family structure today is much greater than before. My belief is this contributes to some of today's problems in society.

Is there anything you would do differently in parenting in looking back?

Possibly adjust my expectation on demanding perfection. With that said, I'd rather error on the side I was on vs. the opposite.

Do you believe that the generations following ours will be, in general, better off or worse financially when they get to our age?

In general, I'd say worse. The wealth gap will continue to broaden in the foreseeable future. Our nation's debt will continue to be a heavy burden on generations to come with possible changes to programs such as Social Security and Medicare potentially being negatively affected at some point.

Do you believe younger generations will live in a better country and world in the coming decades, versus what our generation experienced as we aged?

No. Listen to the news. More is being reported today than yesterday, or at least that I notice. People are feeling more entitled. People are voicing their opinion more. People are less respectful. Politics are toxic. Years ago, once this trend began, I felt we needed another 9/11 type event to pull people back together. Two years ago, along comes Covid and at first, I was thinking that might be "that event". As it's turning out, Covid has increased the downward trend in how people and societies are behaving. I feel for the next set of generations.

Did you worry too much or too little about your parents as they aged?

Both my parents are deceased. My mom passed in 2001 after an 18-month battle with breast cancer. My dad passed in 2012 of COPD. To this day I regret:

1. Not taking seriously enough and paying more attention to my mom at the time of her illness. I was in my mid-40s, working and raising a family. I realize now I should have spent more time with her.
2. I regret not telling both my mom and dad, in particular as they aged, that I loved them. I realize in my own aging process how much that would mean to me for my kids to tell me that....so it likely would have meant something to my mom and dad.
3. Not giving a eulogy at my dad's funeral service (nor did my two older siblings). He deserved that, and I feel I've let him down, so much so that I have shared this with both my son and daughter as a "lesson learned". This would be near the top of my list of things to take a mulligan on if given the chance.

Were you a caregiver when your parents were aged?

I was fortunate that neither of my parents needed to use assisted living and/or nursing care. With that said, as my dad aged and lived alone, I would sometimes take a few meals to him and take care of the lawn. At the time, taking care of the lawn was a burden to me and I didn't look forward to it as it cut into my own time. In the end though that was a small sacrifice to do what was right.

What are you planning to have happen with any funds or possessions after you die?

At this time, Katie and I plan to leave anything we might have left to our two children.

Do you remember your parents or older relatives talking about the Great Depression?

I don't recall much in the way of discussion with parents about the Depression. However, with my mom being a stay-at-home mother and therefore only one household income, with four children, my parents were careful not to spend much. Whether by coincidence or as a result, in my earlier years (and even today to some extent) I was very conservative with my spending and tried to save as much as I could. My two children seem to be following in those same footsteps.

How would you characterize your contributions to your employer / customers / clients / society during the time of your career? What are you most proud of?

I'm most proud of the fact that I was willing to do whatever it took to get the job done. I often viewed work (projects, tasks, etc.) as a competition and I always wanted to be on the winning end. I take great satisfaction in that. I also felt I built a solid reputation in my young professional career and there was always an obligation and desire on my part to maintain, if not build upon, that positive reputation. To do otherwise would be a failure.

How did music impact you growing up?

I love music. I listened to rock and roll growing up and part of it I feel stems from the fact I had three older siblings. The Beatles were big in my household as a young child and to this day they're probably my all-time favorite group even though I might not listen to them as much now. I listen mostly to classic rock and Motown and tend to listen to the music of decades ago vs new music. I am not really into country. I have playlists on my phone based mostly on genre. What mood I'm in at the time dictates which playlist I pull up. Music (songs) tends to remind me of past experiences and provides me an opportunity for reflection. I often say (to myself if nobody else) "music is good for the soul".

Boomers have, and had, a reputation for drinking beer/wine/alcohol. Did you drink growing up? Has that changed as you aged, and if so, how?

Other than one or two beers in high school, I didn't start drinking until college. I drank beer and on occasion my friends and I would drink shots, usually Old Grandad or Wild Turkey bourbon. Over the years I have many great, and not so great, memories where alcohol was involved. I never tried pot or other drugs. I just didn't feel that was a road I wanted to take. I am not so sure I'm in favor of legalizing recreational pot, and if it were to be legalized in the states I live, I'm not so sure I'd partake, although you don't have hangovers from what I'm told.

How would you describe your adult friendships? How important are your friends vs family?

As stated previously, I'm a pretty private person and am guarded in what I say or do (with exceptions). Therefore, I've always maintained a small inner circle of friends that I feel comfortable with. My family and this small inner circle are very important to me. They provide me a foundation (among others) by which to live. I have many casual friends but am guarded in what I say to or do with them. The amount of time I spend with others is about right at this point. With this said, I suspect the line at my funeral will not be all that long.

What do you recall about the press (TV and newspapers mainly) when you were a teenager and in your twenties? How does that compare to now?

Right or wrong, I didn't spend much time during this timeframe paying attention to the media and the news they reported. I will say over the last few years, that the media, or my perception of the media, is that they have become more selective in what they communicate. Too much of it in my opinion is biased to fit their narrative. Over the last 12 months, I have reduced how much news I watch on TV, especially cable news networks. I'd much rather hear more about real news with facts to allow me to form my own opinion. I realize this doesn't sell though, which is unfortunate we've come to this. I feel too many people fall prey to and develop their opinions on misinformation.

What about 9/11? How did that affect how you think about our country and about terrorism?

9/11 was a very shocking event. My wife and I were stunned and glued to the TV for the news. It was an eye opener in that it made us realize how vulnerable we were on our own soil. I'm sure most of us never thought something like that could happen here. I'm more concerned now about cyber warfare attacks (power grid, financial markets, etc.) than traditional warfare. It's a frightening world we live in.

Is there anything you would offer in terms of your thoughts about minority / women's / men's rights and equality?

In general, I have no issue with equality in whatever aspect there is. I do take issue however with those that feel entitled and expect things to be given to them compared to earning it.

How do you feel about U.S. immigration, the border wall, and our illegal alien policies?

In general, I'm not opposed to immigration but there has to be a process to vet and allow select people to come into the country. I also feel there should be levers to be pulled temporarily to halt that process during certain/select critical times. How to define, execute and monitor this I'm sure is not an easy thing. I don't have that answer.

Surveys show that non-Boomers are much more positive about socialism than Boomers. In fact, one study showed that Millennials and Gen Z think slightly more positively about socialism than capitalism. Why do you think that may be?

These generations tend to have a more feelings of entitlement than previous generations. This is likely based on things being given and/or available to them. While I don't like or agree with it, I can't say for sure I wouldn't feel that way too if I was in their shoes. This is not to say everyone in these categories thinks this way. There are many good people in the world that "do the right things". As a society, we tend to hear more about the former and therefore develop our opinions accordingly.

Are we as a society too hard or too easy on convicted felons?

Repeat offenders should have stiffer penalties than first time offenders.

How do you feel about the second amendment and gun rights?

I'm not a big fan of guns. I also understand the position that 'guns rights' advocates take. I don't know what the answer is to reduce the risk that guns can fall into the wrong hands.

How do you feel about the US role as being 'watchman of the world'?

I'm not smart enough to have a strong opinion on this. There are times I go back and forth on this based upon the current situation and/or need. I'm sure there's no easy answer to this. One could argue that looking out for all of humanity is not necessarily a bad thing. I've told my children, especially in their late teenage years, I would help them *if* I saw they were helping themselves first. That philosophy could apply here too.

Do you feel that we are taxed too much or too little? Do you believe that the rich need to pay more or fewer taxes? Do you believe that the poor need to pay more or less taxes?

I'm of the opinion that as long as one (rich or poor) complies legally with income tax returns then what they owe is acceptable. I think what you hear in the media when people complain about the rich is more of a softer issue.

How do you feel about the compensation of our political representatives at the state or national level, including benefits and pension?

Too high……but I don't have any data to back that up.

Should we have more or fewer governmental programs to help the underprivileged?

I'm sure there's many people out there that legitimately need and rely on these programs and there are many who take advantage of them. I suspect this has been true forever. To find those in the latter category I'm sure would take many resources and those are likely not available to execute it properly.

Do you consider yourself to be a conservative or liberal or somewhere in between? Why? Have you changed throughout your life, and if so, how?

I think of myself as a moderate (in between). I try to see both sides of things and base my opinion on that, as opposed to what I think many people do in that they try to justify their position on being one side or the other and only that.

The press talks a lot about the growing disparity in income – is that a big problem in your opinion?

It's probably bigger than I feel it is. This is based primarily on the fact I'm on the good side and therefore have more flexibility on how I live my life.

Are you more worried about the environment now vs. when you were in your teens or in the middle of life?

Most definitely. I never paid much attention to this before as there were other priorities for me.

Do you think the country is headed in the wrong or right direction?

I'm concerned about the toxic world we live in, especially in the U.S. Our politicians are getting farther apart, people are able to more easily promote their thoughts and opinions than ever before with social media tools, the media seems to be more biased than ever before. All this creates more friction and tension which I'm not sure we can sustain without something significantly negative or catastrophic happening. I feel it will get to the point that some very good people will not want to be in a public position to subject themselves to the negative comments and hate that I'm referring to.

Do you have more 'stuff' now than when you were younger? Do the younger generations have more stuff than your generation?

I have more……I'm older. I'm sure there will come a point in time when I will feel it's time to get rid of things that I then realize don't have the same value that they once had. This will also aid my children when they have to get involved in handling my estate and possessions.

Many Boomers believe that education is very important for the younger generations. Is advanced education more or less important than it was when you were growing up?

If you're referring to formal education such as college, I feel it's probably less important than before. There are many more ways for people to earn a living, have a career, etc. without. An example of this is the use of technology (social media, etc.) that didn't exist before. How many times do you hear of or read about a high schooler or someone in their early 20s making decent money off of Tik Tok, Instagram, etc.

Tell me about your health care coverage and your thoughts about the benefits you get vs. what it costs.

Having just gone on Medicare I don't have many data points yet to form an opinion on this. I will say I like the reduction in my out-of-pocket premiums compared to pre-Medicare.

Relative to other concerns you have, where does your health and your family's health rank?

It's good. With that said, as I am a fairly active person, I am not looking forward to the day when my health will get to the point where my style of living/activity will be significantly compromised. It will be mental torture for me. I just hope that situation occurs gradually over time allowing me to more easily transition to a slower life style vs a catastrophic event that would "flip a switch" overnight. We take too much for granted.

How do you feel about social security and the upcoming shortfall of funds?

I'm not yet collecting social security. I'm hopeful it will be available once I claim and receive benefits. I contributed to it some 35 years. I'm sure something will need to be done soon to sustain its longevity and I suspect it will need to be a combination of things. There's no one quick fix. I would like to think the solution would be to grandfather those already collecting benefits but that would require a much longer timeframe to ensure its longevity.

IN SUMMARY

Roy's story is an interesting one. You might say that he is a typical Boomer who led a 'jock' life, focused upon sports and being a 'guy's guy'.

But in getting to know more about his story, he is far from that.

Here is a Boomer who probably grew up with more pressure to perform and to live a noble life than most of us, given the reputation his father built in basketball, although Roy is quick to point out that the pressure he felt was mostly self-imposed. He lost a brother at a young age, which was, in many ways, devastating to him and his family. He studied hard, began his professional career, stayed loyal to one company for 35 years and had a very successful professional life, got married and has stayed loyal to his marriage and wife for over 40 years. He has lost his parents, and now is a family man with a wonderful wife, two children and five grandchildren that he talks about all the time.

Roy keeps a small circle of friends, not someone who might have 500 Facebook friends like some! His family is very important to him. Who could ever argue with having close friends and family to make life meaningful?

He takes pride in trying to stay informed and initially stays neutral on issues within the country today, then listens to both sides before making up his own mind. This is a bit different than many who already formulate an opinion on issues before considering all the facts or arguments.

Like many Boomers, he is a saver, and cares mostly about the welfare of his kids, grandkids and spouse after he is gone. He seems to have found a place of comfort in his life, satisfied with what he has accomplished and the way he has lived his life. He has few if any regrets.

As a friend, he is one of a few people that I can talk to about virtually anything on my mind. I think that is because I value his opinion, and respect his maturity and where he has landed in life.

For those in non-Boomer generations, I hope you can appreciate Roy and his story, realizing that he is more typical than not of Boomers; self-sacrificing, caring for others, independent, and living a life he takes pride in, mainly because it matters to him, as it matters to others in his circle.

CHAPTER 8:
Ernie Lallo, The Italian-American Lawyer Who Loved Frozen Yogurt

BACKGROUND

I first met Ernie in Florida, as in retirement I began playing golf with a group of guys called 'Russo's Raiders'. (Joe Russo and his life story may be a subject for a future entire book!) Ernie is a good golfer, and is one of those people who you remember as being iconic just due to his outgoing personality and his energy.

I learned over time that Ernie was a St. Joseph's graduate in Cleveland, a very large boys-only high school known for being a sports powerhouse. I also found out that he came from a middle/lower class, relatively poor, large blue-collar Italian family. He had financial success as an attorney and as an entrepreneur, investing in a frozen yogurt company in its growth stage. I recall meeting some of his family members who came to play golf with Ernie, and it became evident that he had a family with very strong ties.

In getting to know Ernie, I quickly learned that he had no shortage of opinions on any topic you wanted to discuss! We have had good discussions and debates about various topics. It is always fun talking to Ernie, as he is a very animated person and you always learn something.

EARLY LIFE

Ernie was born in 1954 in Ohio.

He was born the youngest of four siblings. His father was a factory worker and his mother was a homemaker. He was born and raised in Cleveland's 'Little Italy'. Both his parents were first-generation Italians in America, who spoke Italian before speaking English.

His father often worked overtime to make ends meet, and growing up, most of the family's earnings went to help the household. "The most significant influence in my life was growing up with my maternal grandfather who lived with us after my grandmother died. This is typical for Italian families, the grandfather lives with the oldest child, which was my mother. My grandmother passed away three days after my first birthday. Papa Latino then died in 1972 when I was 18 years old.

What made his grandfather so memorable growing up?

"His name was Antonio. He was very industrious, self-taught how to read and write English, however, he spoke Italian at home. He was a hunter and fisherman, he picked dandelions and mushrooms for food, and was totally focused upon family. He came to America with two of his sisters leaving the balance of his family in Sicily. He would teach us little lessons through our lives. One time I remember getting chastised by Papa Latino because I did not replace my bath towel on the rack, that way nobody else would use the same towel after bathing! To this day, guess who always hangs up his bath towel now? He was very proud of me as I grew up, but was devastated the time I got arrested for hitchhiking, since I did not have a car to drive. He was just appalled that I got this ticket and after he died, we found an envelope with $300 in it, and the envelope said 'For Ernie's Car'.

Ernie describes their early home life as eight people living in a home the size of his garage, with one bathroom.

One of the most memorable events in his life occurred when Ernie was about seven years old and his father was laid off from his job due to an economic slowdown. "It was a very tough time. My dad sold peanuts on the corner after dinner. My grandfather picked dandelions and mushrooms, caught fish, and hunted rabbit to supplement our food supply. My mom knitted Afghans and sold them. My sisters babysat. My brother washed cars. Even I, at seven years old, worked shining shoes."

That year, Ernie recalls that the only Christmas toy he received was from his uncle's Jewish friend from the Air Force, Irving Cutler. "He bought me an Army Station with accompanying Army figurines, the green rubber kind. I played with that station and staged battles using toothpicks as the enemy since I couldn't buy more figurines. I can honestly tell you once I became an attorney, Itzy Cutler never had another legal bill!"

Towards the end of the recession, his dad made plans to uproot the family and move to California where he could work with three of his brothers in construction. Three days before his planned departure, he was called back to his first employer. Had he not, everything in the family's life would have changed.

Ernie remembers a variety of jobs growing up, and in addition to shining shoes at age seven, he delivered newspapers at ten, washed pans and mopped floors at a pizza shop at age twelve, worked as a bus boy at thirteen, clerked at a grocery store at sixteen, and worked full time in college. "I worked in a large grocery chain from when I was a junior in high school through college. In that grocery store job, I learned the value of teamwork with my co-workers and cooperation with my managers, which paid off when I needed to customize my college class schedule and my work schedule. I learned the value of the collective voice of the Retail Clerk's Union, which provided me with benefits unheard of today." Also, in college, Ernie worked in a paid capacity as a field coordinator in the Ohio Governor's race.

Ernie describes his parents as being 'very ethnic Italian-Americans without a prejudiced bone in their body', and remembers his mother as being very gregarious, social, and religious. "My dad respected authority almost to a fault. My mom was a peace-maker, gave everyone the benefit of the doubt, and was very giving of herself. She often would say 'never burn a bridge'. Dad was quiet and often worked seven days a week, twelve hours a day, in part because of his unemployment period of the early 60's and because we needed him to. He was totally dedicated to his family and rarely spent any time on himself."

How about his parents child-rearing style? Did he and his siblings fear spanking when he was young?

"Of course. Especially as a toddler and a very young child. Once we were 6-8 years old, fearing physical punishment evaporated. It was an extremely rare occasion either parent would use physical punishment, however Italian moms were prone to using the 'wooden spoon' as a threat."

What was his neighborhood like?

"I grew up in a very protective ethnic neighborhood, where outsiders were treated with disdain. Many would label Little Italy as prejudicial, but what we really wanted was to be left alone. My mom despised that part of the ethnic atmosphere, especially during the racial unrest of the 1960's. Both my parents were inclusive and believed everyone should be treated equally. One major difference in our opinions was the Vietnam War, where I questioned every aspect of it, while my parents did not question authority. This aroused my independent thinking as a very young child which only grew as I aged."

In Ernie's family, every Sunday and holiday meant being with family. "Who else but Italians know their third cousins, and everyone over forty was either called Aunt or Comare? The tables were crammed in alternating basements where the hosts tried to outdo last week's meal, which would always last from after Sunday Mass until 6:00 p.m. Today we make every effort to keep our family together especially during holidays and special events. It is nothing to have fifty to sixty people over at our house for Thanksgiving dinner."

Ernie reflects back as being grateful that his grandfathers 'caught the boat' to America. He is one of 38 grandchildren on his paternal side. His paternal grandfather was an immigrant steel worker. "On my maternal side, my immigrant grandfather was a ditch-digger working for the utility company. All my uncles were blue-collar workers and most of them served in the Armed Forces. My cousins thrived and worked as steelworkers, tradesmen, nurses, teachers, professionals, and business owners. For me, America was truly a land of opportunity. Where in the world can a grandchild of an immigrant steel worker and a ditch digger grow up to be a successful attorney and businessman?"

How does he feel about the entire family now, looking back on his generation and the two prior generations? "Within two generations, I feel as though my extended family has contributed much to American society, and I am very proud."

In high school, Ernie remembers his all-boys high school experience as 'being with 2200 other boys', and that dances and sports events were 'where we got to see girls'! He was a class officer for three years and on the student council. He coordinated the Student Exchange Program and visited over forty schools his senior year. Also, Ernie was involved in a voter registration effort in response to the passage of the 25th Amendment, which enabled 18-year-olds to vote. That effort registered over sixty thousand recent high school graduates from across Northeast Ohio, and enabled the start of a lifelong relationship with a prominent politician who would later become Ohio Lt. Governor, Peace Corp Director, Ohio Governor and Ambassador to India. "I loved high school and remember special times such as co-ed Christmas caroling with neighboring schools, and going to football and basketball games along with rallies. I remember taking public transportation, hitchhiking to school and work, and eventually driving a beat-up 1964 Buick Special, without a floorboard, around town."

But a moment he most fondly recalls was when, in the fall of his junior year, he was visiting Notre Dame Academy. "I remember seeing this drop-dead gorgeous girl with great legs playing soccer, and a few months later going on a blind date with her. Within fifteen seconds of dancing with Helen, I knew she would be my life-long soulmate. Fifty-one years later we are still together. I would go back to that high school time in a heartbeat. I would not do anything differently."

At the time Ernie turned 18 years old, the military draft was still in place, but Ernie recalls that the number of draftees had fallen off at that time as the Vietnam War was beginning to wind down, and his draft number was somewhere in the middle of the pack, thus he was never drafted.

ON TO COLLEGE

Ernie recalls his college experience as not quite as good as high school. "I went to a local college and attended full-time, worked full-time, was active in various political campaigns and lived at home with my parents. This did not leave much time to socialize and live the college experience. That being said, I had a blast with my fraternity which was made up of all commuters. I learned a great deal from my political science department which prepared me for law school (my vocation) and politics (my avocation).

During his sophomore year, he proposed to Helen and became engaged. "I bought her a ring for Christmas for $300. I asked her dad, Pavel, if I could marry his daughter before I gave it to her."

Just a bit of background on Helen's father; he had been born in Slovenia, which was then Yugoslavia. During World War II, he was pro-democratic and fought against Tito's communist regime, ultimately being captured in Slovenia and sent to a labor camp in Arezzo, Italy. Ernie had noticed that Helen's father never ate onions. One day, he asked him why. "He said it was because one year, while in the war camp, his Christmas meal was half an onion. His cell mate died that day, so he was able to eat the entire onion. He swore that day he would never eat another onion."

At the end of the war, he was liberated and sent to Austria. His fiancée in Slovenia discovered he was alive, and interned in Linz, Austria. She left her family travelling by every means possible, eventually finding him, getting married and having their first-born son in the camp before immigrating to America. Pavel hated Italians because of the war and his time in the labor camp, so Ernie was worried about the response he may get when this long-haired, antiwar protestor, farmworkers-union-supporting Italian approached him about marriage.

"With a tear in his eye, he answered 'Absolutely! You fight for what you believe in and I know you will take care of my daughter.' We became very close."

Despite all the expensive jewelry Ernie bought over the years, that $300.00 ring has never left Helen's finger.

Ernie and Helen were married the summer between their junior and senior year. They had been living at home before then. But they found an apartment near his job and near his wife's parents, with rent being $150. "It was a great place for us. But after our honeymoon, the owner tripled the rent!" His father-in-law was upset, and loaned them the money to put a down payment on a house, as he did not want them wasting money on rent.

"Helen was making $600 per month teaching at an elementary school, and I had to quit my grocery store job when I started law school at Marshall / Cleveland State. Money was tight, we were frugal and never splurged."

Ernie chose the CSU Law School because it was close to home and Helen's family. "We considered going to law school and living in Columbus. We even arranged a teaching position for Helen in the Columbus schools, and I was to be a Page in the Ohio Senate. In the end, though, we wanted to stay home."

In looking back, what would you say about your wife, Helen?

"I made a toast at our 40th anniversary which I think says it all. I said 'When she wakes up in the morning, she is the last person she thinks about!' She has taken care of her parents, her kids, her grandchildren, and of course me. She never cares about herself. She has a tireless work ethic inherited from her parents. She is the most unselfish, loving, humble, caring, empathetic and compassionate person on the planet."

ON TO A CAREER

Ernie's first professional job during law school was as a law clerk for a solo practitioner who specialized in personal injury and representing injured workers. He worked all hours of the day and weekends to accommodate his law school schedule. Typically, he went to classes early in the day and then again at night, and worked during the day and on weekends. "Many a night Helen and I ate our dinner on TV trays watching Johnny Carson. The attorney I worked for taught me how to hustle, network, and treat every case as if it was the most important one in the office. I had to learn to complete a task with no excuses or delay."

When Ernie finished law school, the owner started developing property in Florida, and Ernie began working alongside his future law partner, basically running most of the business while the owner was away. "I did not like where the law firm was headed, there were some older guys there who were great but taking the business in a direction I did not like. So, I flew to Florida to meet with the owner, we met in a deli for lunch, and told him I either had to quit or to buy him out. Without hesitation, the owner said 'Then buy me out!' Right there in the deli, on a paper napkin, we made a six-figure deal. Forty-three years later, my partner and I were still partners and running our law firm."

Ernie's law practice centered on representing injured workers. His satisfaction came from helping the most seriously injured, or their dependents in cases of work-related deaths. "What I achieved for these folks was a lifetime of financial security. It was very rewarding. I am most proud of my involvement in defeating an employer-influenced legislation which decimated workers' rights and benefits. Recently, my son took over the business, although I am still active."

"Once at a paid vacation for staff in the office, I made a toast and said 'I have lived a very charmed life, when I wake up in the morning, I never worry about what my wife is doing. At night when I leave the office, I never worry about what my partner is doing.'" Ernie raves about his employees, most of whom worked their entire lives with his firm.

THE FROZEN YOGURT STORY

During his early career, his cousin, who was a bricklayer, was in Florida staying in a house they owned and used for family vacations. Ernie was about 28 years old at the time. One day, his cousin called him and told him that there were people lined up for blocks in the local town, waiting to get a frozen yogurt from a chain store he had not seen before. Ernie asked him "What the hell is frozen yogurt?"

The next day, his cousin sent him a brochure about the company, and indicated an interest in opening a new store, and that he needed an investor. "We flew to the company headquarters and negotiated a seven-figure development agreement for four counties and twelve stores in northern Ohio. While we were there, I said to my cousin, 'I probably should taste this stuff before we finalize things!'" So, they walked outside and found a local store and Ernie had his first taste of frozen yogurt.

OK, I must interject here. Here was this very intelligent guy, fresh out of law school, running his own business, and he flies to across the country to a company's headquarters, and invests a LOT of money in a company and a product, a product he had NOT EVEN TASTED YET! Who does that? Ernie did.

"I handled the legal work and some administrative stuff, and Tony ran the stores. At the time, there were no other frozen yogurt companies. This one had a patent on the process to make it. The stores were making enough money then that we could pay off each new store in a year. We kept investing in new stores, and ended up opening fourteen stores." Others wanted to buy their stores, but they declined, thinking that they wanted to own and run them all.

Suddenly, the market changed due to new competition. New competitor stores started opening very close to their existing stores, and financially things started to decline. "Eventually, we sold the stores back to the company. I was active in the company, and for a time was chairman of the franchisee association. There were 80 locations in the chain when we invested in the stores. At its peak, there were over 1,750 stores. I actually made most of my money in the market, buying stock along the way. In the mid-eighties, this company had the best-performing stock on NASDAQ two years in a row. We did not really make money in the long run operating the stores. As a side note, as chairman of the association, I was able to attend many corporate meetings and functions. As a result, on many of those occasions, I interacted with the wife of the Arkansas governor, and board member, Hillary Clinton.

FAMILY LIFE

Ernie and Helen are parents to four children, who all live within 20 minutes of their home, and they range in age from 38 to 43. Joe, a Kent State graduate, is a union masonry contractor and has two children with one on the way. Melissa graduated from Miami of Ohio. She is a director/media strategist with a major marketing firm and is the mother of two children. Matt is an attorney, local Law Director and the managing partner in Ernie's law firm. He graduated from Miami and Cleveland State Law School and has two children. Ernie's "baby daughter" Michelle is a Kent State Fashion School grad who left a management position at a major retailer to raise her three children. She now works part time for both her brothers' companies. "All four children have stable, successful marriages and careers. We have nine grandchildren. We are very close."

So how does Ernie describe how he and Helen raised their children relative to how his parents raised him and his siblings?

"I provided financial security for my children and gave them opportunities and support to succeed. All my children were taught that everything is earned. I taught my girls to think independently and speak up. I hammered home to my boys to be respectful, gracious, and kind. However, my wife really ran the household."

Ernie believes that compared to his parents, he and Helen are and were more indulgent with their children. "I am not as dogmatic as my parents were, and I encourage independent thinking and the questioning of authority. I would not say I consciously have a different parenting style than my parents, it's just that we are so different in terms of income status, education, opportunities, and social environment. I often said that our children are 'victims' of our lifestyle. They travelled the world, rode in nice cars, lived in a large home, and had a landscaper and housekeeper. However, we made every effort to push them to work hard and appreciate things, to be grateful and to exhibit grace and humbleness. We made it clear to them growing up that they must study and work hard to achieve what we did. My parents didn't have much choice on how to raise us. They were preoccupied with survival. In some ways, we had it harder. It would have been easy to raise lazy ungrateful privileged children, but we made it our everyday goal to keep the kids grounded and cognizant of the good life and blessings they were afforded."

What happened to his siblings?

"My sister, Linda, who passed on October 26, 2022, had polio at a young age, but went on to become a nun for 8 years, and was one of the Medical Missionary Singing Nuns, they became fairly famous, travelled the world, and cut an album (Joy Is Like the Rain) that was very popular. She had to leave the convent because she could not go on missions due to her polio. She eventually married, had four sons and was an administrative assistant at Ohio Wesleyan College. My brother Jim worked for a steel company as a boilermaker, retiring on disability. He has four children with three different wives. My other sister, Susan, recently passed on January 2, 2023. She was a housewife raising her two children, then began her career as a bookkeeper. They all were fairly local and we stayed close after our childhood."

As Ernie's parents aged, he and his family were involved in their care. "Dad died seven years before Mom, and we took care of mom for a short while after her latest cancer diagnosis. However, she insisted on entering a nursing home because she did not want to 'burden' us. This was because my mom took care of her mother, who had cancer for a year, when I was a newborn, and she did not want us to go through that scenario. The time we were able to share with my mom was rewarding. My wife had a lot to do with that. She is very compassionate and patient with the elderly. She was her mother's caretaker for quite some time, and exhibited the patience of a saint."

UPON REFLECTION

What does semi-retirement look like now for Ernie?

"Life is very different if I am in Florida during winters or in Ohio during the rest of the year. I golf more in Florida, but in Ohio I attend more events of grandkids and help out my children wherever possible. I work a couple of hours daily for our law firm, continue sitting as an acting judge in our local municipal court, and continue working on various political campaigns. We take extended vacations and I enjoy spending time on planning them. I am still sorting this retirement thing out. My intentions are to stay relevant, probably teach a college class in politics, business and/or law, and become a mediator - arbitrator."

In looking back, what was his primary philosophy of life and what most contributed to his success?

"Everything I have experienced in life such as education, career, marriage, family, friendships, I have reaped what I have sown. I lived by my credo that in order to be successful in any aspect of life, you must work tirelessly, sacrifice and be totally unselfish. I am the product of a first-generation blue-collar family and was able to prosper in my legal career and business pursuits. Other than a few irrational investments, I would not do anything differently. There is one caveat to success, and that is there is an element of luck. I once heard luck defined as 'when preparation meets opportunity'. Preparation came from my work ethic inherited from my parents and grandparents, and opportunity came by growing up in America."

How does he think he will be remembered by his children and grandkids?

"I want to think my children will remember me as someone whose main goal in life was to leave the world a better place than I found it. My kids will remember my dedication to our family and my unconditional love for them. On many occasions, they heard me say "My love for you is unconditional. I have no agenda other than your well-being. There are 8 billion people on this earth. Other than your mom, no one loves you more than me."

POLLING FOR OPINIONS

If forced to list only three of the most important lessons in life you have learned, which might benefit others, what would they be?

1. You reap what you sow.
2. Rue is the most destructive and poisonous human emotion.
3. Give of yourself (time, attention, advice and money)

If a Millennial or Gen X or Gen Z person was sitting next to you on your death bed, and they asked you "What is the meaning of life? What is it all about?" What do you think your answer would be?

The meaning of life is to go through time seeking a balance between reaching goals and enjoying success of achieving those goals.

How would you compare the values of yourself to your children?

They are quite the same. We lived our values, so they acquired most of them through osmosis!

How would you describe your Grandchildren relationships?

They are great, primarily due to my wife. (I am always trying to improve) They are at a young age and understand that we are loving, supportive and care about them before ourselves. They, like their parents, come first before anything else in our lives. My wife showers them with time and attention. I go along for the ride.

How would you compare the relationship you have with your children, vs. the relationship between your parents and you when you were their age?

We are more open with them. It feels like we have more in common with our kids than our parents did with us. It seems growing up we were given more space. We, on the other hand, are more like helicopter parents hovering over our children and grandchildren, which I sometimes wonder is the right thing to do.

Do you still help your children financially as adults?

My kids are all doing very well now, so no, we don't gift them funds today on a regular basis. But when they were growing up, all our children had a new car when they turned 16, but had to maintain it and were advised this would be the only one we would provide. Their private high school tuitions along with all college tuitions and costs were paid by us, but they had to work to pay for entertainment, travel, etc. They all had large weddings that were fully paid for. We lent each of them their down payments (interest free) for their first homes which have all been paid back. I did subsidize both my girls' rent payments when they went to Chicago for their first jobs. It was more for my piece of mind, because affordable rent was impossible in a safe and decent neighborhood. They both eventually came home to raise their families in Ohio.

Do you think you worry too much about your children?

Without a doubt. I obsess over their emotional and financial well-being. I think I have all the answers and cures. My mom constantly worried about us, she prayed every day for us. She would say in Italian, "Please God, watch all children, but especially mine". I think I worry more about my kids because in my mind, they have more challenges in today's world than we had. This very well may be a perception of mine, but is how I feel. My mom was an obsessive worrier, and I am like her, so my wife says.

You said that you did, when very young, fear spanking from your parents. How did you raise yours in terms of spanking?

My kids didn't have the same fear, but we would on very rare occasions spank them but only as a toddler. I would say my children treat theirs similarly. Thankfully, nobody in our family uses physical punishment and never once after a child passed toddler age. I believe these changes are for the better. Violence begets violence. It fosters disrespect for the human condition and is the easy way out to enforcing discipline. That being said, we try to teach our kids and grandkids that bad behavior does have consequences. Just not physical consequences.

What are you most proud of from the years raising your children?

How we instilled in our kids the value of being a close family, developing a social circle of true and unending friendships, and loyalty to your family, church, and community. We taught our kids to respect themselves and others.

Do you think that society does or does not value enough a parent who stays home with children?

The issue is not how much time a parent is at home, as much as what they do with their time. We were lucky enough for my wife to stay home and raise our four children. And yes, I do think that society does not value enough a parent who stays home with their children.

Do you believe that the generations following ours will be, in general, better off or worse financially when they get to our age?

My family will be better off financially since they have all had a great start in life. They all have good jobs/professions and to some extent will inherit some money. In general, there will always be opportunities to succeed in this country. The difference is the rest of the world is catching up, so the competition becomes greater.

Do you believe those generations will live in a better country and world in the coming decades, versus what our generation experienced as we aged?

No. We are becoming more isolated and selfish. When we grew up, we were more communal and interactive, and the younger generations, maybe due to social media, seem to be more isolated. "The common good" is no longer what it used to be. We are intolerant of others. There are less traumatic events and or causes that would make people come together. We have too much free time on our hands. We do not have as many common goals as we had in the past. We have collectively created distrust in our institutions and are headed for civil unrest unless some things change.

What are you planning to have happen with any funds or possessions after you die?

We plan to distribute our estate through a trust to preserve some assets for the grandkids as well as our kids. We will also donate to Catholic education, food banks and shelters. Leaving money is the least of my priorities. I want to leave a legacy of humility, grace, charitableness and gratitude that future generations may emulate.

Do you remember your parents or older relatives talking about the great depression?

My parents often spoke about the depression. For the most part, they struggled to make ends meet. They lived in a family environment that provided a sense of security. As immigrants, they all struggled and worked hard, and managed with little, so the changes that the depression brought on were not as drastic. I have a hard time believing a great depression could happen again since we have many more safeguards in place.

How did music impact you growing up?

Music had a great impact on me growing up during the Vietnam War era. I listen almost exclusively to music from the 60's and 70's today. They are a reminiscent of a great time in my life and it is wistfully nostalgic. Some of my favorites back then were Crosby/Stills/Nash, Joan Baez, Joanie Mitchell, Arlo Guthrie, Bob Dylan, James Taylor, Jackson Brown, Carly Simon, and Judy Collins. The music put you in a place that you could remember forever. To this day, Chicago's Color my World will send me back to my first dance with my then blind date, now my wife. Today, I listen to mostly Cat Stevens, Neil Young, The Beach Boys, Paul Simon, CSN, Judy Collins, Stevie Nicks, James Taylor, Earth Wind and Fire, Chicago, Joanie Mitchell, Steely Dan, and The Beatles. The Beatles had a profound impact on me especially the first few years of high school. They changed with the times as we did. Without a doubt, CSNY's 'Ohio', 'Teach Your Children', 'Our House', plus 'After the Gold Rush', 'Harvest Moon' and 'Sweet Judy Blue Eyes' all express various attitudes and emotions experienced during my teenage and early adult life.

Boomers have, and had, a reputation for drinking beer/wine/alcohol. Did you drink growing up?

Not really. I can count on one hand the times I have been drunk throughout my life. I can't physically handle it, so I don't do it. I do have an occasional cocktail and we certainly enjoy wine with dinner. I never used any type of drugs. I don't mind if marijuana is legalized, because I believe the science that its long-term side effects are no greater than alcohol. Who am I to tell somebody how to relax or enjoy themselves?

How would you describe your adult friendships?

I have many great friends from different aspects of my life. Some I grew up with in the 'old neighborhood', others in high school, college and law school. We have many good friends from country club associations, and great friends from being involved in my kids' grade school and high school parent-teacher organizations. We have formed friendships with people associated with my law practice, my wife's involvement in various social activities, our exurban neighborhood where we lived for thirty-one years, and fellow parishioners from St. Gabriel Church where we have belonged for 41 years. Also, we have friends from political campaigns. We recently caught up with my old boss/mentor from the Governor's campaign forty years ago who I consider a dear friend. At dinner, I made a toast to him and started it by saying "I have few regrets in life and one of them is not spending more time with you." Time and distance stop us from spending more time with many of our friends. And it seems the older we get, the more difficult it is to devote time to our friendships.

Has your time spent with friends changed as you have aged?

Many relationships cooled as we have less in common, and others have cooled because of the toxic political environment. Others because we spend more time with our children and grandchildren. We have less time because we split it between Florida and Ohio and travel more. It's just harder to make time. Some friends have reached an age where they are more physically challenged, and therefore miserable, depressed and angry. I try very hard to overcome these obstacles because I am probably exhibiting some of these characteristics, and out of loyalty to these lifelong friends.

In what ways have you changed as a result of losing someone close?

When I lost my dad, I appreciated my relationship with my children, and I hoped they would love me as much as I loved my dad. When my mom died, I became an orphan (at 45 years old) and lost the one person who would unconditionally love me. Within a span of sixty-eight days, I lost both sisters to cancer. It was devastating to lose two women who loved me throughout my entire life and treated me always as "their baby brother". My wife is the one who experienced an excruciating life-altering change with the tragic loss of her brother in Vietnam. Ironically, Josef was the child born in the Austrian DP camp and brought to America in the arms of his refugee mother, only to die for their new country. His death dramatically changed my wife's entire family forever.

Were there any specific historic events that impacted you?

The Cuban missile crisis made us all a little paranoid of potential world destruction, as we are now seeing in the Ukraine conflict. The Vietnam War made me question government authority and political motives. 9/11 made us, as a whole nation, much less secure and realizing that we are not invincible. January 6 shook me to my core. The internet has changed everything, and for the most part badly. I will not use Facebook or social media. The internet has given voice and legitimacy to extreme viewpoints, and I don't know how we can rein these in. I'm more pessimistic about the future because I don't know how we can get back to the middle. The damn smartphone has become an appendage and we don't know how to interact with each other.

What do you recall about the press (TV and newspapers mainly) when you were a teenager and in your twenties? How does that compare to now?

We all listen to what we want to hear. Some say that the press has been liberal for years. There has to be a way to filter fact from fiction, but it is so frustrating today compared to the press when we grew up. I don't know what the right answer is. 24-hour news dilutes what we have to listen to now and most media are echo chambers. It is all about ratings, not facts. I feel sorry for people who don't know any better, who believe all of what they see or hear in the media.

What about equal rights progress or lack thereof?

I believe America has come a long way in leveling the playing field for both racial minorities and women. This certainly was not the case growing up in the 60's. I grew up in a neighborhood that was front and center during the race riots of 1966-67. I clearly remember gun-toting National Guardsmen driving through my street, Army jeeps stationed on every corner, and my grade school being sheltered in place while riots occurred outside. I remember black men being beaten for entering our neighborhood, but I also remember my sisters being harassed by groups of black teens while walking to high school. I can remember being taught to not chase a ball that flew over the railroad tracks since it was on the "wrong side of town."

How do you feel about U.S. immigration, the border wall, and our illegal alien policies?

I believe America should welcome people who are desperados and are searching for a better life just as we did 100 years ago. I believe America should welcome refugees and those seeking asylum, to provide these individuals with an opportunity for a better life. Most immigrants are looking for an opportunity and would make this country stronger and more prosperous just as our ancestors did. The problem is, we have made many of these people attempting to enter our country illegal. Obviously, those who crash the border, sneak in, etc. clearly have no place in our country. However, asylum seekers, refugees, and those simply wanting a better life are a different issue and should be accepted as was done throughout our history. With that being said, we do need to reform our immigration policy to control the influx of immigrants and not overwhelm the system. The problem is both sides need to compromise and make reforms that will have objections by the bases. In other words, elected officials need to GOVERN not continually run for re-election.

What would you say about Gen X (born 1965-1979), Millennials (born 1980-1994), or Gen Z (born 1995-2015) as generations compared to Boomers?

What I say comes from my own experiences. My life story affects how I see other generations, so obviously, I don't see them working as hard, I don't see them fighting for a cause nor the common good. They are more "spectators" than participants. I challenge them to develop a communal sense of respect for themselves, each other and our institutions. I hope they understand and learn from the past and figure out ways to make our world a better place for the future.

Surveys show that non-Boomers are much more positive about socialism than Boomers. How do you feel about socialism vs capitalism?

I'm clearly a capitalist but we certainly need social safety nets, we need to help the poor, sick and the elderly. We did need government to step in when businesses couldn't do the job. (i.e., pandemic related issues, natural disasters, unnatural supply chain problems, etc.) It is a delicate balance. I sat on the board of Lakeland Community College and saw firsthand that subsidized post-high school education can help the community in so many ways. Subsidized childcare helps lower income families succeed and become independent of government aid. Thus, there is this delicate balance where we don't want to provide simple handouts without conditions and limits (i.e., PPP distributions, child tax credits). I myself was a recipient of a 'handout' - Ohio Instructional Grants which helped pay for my college education and I believe I have paid back my 'handout' and more.

What are your feelings about 'green initiatives' and the state of our planet?

Actions to improve the environment cannot hurt. There have been amazing developments in various technologies, yet we still have combustible engines. If we lead on new technologies, and create new products that are greener and more competitive, other countries are going to have to follow our lead.

How do you feel about the second amendment and gun rights?

I strongly believe and will protect the exercise of <u>all</u> the rights found in all the amendments to our Constitution including second amendment rights. However, no right is absolute and that also goes for second amendment rights. Even though I never owned a gun, I have no problem with people owning guns and weapons but there must be a way to keep guns out of the hands of the mentally ill, criminals and those with violent tendencies. We do need to limit capacity and there is no reason in the world assault and military style weapons should be in the mainstream. Does our country really need more guns than people?

What about the growing national debt?

Younger generations are the beneficiaries of all the debt spending that has occurred for years, that spending went to things like national defense, social programs, schools and infrastructure. Both political parties have overspent for decades, and it didn't matter which party we voted for. So why is this the fault of the Boomer generation? Many times, government overspent to stimulate the economy when times were tough and everyone benefited.

Why are politicians so divided? Has it really changed, or has it been like this for a long time?

We are divided for three main reasons. First, gerrymandering makes it far easier to elect extremists from both sides so that moderate views are eliminated. This causes compromise to become a sign of weakness, a dirty word. Second, social media and its algorithms create a saturation of slanted information/half-truths that feeds the consumer biases and create immovable barriers to understanding an issue and/or other opinions. Third, 24-hour news cycles and echo chamber media give people only a view point they want to hear and often a very slanted view to distort reality.

Do you consider yourself to be a conservative or liberal or somewhere in between? Why? Have you changed throughout your life, and if so, how?

Most of my conservative friends call me the "Limousine Liberal". Socially, I am a liberal however, fiscally I am more middle of the road. I have always believed "live and let live". I feel I am tolerant. At the end of the day, I consider myself a progressive-- I look forward. I have never changed.

The press talks a lot about the growing disparity in income – is that a big problem in your opinion?

What we want to avoid is to create a class of oligarchs in this country who would wield an outsized influence on political and business decisions. How we do this is a difficult question to answer.

Do you believe the US should be more focused upon our country mainly, or more focused globally, in terms of how our tax dollars are used?

It's crazy how I think my answer changed a bit after the Russian invasion of Ukraine. The U.S. is carrying the ball on spending for Ukraine, but every day Europeans are paying the price in higher food and energy prices.

Do you think the country is headed in the wrong or right direction?

I pride myself on being an eternal optimist. However, we must fight daily to keep this country from heading in the wrong direction. The attack on the news media as fake news, creating distrust in our national institutions such as the justice system, FBI, CDC, etc. deteriorate our faith in our government.

The attempts to change the results of the 2020 election have shaken me to the core. Throughout my life, I've been on both winning and losing ends of elections. I have learned that no one must agree with the victor, however, we must agree with the results and the proven process. There's nothing wrong with working to win the next election, but not change the results. I'm very afraid of the fear-mongering and authoritarianism, although this too comes and goes through time. On the positive side, the economy is strong, we recognize we need to be more independent when it comes to strategic manufacturing, energy sources, etc. We are realizing the need to step up our efforts for green/renewable energy.

Changes in our country are normal. Most things in life are on a pendulum and when one side swings too far from center there is enough force to bring it back to the middle. But we must be vigilant of the process and hold dearly our freedoms.

Do you have more 'stuff' now than when you were younger? Do you want to get RID of stuff, or GET more stuff?

Absolutely getting rid of stuff. Two years ago, we downsized our house, and got rid of truckloads of stuff. Younger generations have way too much stuff too. We need to make our lives simpler, and keep getting rid of stuff. Do we really need a GPS watch, a GPS device that talks to you, a laser rangefinder, and golf cart GPS to find the distance to the hole? Do we really need 6 TV's in our houses? How about eight pairs of golf shoes and ten hats? When my father died in a nursing home, everything he owned in the world fit into a shopping cart.

Tell me about your health care coverage and your thoughts about the benefits you get vs. what it costs.

Medicare with supplement policies is great. Before that I had great coverage through my office plan, but it was $1100.00 per person. All my various surgeries were fully paid and a blessing. Everyone should have the same care.

Relative to other concerns you have, where does your health and your family's health rank?

After recently losing both sisters to cancer, I've become increasingly aware of life-threatening diseases. As of now, I thank God all my children and grandchildren are healthy. My wife and I have chronic minor conditions that don't impair our lifestyle.

IN SUMMARY

There are many different kinds of 'American Success Stories' in this book, but Ernie's story might be one of the most extreme in terms of his transformation from his early years, polishing shoes at age seven to help his family survive, to his current status as a successful businessman, semi-retired, with a long track record of financial success, community involvement, and dedication to family.

Boomers who have this sort of career and financial success might typically be conservatives. Ernie is not.

As I worked on his story, and focused upon his 'POLLING FOR OPINIONS' answers, I found myself wondering why Ernie's beliefs about key issues were in many cases different than mine, and why he is mostly liberal, while I am mostly conservative. We are close to the same age, we both have similar stories in terms of growing up in relatively poor families yet achieving some level of career success, we both had close families, we both had siblings and children and grandchildren, we both have a bit of a passion for golf, we believe in personal responsibility, we value our families and friendships, etc.

Then it occurred to me that a key difference in our lives was that Ernie grew up with a very close and strong exposure to his family's 'first generation' immigrants. He lived and was close with his maternal grandfather, and is grateful for all of his grandparents 'catching the boat', in Ernie's words. In my upbringing, I never knew either of my grandfathers, and my grandmothers who I did know were at least two generations away from the first family immigrants.

It hit me how profound these differences may be. Ernie clearly was influenced in his development in many ways by the grandfather who lived with them. One of the first things Ernie said when I started the process of capturing his life story was - "I could tell you dozens of stories about my grandpa Antonio, and I will share those when we meet for the interview." Since then, I have found that some of Ernie's favorite stories in life are about Antonio. He repeats them often. My conclusion may be invalid, but I believe that Ernie's feelings about some of the "POLLING FOR OPINIONS' questions may arise a bit from how he feels about immigrants and what they had to overcome once they settled here.

Given my lack of exposure to any first-generation immigrants, I certainly do not have that closeness or experience. I usually find that when I am discussing some of the larger issues going on in our country, I usually think about the impact to our current citizens. A not uncommon comment I make is something such as 'The taxpayers are getting the short end of the stick again given the direction we are headed.' Whether it is the national debt, or who must pay for food, housing, medical care, etc. for millions of illegal immigrants flooding our borders each year, to our country's history of giving billions of dollars to overseas interests, my first thought sometimes is 'that is a lot of money and sacrifice that our taxpayers have to shoulder, when we have our own problems at home that need funding.' Could it be that I am being overly protective of Americans who need assistance, or Americans who are paying taxes that fund various needs?

Ernie, given his background and experiences, likely does not have that concern. He is much more open and accommodating to those outside our country or wanting to live here, and to those in other countries that need assistance and help.

One other difference is that Ernie, in his law practice, represented individuals and families in lawsuits against employers in the main. My career was spent with one of those employers! So of course, our perspectives about corporations may differ quite a bit. It could be that our professional background difference is the primary source of our diversity of opinions on key issues, versus exposure to first generation immigrants, but it is impossible to know for sure.

It has been a great experience to have made a new friend, even with the differences in some of our views. It convinces me that any of us can openly discuss our differences and still remain friends, as long as we remain respectful. To me, developing an understanding about the linkage between our backgrounds and our current opinions and views is fascinating.

In my view, Ernie is exceptional in many positive ways. How can you not admire his work ethic throughout his life, his focus on family, his focus on the underdog, and the love he has for his wife, siblings, parents, children, grandchildren, and friends? Ernie is a smart guy, but I know plenty of Boomers who are equally smart, yet have not had his level of success across a spectrum of things in life. I attribute that to his work ethic, energy, and the direct influence of his parents and grandparents, who had very strong opinions and beliefs.

Thank you, Ernie, for sharing your story with me and the readers. It is one that we will all remember for some time!

CHAPTER 9:
Cathy:
The Professor from Ireland

BACKGROUND

I first met Cathy at a university event while I was still working as an executive at my company. I was invited because I was a graduate of the university, and the people attending were comprised of managers and executives of other companies, as well as professors and administrators who were involved with the information systems and related majors.

Anyway, I enjoyed the discussion and volunteered to continue to attend and to get more involved with the curriculum committee. Cathy was very outgoing, friendly, and organized. She was leading the group, planning meetings and content, and clearly had a strong interest in the future careers of her current and former students.

I always respected her for her openness, wisdom, experience, and ability to get things done. Clearly her students had a great deal of respect for her as well. I wanted her story to be in my book because I knew she had been born in Ireland, and I thought that learning about the life of someone who was born outside the U.S. would be interesting, as well as hearing about her migration to the U.S. and her contributions to students and the university.

HER STORY

Cathy was born in 1954 in Cork City, Ireland, the eldest of four children, with one sister and two brothers. Cork is the southernmost county in Ireland and Cork City is the second largest city in the Republic.

Her father worked in sales for a large distillery company, and her mother (her Mum) did not work outside the home. Cathy recalls that she brought her lunch milk to school in whiskey or gin bottles!

She and her sister attended a 'lay girls' school (which did not teach science or advanced math) while her brothers attended a Christian Brothers' school. Because she wanted the option of going to college and studying engineering, she switched schools for her final year of secondary school (the Irish equivalent of high school). "All the other students at the new school had taken the 'Leaving Cert' before and were just repeating a few subjects to get the points they needed for what they wanted to study in college. I was taking a full course load, probably English, Irish, Latin, French, math and, for the first time, physics, chemistry, and applied math. Neither my parents nor any of my siblings went to college."

I am including a lot more in her story about her upbringing and what life was like growing up, simply to share how her life might have differed from growing up in the U.S.

Cathy's mother was a wonderful pianist (you may notice that most Boomers I am writing about had a piano at home), and Cathy studied under her mother's teacher for a while, later taking lessons from a woman who taught singing and permitted Cathy to play film themes in addition to the usual classical pieces. "I remember Mum and Dad having singalongs with their friends in our living room."

Her dad's job as a traveling salesman and later as a regional sales manager created some memorable experiences for Cathy and the family. Included was a role presenting prizes at greyhound races and horse races and attending the annual Cork Film Festival. She was sometimes permitted to accompany him if her mom couldn't attend. Her dad used to tell a story about a distillery meeting where he admitted that he would have preferred to be a doctor and, at "the golden gates," been able to tell St. Peter that he had saved lives instead of selling booze for a living.

"He was offered a promotion which would have required moving to Dublin, but chose not to disrupt the family, and declined the promotion."

Her dad used to drive the kids to school, and they would take a double-decker bus home.

Cathy recalls holidays, as well as Sundays, when the family would visit relatives. "Some traditions included visiting my grandmother's (who was my mother's mother and my only living grandparent) on Sundays, along with many aunts, uncles, and cousins. There was lots of room to play outside, and during cherry blossom season, one of our favorite activities was to have make-believe weddings using the cherry blossoms for petals, hair ornaments, and bouquets. We would also visit Gran on Christmas Eve, and with many extended family, exchange Christmas presents at a cousin's house on Christmas Day. Our Christmas dinner included turkey (with stuffing and gravy), ham, potatoes, and vegetables. Dessert was fruit salad laced with some kind of liquor, and plum pudding with whipped cream and brandy butter."

Her dad was a year-round golfer, and was expected to win the Christmas turkey playing golf, and no doubt stopped briefly at the '19th hole' before coming home.

"Mum and Dad would ceremoniously bring the plum pudding into the dining room with some holly and whiskey on top, turn off the lights, and set the whiskey aflame with a match."

At Easter, the children were given large hollow chocolate eggs filled with individual chocolates, and Lindt chocolate animals such as bunnies or chickens. "We usually had leg of lamb for dinner on Easter Sunday."

"We went to Mass as a family every Sunday and holy day. Mum always entered the pew first, then the 4 children, and Dad came in last."

Cathy talks about growing up and what was going on politically and in the news. "When I was growing up, the main sources of news in our home were newspapers, radio (both Irish and English stations), and eventually RTE, the only available TV station. Mum read the paper pretty much every day, and Dad regularly listened to the radio and read the Sunday papers. Both watched the news on TV in English. There was a separate Irish version but most of us would not have understood it even though, in those days, you couldn't pass your exams without passing Irish. The troubles in Northern Ireland were in the news a lot. While some people view the issues as Protestant versus Catholic, to me the cause seemed more like a consequence of British colonialism. We used to say that Ireland was England's first and last colony."

Cathy sheds some light on how her parents and friends felt about neighboring countries. "Mum & Dad had some close friends from England, and many Irish people lived there, but the situation was complicated. I'm fairly sure Mum & Dad were not happy with England's policies towards Northern Ireland and its support of Unionists such as Ian Paisley. I think everyone in Ireland (including my parents) loved the U.S. and everything it stood for. Most people had relatives who'd emigrated to the U.S., and there was great excitement when JFK visited and, of course, great upset when he was assassinated."

Cathy talks about how her parents influenced her growing up. "I was influenced by my parents' religious convictions, the value they placed on education, and what they taught us about the importance of doing the right thing and always telling the truth. Now, I hate lies and start out trusting everyone but, once I discover that someone has lied to me, I'm very slow to trust them again. I share Dad's love of meeting interesting people, especially from other countries. He used to tell us that 'what's worth doing is worth doing well', which may have something to do with why it often takes me so long to complete tasks."

"Mum and Dad were devout Catholics but kept their religious beliefs private and had close friends from other religions. Dad was more traditional, and Mum was more progressive and thought tolerance was very important. Irish politics and laws were heavily influenced by the Catholic Church, and birth control, divorce, and abortion were all illegal. Times have changed since then and, in 2015, Ireland became the first country to legalize same sex marriage!"

"I'd rate my relationship with my parents as excellent, and appreciate growing up in a loving, stable home. We didn't really talk about love, or display it overtly, but it was there. Whereas some children seem to view their parents as friends, our family wasn't like that; our parents were our parents!"

Even though the family did not live right on the coast, there were beaches about 20 or 30 minutes away, and the ones they liked best were 40 miles away in Ardmore, County Waterford, a one-hour drive. "Sometimes we would rent a small house in Ardmore for a month in the summer. We had lots of fun with other families we knew well, playing tennis or rounders on the sand, climbing the rocks, and swimming in the very cold Atlantic. We often had picnics. I especially liked swimming when the tide was in (and diving off the rocks), or reading a good book while sitting on the rocks and listening to the sea."

"For birthdays, we might go to a movie (perhaps starring Elvis Presley or Cliff Richard) with a few friends and have birthday cake afterwards. St. Patrick's Day was a state holiday and church holy day. After Mass, we'd pick some shamrock to wear (it grew wild among the grass) and go to the parade where the highlight was the American high school marching bands. Unlike now, I think the pubs were closed!"

Cathy remembers one time when her family moved to a different house, which meant that she would be moving away from her friends. "The new house had a magnificent view of the River Lee and Blackrock Castle, but I was so upset, by way of protest, I chose the only bedroom without a view!"

"The house had an upstairs "hot press" which is like a tiny room or large closet containing shelves built around a water tank. We'd store clean towels and linens there, and to heat water for a bath, have to flip a switch an hour beforehand. We might also put our bath towel near the tank to have it nice and warm. Since we did not have a shower, we'd wash our hair in the kitchen sink."

Cathy's experience in secondary school was OK, but in her words, it was a small school run by 2 unmarried sisters. "I think there were 8 of us in my primary school class and 16 in secondary school. Our subjects (we had no choices) were English, Irish, Latin, French, Math, History, and Geography, and also Art at which I was terrible. I played field hockey but don't think our school teams ever won a match. We were ecstatic if we had a draw or only lost by a few goals."

Cathy also joined the Girl Guides (like Girl Scouts in the U.S) which met on Monday evenings and was fun for her.

In secondary school, which was an all-girls school, Cathy was a good student except for art. "I can't think of anything I could have done differently, but if the option of a mixed school had been available (only the Protestant Grammar School was mixed), I think I'd have preferred that, especially if it included science and advanced math."

When she was younger, she had thought she would like to be a teacher but, near the end of secondary school, she started thinking about engineering even though she knew very little about what that meant. "My rationale was that I liked math, engineers were likely to be employable, and there'd be boys!" Cathy completed secondary school in 1971.

ON TO UNIVERSITY LIFE

Cathy applied and was accepted into University College Cork (UCC) and studied engineering, a 4-year program that in the U.S. would be considered 'lockstep'. "There were over 100 students including 3 girls. The first 2 years were common to civil and electrical engineering, and, after that, I chose electrical and became the first female to do so at UCC. I lived at home throughout those 4 years."

She spent the summers after her 2nd and 3rd years at UCC working as a "set up" girl at a Cape Cod restaurant and as an international exchange student at a communications company, both in Massachusetts. At the restaurant, she set tables after the busboys cleared them. "We had to change the tablecloth without exposing the table underneath!" At the time, it was a common practice for Irish students to take summer jobs in the U.S. and elsewhere.

"I think the majority of my classmates emigrated after graduation, as there were very few jobs available in Ireland for new graduates. But I found a job as an instrumentation sales engineer at a telecom company in Dublin. I had applied for an engineering job but the engineer who interviewed me didn't want to hire a female, so since my grades were good, he referred me to the sales department which was not an ideal place for a new grad to start a career. I was not permitted to sell inside Ireland. When I first moved to Dublin in 1975, I was pretty homesick and made the mistake of frequently coming home to Cork on weekends. It took spending weekends in Dublin to make new friends there." While with the company, she travelled to England, Belgium, Germany, and Switzerland which was very exciting for her, but she was not motivated by sales commissions. As the only female employee who wasn't a secretary, and the only engineer who wasn't a guy, she thought that the secretaries resented her and were less eager to assist her. "This was unlike when I came to my professor position seven years later, the department secretary was like a cheerleader for the female faculty!"

"I left after one year to pursue a masters' degree in bioengineering in the University College Dublin chemical engineering department. Since this only required research and a thesis, and I wanted to learn something more about bioengineering, so I attended some night classes at a nearby vocational school."

During that time, she applied to bioengineering programs at U.S. universities and was accepted by Penn State in 1977. She did well on her courses but not on her candidacy exams. "I switched to industrial engineering, specializing in operations research (OR), and received my Ph.D. in 1982. I loved OR as it was like solving puzzles."

Cathy found that during her time at Penn State, she began to start questioning her Catholic beliefs. She was exposed to other religions, and "This made it hard to continue accepting that Catholicism was 'the one true church'. Religion became very confusing for me and gradually I became agnostic, although I'm always grateful when others pray on my behalf, especially an episcopal priest and his wife who have become very close friends."

ON TO A CAREER

After interviewing at, and receiving offers from, the University of South Florida in Tampa, SUNY Buffalo, and Princeton, Cathy was then hired at a state university in Ohio, where she taught a mix of OR and information systems (IS) classes. At the time, universities were having difficulty finding IS professors. "I probably got the job because, even though I had no background in IS, my dissertation mentioned computer networks."

During the summer of 1983, she attended the Information Systems Faculty Development Institute at the University of Minnesota in Minneapolis, a program for IS faculty from non-IS backgrounds. "Over time, I taught fewer OR and more IS classes and eventually phased out of OR completely."

In 1986, a colleague founded the Center for Information Systems and she joined, along with various corporate members and faculty, staff, and students. "While the emphasis changed over the years, the goals of CIS have included keeping the curriculum relevant, giving scholarships and other awards to students, helping students find jobs and internships, attracting students to the IS major, providing networking opportunities for members, encouraging Ph.D. students to do applied research, and helping the student association find speakers for their meetings."

Later in her career, she chaired some CIS committees and became the CIS co-director along with Ryan Conlon, a retired IT executive. To help bridge academia with the "real world," they had previously decided that the Center and its committees be jointly led by someone inside and outside the university, hence the co-chair and co-director positions. "I retired as a full-time faculty member in 2015 but continued as CIS co-director until 2018."

"Since then, I've tried to keep busy by volunteering as a math tutor, attending classes through the senior guest program, and spending time reading, swimming, and walking. I also enjoy getting together with friends to share good conversation, good food, and good wine!"

FAMILY LIFE

Cathy met her husband Mike in 1987, and Mike had a daughter Dara from a prior marriage. They were married twice in 1988, both a civil wedding in the US and a Catholic wedding in the chapel at UCC.

"At the wedding in Ireland, even though I was the first female EE grad from UCC and a professor, I was given a leaky pen to sign the marriage register which had my occupation listed as 'spinster'! I didn't fight it to get it changed, I thought it was funny."

At the time, Mike worked in healthcare marketing and had been a volunteer firefighter/medic. He later started a successful wheelchair transportation business which they named, over some wine, Emerald Transportation after the Emerald Isle.

"My parents loved Mike but, being Catholic and living in a country where divorce was illegal, didn't think we could get married. To make it easy for my family and me, even though he wasn't Catholic, Mike volunteered to apply for an annulment, which was ultimately granted. In the meantime, we had a secret civil wedding in Ohio with just a judge and our 2 witnesses. Four months later, a bishop who golfed with Dad married us in Ireland. I like to say that I'm Mike's 2nd and 3rd wife, and he's my 1st and 2nd husband!" Cathy and Mike just celebrated their 34th wedding anniversary.

In 2008, Mike was diagnosed with melanoma, for which he had some surgeries and other treatments. In 2010, there was a concern about the original melanoma site on Mike's leg. Mike's dermatologist suspected shin splints, and told him that a biopsy could wait until after Cathy's mother's 90th birthday party in June. "So, we travelled to Ireland, joined by Dara who was wonderful with Mum, especially at helping with a wheelchair we had bought. The party was a great success. Unfortunately, when Mike had the biopsy after we came back, it was positive, and there were new tumors. His oncologist was wonderful but Mike's situation had become too serious for him to treat, so Mike went to UPMC in Pittsburgh, which has world-renowned melanoma specialists. Mike spent the fall of 2010 participating in a clinical trial, at a time when melanoma research was only just starting to make progress. We would attend symposia where the presenters were excited about survival times on the order of months. The trial concluded in December but, 2 months later, when Mike started acting strangely at dinner one night, I called 911.

He was diagnosed with a brain tumor, a melanoma metastasis which thankfully was operable."

However, he had a brain bleed that night requiring another brain surgery the following morning. "I don't think I'll ever forget ignoring the speed limit as I rushed to the hospital in the hope of seeing him before they took him back to surgery! Afterwards, he needed speech therapy to re-learn how to read and write, which he hated. He also went back to UPMC for radiation treatment and, later, took oral chemo."

Miraculously he defied all the odds, and today looks the picture of health. "Needless to say, that period was one of our greatest challenges, if not the greatest, and a wakeup call in setting priorities."

Cathy is very impressed by her stepdaughter Dara's many accomplishments and the challenges Dara has overcome. "Dara lived with us through high school. After that she attended Kent State's gerontology program, qualified and worked as a professional firefighter/medic, became a nurse, moved to Columbus, got married, had our 2 grandchildren, and now manages multiple ICUs (primarily for Covid during the pandemic), on top of all her family responsibilities."

Before the Covid pandemic, Cathy and Mike used to spend most Fridays babysitting (which Mike refers to as performing "security detail"!) their grandkids in Columbus, but then went 18 months making the best of FaceTime instead of seeing the grandchildren in person.

LOOKING BACK

Cathy gained a lot of job satisfaction from her work with students throughout her career, and a lot of enjoyment from her role as a grandmother. "A highlight was helping students through my work with CIS, my volunteering as a math tutor and, best of all, my role as 'granny'!"

When asked about regrets, if any, Cathy would have (1) been a better stepmother, (2) taken more vacations with her husband while she was working, "especially to places other than Ireland which I usually visited twice a year" (3) missed fewer family milestones in Ireland, and (4) provided more help to her siblings in Ireland as her parents got older.

"I hope I have been a decent role model and set a good example for Dara and our grandkids, and also for the students I taught at KSU and those I tutored, especially at the Tallmadge High School and Students with a Goal (SWAG) in Akron. Some former students who are female told me they liked having a female professor, as all the OR and IS professors hired before me were men."

POLLING FOR OPINIONS

What are the best life lessons you have learned that might benefit others?

1. Family, friendships, and both mental and physical health are precious; appreciate and nurture them.
2. Have a good sense of humor that includes the ability to laugh at yourself and not take yourself seriously.
3. When things don't go your way, look for silver linings and lessons to be learned; develop the ability to adapt.
4. Make sure your opinions are informed, respect the opinions of others, and be willing to revise your opinions in light of new information.
5. When deciding whether to accept a job offer, consider more than just the pay and benefits.

If a Millennial or Gen X or Gen Z person was sitting next to you on your death bed, and they asked you "What is the meaning of life? What is it all about?", what do you think your answer would be?

To do your best to help others and be kind to everyone including yourself, i.e., to follow the Golden Rule!

In looking back on your college experience, how do you feel?

I would rate it a 10. At UCC, a 4-year program, there were only two other girls in the class of over 100, and one was dating one of the guys, so the other girl and I did a lot together, as well as with other guys in the class. We worked hard and played hard. As one of the few females, I felt pressure to get good grades, especially since our results for the year were posted in a very public place. We were never given a breakdown by course or any kind of numeric score; instead, our names were printed in rank order, grouped by First Class Honours, Second Class Honours, Pass, Repeat, and Fail.

Years later when I was at Penn State, I finally saw all my UCC scores and, considering my low scores on Mechanics of Machines and Thermodynamics and that I always ranked near the top of the class, there was definitely no "grade inflation" then!" My masters involved no coursework, just research and a thesis, and only took one year.

After initially receiving my Ph.D. candidacy exam results, I was very upset at the prospect of returning to Ireland a failure; I remember how miserable I felt at a singalong one Saturday night when people sang "This Land is Your Land" and thinking "this land" wasn't mine! For my entire 5 years at Penn State, I lived in a graduate dorm where there were many international students. The days were busy with classes and research but, after dinner, I'd study for a few hours and then go out to a bar with friends. This was all very exciting after a sheltered Irish upbringing. It was the time of the Iran Hostage Crisis, and I had quite a few friends from Iran and other middle east countries.

How would you describe your Grandchildren relationships?

We have 2 grandchildren, Conrad who was born on St. Patrick's Day, and CJ (Colleen Joan) who is 2 years younger. We spent a lot of time with them before Covid, and I always enjoy 'playing' at math with them on the Khan Academy. We've also enjoyed taking them to places such as the Ohio State Airport, COSI, the U.S. Air Force Museum, and (primarily for Mike!) a toy shop and classic car dealer. The kids and I had fun playing hide and seek while Mike looked at cars!

Did you ever fear some sort of physical punishment (e.g., spanking) from your parents if you misbehaved?

If we had been very bold, Mum would either threaten to spank us with a wooden spoon (which has become a family joke) or to tell Dad when he got home from work. I certainly don't remember having much fear about either. I'm pretty sure our grandkids neither receive nor fear any physical punishment; when they misbehave, they're likely to be put on timeout or sent to their room.

Do you believe that the generations following ours will be, in general, better off or worse financially when they get to our age?

I'm concerned they will be worse off because people seem to spend more now and assume they're entitled to have more things, even when that means going into debt. Perhaps this isn't politically correct, but I find that some Americans overuse the word "need" as opposed to saying they would like to have something! I'm also concerned about the national debt catching up with future generations.

Do you believe those generations will live in a better country and world in the coming decades, versus what our generation experienced as we aged?

No, I don't. I'm extremely worried about climate change, the current state of education (especially STEM), political extremism, gun violence, cybersecurity threats, the growth of authoritarianism, global corruption, the ever-growing national debt (as well as the debt taken on by individuals), and the number of people on welfare.

Did you worry too much or too little about your parents as they grew older?

I worried about Dad's Alzheimer's, and its impact on both of my parents. I also worried about Mum living alone until after her 90th birthday, and think my worrying was justified. Since I lived so far away, my sister and her husband (Colette and Dave), and also my brother and his wife (Rory and Ger) had the bulk of the responsibility of caring for Mum and Dad as they got older. As Dad developed Alzheimer's, his personality changed from that of "the perfect gentleman" to becoming aggressive and paranoid. Over the duration of multiple visits, I learned that you can't take care of others if you don't take care of yourself, a lesson that was helpful when Mike became sick but hard to put into practice.

What about your first few jobs and what you learned from them?

While I earned pocket money for babysitting, helping with neighbors' dinner parties and, one summer, washing hair at a hairdresser (hair that was dyed or permed felt yucky!), my first job with a regular paycheck was in the boys' department of a Cork department store. I earned £5.50 per 40-hour week! From that job, I learned that I preferred something more challenging and less repetitive. Later, at my first professional job, I learned that, for me anyway, it was important to have job satisfaction. I also learned that a career has forks, and when choosing which direction to take, some decisions are more easily backtracked than others. I think dedication between employers and employees is more about the people involved than the organizations. I felt a greater responsibility to my colleagues and students than to the organizations where I worked.

Do you remember your parents or older relatives talking about the Great Depression?

I don't remember hearing anything about the Great Depression while growing up in Ireland. However, we had a family friend from Holland who was in the Dutch Resistance during World War II and saw people starving; she influenced us never to waste food, something I try hard to follow. However, I think both of my parents experienced rationing of things like tea, sugar, and petrol during WW2.

Any recollections of your key contributions as a professional?

I've loved when former students told me that something they learned in my classes helped them in their jobs, or that they thought I was a good teacher. I still keep in touch and have friendly relationships with some. I'm also glad that through CIS, I was able to help students find jobs and internships and receive scholarships and other awards.

How did music impact you growing up?

While growing up, in addition to studying the piano, I listened to pop records (a mix of Irish, British, and American), went to some choral festivals where the Russians always stole the show, and attended some concerts of which the most memorable was the Bee Gees. Showbands were popular, and I also enjoyed the Chieftains (especially Derek Bell), the Dubliners (especially Luke Kelly), the Clancy Brothers & Tommy Makem, and Christy Moore who performed Irish music. I also listened to the Beatles, Herman's Hermits, the Foundations, Petula Clark, Mary Hopkin (my mother loved "Those Were the Days," and I remember listening to it over and over in order to transcribe the words for her), Cliff Richard, and Tom Jones; the Welsh had wonderful singers which were fun to observe at international rugby matches. Among American performers, I liked Elvis Presley, Simon & Garfunkel, the Eagles, Diana Ross and the Supremes, and the Beach Boys.

When we were in Ardmore during the summer, one of my favorite pastimes was to go to pub singalongs in the evenings where I drank ginger ale with a little Rose's lime juice added. Two of my favorite audience participation songs were "Whiskey in the Jar" and "Will Ye Go Lassie Go".

I love going to symphony concerts in Cleveland, Akron, or Canton, as well as to Apollo's Fire performances and to hear Irish traditional or Russian balalaika music. I associate disco with my time at Penn State. On Friday nights, my friends and I would go to Mr. C's and drink happy hour cocktails such as Tequila Sunrises and Harvey Wallbangers which were all new to me, and be amused by the effects of the crazy strobe lighting on peoples' clothes.

Boomers have, and had, a reputation for drinking beer/wine/alcohol. Did you drink growing up?

When I was very young, Mum & Dad would let me have a sip of sherry on special occasions, but that stopped after my confirmation at age 10 when it was customary to take an abstinence pledge until age 18 or 21, I'm not certain which. It seemed like girls were more likely than boys to keep their pledges! I think my pledge lasted until the summer of 1973 in Cape Cod, when after work at night, I often went out to a bar with friends and started sampling sweet drinks like Singapore Slings. After I got back to Ireland, I think I drank Dubonnet for a while. Most of the alcohol I've consumed since coming to Kent has been wine. I used to teach a lot of night classes and, when I'd get home around 9 or 10 pm, Mike would often have a snack and glass of wine ready to help me unwind.

I never tried drugs. I'm in favor of legalizing marijuana in the hope that would help friends and others who suffer from chronic pain. I don't feel well enough informed to have opinions about other drugs.

Tell me about your life post-retirement.

As it turned out, the timing of my retirement worked out well. My sister's husband's cancer had advanced, and it allowed time for me to travel to Ireland to provide moral support for Colette while Dave was still alive as well as after he died.

Since I'm not good at sitting around idle, I also enrolled in the university senior guest program and have thoroughly enjoyed taking classes in Physics, Music, History, and Political Science; I'm currently taking an accounting class, my first business class in spite of 36 years working in a business school. I also started volunteering as a math tutor and was able to enjoy swimming more regularly and without having to watch the clock.

How would you describe your adult friendships?

I am extremely happy with my adult friendships, and consider my adult friends one of the best parts of my life, especially since my siblings are so far away. I feel closest to my sister (even though I haven't seen her in person since before the pandemic), but also very close to at least 4 friends in Ohio who have been incredibly helpful to Mike and me, especially around the time of his cancer surgeries and treatments. Since coming to the U.S., I've found it much easier to have close female friends, possibly a consequence of living in college towns where the level of education is likely to be higher. As for the amount of time I spend with friends, some weeks I'd like more (but busy schedules get in the way, especially for friends who are still working) and other weeks less, so overall the mix seems about right.

In what ways have you changed as a result of losing someone close?

I only had one living grandparent, my grandmother, who was also my godmother and died just before my 21st birthday when she was in her 90s; Dad died in 2009 when he was 84, and my mother died the following year just after her 90th birthday. While very sad and upsetting, I don't know that my grandmother's or parents' deaths changed me, certainly not as much as Mike's melanoma. However, I do find myself lingering when I come across photos of lost loved ones, so dusting our house sometimes takes longer than it should!

Consider for a moment all of the history of the time you were growing up. Do any historical events linger in your memory?

My memory of the JFK assassination was vivid. Irish TV was interrupted with the announcement and everyone was very upset especially since up to that point, he had been the only U.S. president to visit Ireland. Also, the Nixon impeachment and Watergate lingers in my memory. When I worked in Massachusetts in the summers of 1973 and 1974, people had bumper stickers boasting about being the only state that hadn't voted for Nixon.

Computers caused a lot of change at work, including word processors, spreadsheets, and email. The Internet caused major changes in enabling so many capabilities that we all use.

I also remember we had milk and bread delivery. We had a milk man who also delivered the newspaper, and a bread man. The milk came in 1 pint glass bottles with cream at the top, we'd return the empties, and we had a little dial to indicate how many new bottles we wanted.

Having FaceTime especially has been fantastic for staying in touch with my family in Ireland. I remember when phone calls were about $1 per minute so we'd either keep them short or write letters. Now we can chat as long as we like with the ability to see each other and with no worries about cost.

What do you recall about the press when you were growing up? How does that compare to now?

I think I paid less attention to the news when I was younger than I do now. I had less free time so I probably just watched the nightly news on TV, or I might have read a news magazine. When I was young, the news we received came from Ireland and England, so I don't feel able to make a fair comparison with the U.S. news I receive now.

What about 9/11? How did that affect how you think about our country and about terrorism?

I remember 9/11 very well. I was scheduled to teach that day, and 2 of my nephews, who had spent the summer working in the U.S. (at a seafood restaurant in Cape Cod and as a geneticist in La Jolla), were supposed to visit shortly afterwards. Neither nephew made it to Ohio. I remember trying to locate the two boys and being glued to the TV. It was all so terribly upsetting that, after a few days, I needed a break from news. Having grown up with Northern Ireland regularly on the news, I was aware of what is now called terrorism, although when the term was first used, I found it strange. I also find "Homeland Security" strange. When living in Ireland, I would have known about the conflict between Palestinians and Israel. In general, and in spite of being aware of the Holocaust, I think Irish people viewed the Palestinians as underdogs and had sympathy for them. However, I don't know anyone who supported acts of violence.

Any observations about minority / women's / men's rights and equality? How would you compare our gender and race equality status now vs. your years growing up?

I think Women's Lib was pretty big while I was at UCC but I didn't identify with the movement. I was probably too busy as a student. Obviously, my gender was a handicap when I applied to my first professional job, otherwise, I might have had a career as a real engineer instead of just engineering degrees. I'm fairly sure that it's been well researched and documented that female faculty at some universities have been paid significantly less than males in comparable positions, and I think it's probable that women were less readily tenured and promoted. I've also seen some females receive heavier teaching assignments than the men. Compared to when I was growing up, I think the situation is much better now. In spite of the above, I feel lucky to have worked with some wonderful people, most of whom were men, and many have become very good friends

How do you feel about U.S. immigration, the border wall, and our illegal alien policies?

As an immigrant, I have some feelings about immigration that are different from many of my American friends. I was lucky to be able to come to the U.S. legally, but that option is not available to most people and, even if it is, it can take an extremely long time. I think the U.S. could benefit from allowing more immigrants, especially those who are skilled in STEM (Science, Technology, Engineering, and Math) fields and those who are willing to do jobs where U.S. labor is hard to find. I'm very concerned about the future of this country as so few people born here are going into STEM, especially at the graduate level. Most of the grad students when I was studying engineering at Penn State were foreign, and Mike's previous and current oncologists at UPMC are from Lebanon. If the U.S. is going to compete with China, it needs to attract more international students and permit them to stay after they graduate. China seems to be doing a much better job of that and likely to surpass America in science and technology innovation, which could be a national, if not global, security challenge.

As for illegal alien policies, I don't think anyone would argue that they need reform, but I don't have a simple solution. I'd like to see the U.S. be more welcoming to those immigrants who would contribute to society and increase the number of admitted refugees/asylum seekers. However, I'd also like if that could be managed efficiently and in a way that keeps violent criminals out. While I don't support breaking the law, it bothers me to hear someone saying that an illegal alien should have followed the rules like I did and come here legally. Since most aliens don't have any mechanism for that, I feel like they're being criticized for not being able to do the impossible. If you don't have degreed technical skills, or you are not seeking asylum, or you don't have an immediate relative in the U.S., you may have to wait an entire lifetime. There a lot of hurdles along the way.

What would you say about Gen X (born 1965-1979), Millennials (born 1980-1994), or Gen Z (born 1995-2015)? Does anything stand out to you as significantly different than Boomers in how they think/act/behave?

I had not heard the term Boomer until long after I came to the U.S., so I don't feel competent to compare Boomers with later generations. One thing that stands out to me is young peoples' addiction to their devices, and how unsafe phone distraction makes driving or just walking. On the other hand, at times I wish we were as tech savvy. As for lifestyle differences, young people seem to possess a lot of things and view them as necessities instead of luxuries. Also, when I was teaching, students behaved a lot differently in class than our generation would have. Students might arrive late, temporarily leave the room during class, and/or leave before the end, and appear not to be in the least embarrassed about doing so. They were also more likely to ask for extensions on assignments or tests, and to contest grades. The level of grammar and math skills also deteriorated over the years. Of course, I also had the privilege to teach some absolutely wonderful and very diligent students who now have successful careers.

How do you feel about the second amendment and gun rights?

While I support the second amendment and the right to defend oneself, one's family, and one's property, I think there are too many guns and that there should be controls (in the form of background checks, tests, and licenses) on who is allowed to use guns and which types. Operating different types of transportation (which I also view as deadly weapons) have varying licensing requirements (e.g., for cars, buses, planes, ships, etc.) and I think guns should too.

How do you feel about the U.S. role as being 'watchman of the world'? Should we reduce our global influence, or expand it?

I have mixed feelings about this. I'm very concerned that, if the U.S. loses its lead in global affairs, the role would be taken over by China or Russia. I'm ok with my tax dollars being used for non-U.S. aid in certain circumstances, such as humanitarian aid, as long as there are controls to ensure the aid is used for its intended purpose and doesn't get in the wrong hands. I have concerns about military aid going to authoritarian leaders/repressive regimes. I'm concerned about the risk of that leading to anti-U.S. feelings and, potentially, acts of terror against the U.S.

What are your feelings about 'green initiatives' and the state of our planet?

I support "green initiatives," and think global warming/climate change is extremely serious and that we should be doing a lot more. I think some countries (e.g., European countries) are ahead of the U.S. The use of plastics has been reduced (e.g., many years ago, to encourage the use of reusable bags, stores started charging for grocery bags and stopped using plastic). Some countries also provide incentives for using electric cars and bicycles, and have increased their use of cleaner energy sources.

Do you feel that we are taxed too much or too little?

I think the super-rich should pay more and have fewer loopholes – and wish our taxes were used more efficiently and effectively.

How do you feel about our political representatives at the state or national level, including benefits and pension, and should there be term limits?

Yes, I think there should be term limits. I don't like that politicians have special life-time health care plans and pensions, even if they only serve for 2 years. I don't have a problem with them getting fees for speeches and books, but do for serving on boards when there's potential conflict of interest. Also, I don't like when politicians benefit from insider trading but make laws that would put stockbrokers in jail for doing so.

Should we have more or fewer governmental programs to help the underprivileged?

I support programs that ensure kids, the elderly, and those who have severe physical or mental challenges have adequate food, healthcare, and shelter. I support providing a decent education, at least through high school. I'm in favor of subsidizing post-secondary education but, in most cases, not with forgiving past student loans, and I don't think a university education is a right, or is best, for everyone. I think cheating within government programs is a problem and would like to see more enforcement.

What about the growing national debt?

I think the national debt is a very serious problem and likely to result in a lower standard of living for the next generations. I also think it's a national security risk.

Why are politicians so divided? Has it really changed, or has it been like this for a long time?

From what I've heard/read, the division started when a republican leader organized separate orientations for newly elected Democrats and Republicans. This resulted in the 2 groups not getting to know each other and not developing relationships outside their own parties. If the 2 groups spent more time getting to know each other, they might have less dislike and disrespect for one another and learn to disagree more agreeably. I think another issue is that there is less moderation and less willingness to really listen to the viewpoints of others or to compromise, and I'm uncomfortable with the extremism I see on both sides. I think the straight vote electoral system, combined with the 2-party system, is another cause of the division. Ireland has a complicated proportional representation voting system

(https://www.citizensinformation.ie/en/government_in_ireland/elections_and_referenda/voting/proportional_representation.html)

which, in my opinion, is fairer; the drawback with PR is that it's more difficult for any one party to get a clear majority, which sometimes leads to the formation of a coalition government that doesn't survive its full term.

Do you consider yourself to be a conservative or liberal or somewhere in between? Why? Have you changed throughout your life, and if so, how?

I am somewhere in between. I have changed from more liberal to more conservative.

The press talks a lot about the growing disparity in income – is that a big problem in your opinion?

Yes, I think it is, and wish I had a solution, but all I can come up with is to improve the education system, especially in poorer areas. From my volunteering as a math tutor, I have become extremely worried about the futures of the kids I saw based on their poor math skills, and I suspect they weren't doing so well in their other schoolwork either. They also seemed to have unrealistic expectations of how they were going to find work and make a living when they got older.

Are you more worried about the environment now vs. when you were in your teens or in the middle of life?

Yes, much more worried, especially after all the crazy weather, droughts, and fires we've seen in recent years.

Do you believe the U.S. should be more focused upon our country mainly, or more focused globally, in terms of how our tax dollars are used?

I think both are important since both, directly or indirectly, impact what happens in this country.

Do you think the country is headed in the wrong or right direction?

The wrong direction. The division, extremism, and lack of competent, honest leadership alarm me greatly.

Do you have more 'stuff' now than when you were younger? What are you doing about it if anything?

Yes, I have more stuff now, possibly because I lived fairly frugally when I was younger and tried not to buy something I was unlikely to need or couldn't afford. I don't like to have stuff I'm unlikely to use in the future, especially if someone else could use it so, when I buy new clothes for instance, I try to donate some old ones. Also, I get more pleasure out of time spent with friends, attending a concert or other type of performance, or travelling for vacation than I do from acquiring stuff. I also think the younger generations have more stuff, possibly a result of entitlement and of a greater willingness to take on debt. Maybe also because more women are working outside the home, so couples have more disposable income. It seems like every time we see our grandkids, they have more new toys to show us.

How important is education now vs. when you grew up?

It is more important now, primarily because of the impact of technologies such as AI, machine learning, and robotics, including the number of jobs that are going away due to automation. However, I don't think everyone should go to college. The country needs people with a variety of skills and, since we're likely to be most successful working at something we enjoy and feel passionate about, I'd like to see everyone getting the level, and type, of education that's best for them. Also, there seems to be a huge shortage of plumbers, electricians, and so on, so I think anyone with an aptitude for a trade could make a lot of money and receive a lot of satisfaction from entering such a field.

Tell me about your health care coverage and its value vs cost.

Mike and I are fortunate to have good coverage. However, I think it's terrible that oncologists and other medical professionals have to spend inordinate amounts of time advocating with insurance companies on behalf of their patients, time that could be better spent treating people and reducing potentially life-threatening wait times. I hope we won't ever get to the point where non-medical people take over from knowledgeable professionals when healthcare decisions are being made for us.

Relative to other concerns you have, where does your health and your family's health rank?

Near, if not at, the top, both physical and mental health.

Can you contrast living in the U.S. versus living in Ireland?

In Ireland, it is a smaller country, so friends and family tend to be closer geographically. Also, there is a lot of scenery variety within a short distance. It is easier to discuss politics openly without dividing family or losing friends. There is a greater awareness of what is happening in other countries. Pace of life is slower, the quality of education in primary and secondary schools is more uniform, and fees are lower. Healthcare is less expensive also.

In the U.S., things are more likely to work, and services are more likely to be delivered on time. The cost of living is lower other than for health care and education. There is magnificent scenery, and there are more sunny days. There is access to world class graduate education. People are more orderly and willing to follow rules, such as standing in line. The U.S. is less reliant on other countries, such as for food or cars. There is more access to advanced healthcare, including clinical trials.

Tell me about your immigration experience.

I had attended Penn State on a student visa and originally went there with no intention of staying in the U.S. after graduation. However, by 1982, I started realizing that my degree was more likely to be employable in the U.S. than Ireland, and interviewed for faculty positions in a mix of engineering and business schools in multiple states. Because of the nature of my degree, I was eligible for "practical training," which is how the university was able to hire me. During my "practical training," I applied for permanent residence which involved a process called labor certification that is intended to prevent aliens taking jobs from people who were born here. However, labor certification is easier in the case of academic institutions who only have to prove that a job applicant is the "best qualified" candidate, as opposed to the "only qualified" candidate in the case of non-academic organizations. After receiving my labor certification, I was called for an interview at the INS offices in Cleveland, at which the interviewer mistakenly thought my attorney was my interpreter! If I remember correctly, there was then a period of a few months where, if I needed to travel outside the U.S. and wished to return, I would have had to apply for "parole". My original "green card" was actually blue and good for life. However, after marrying Mike, I changed my last name and tried unsuccessfully to contact the INS by phone to find out what I needed to do about that.

Eventually Mike and I had to go in person to the Cleveland office where even he felt he was being treated like a criminal and, because of the amount of time that had elapsed, I was fined, probably a few hundred dollars. The replacement "green card" was red and, ironically since Mike was born in the U.S., it was only good for 10 years. In 2000, I decided to apply for U.S. naturalization. I had been living here full-time since 1977 (so half my life up to then) and paying taxes, but unable to vote. Also, not being a citizen had implications for potential future inheritance taxes. However, the primary reason for my decision was that my parents were getting older, and I didn't want to risk being without a passport if I needed to travel home in a hurry. I figured that, living in the U.S., it would be faster to renew a U.S. passport than an Irish one – however that turned out to be wrong, even though I always pay extra to have my U.S. passport expedited.

I completed and submitted the naturalization application form in January 2001 (listing all the times I had travelled internationally over the years was a challenge), and the process took longer than usual because everything slowed after 9/11. I started studying for the citizenship test and found the material very interesting. By that time, all the test questions, and most of the answers, were available online so I felt pressure to do well! My test was in April 2002, thankfully I did score 100%, and my swearing in ceremony was on May 17, 2002. I had to surrender my green card then. However, since the U.S. cannot confiscate another country's passport, I held onto my Irish one, had my U.S. passport application ready to go, and immediately went to the post office to mail it in.

I was very upset for a few days after the ceremony because of the "renouncing" parts of the Naturalization Oath of Allegiance (*"I hereby declare, on oath, that I absolutely and entirely renounce and abjure all allegiance and fidelity to any foreign prince, potentate, state, or sovereignty, of whom or which I have heretofore been a subject or citizen"*), as well as the 1st paragraph in the welcome booklet from President Bush implying that I was no longer Irish:

> TODAY you have become a citizen of the United States of America. You are no longer an Englishman, a Frenchman, an Italian, a Pole. Neither are you a hyphenated-American— a Polish-American, an Italian-American. You are no longer a subject of a government. Henceforth, you are an integral part of this Government—a freeman—a Citizen of the United States of America.

I found it reassuring that the judge who conducted the ceremony considered the oath antiquated. Also, a few days later, a good friend gave me a friendship pin (with Irish and American flags) which cheered me up. I now have two passports and keep both current which is nice since, when Mike and I travel into the E.U. or the U.S., we can always choose the faster line!

IN SUMMARY

Cathy is such an interesting person in terms of her life and experiences. Here is someone who made it a high priority to focus upon education from her early years and forward, and finding her path in life professionally. Eventually, that focus on education brought her to the U.S. where she is now a citizen. She served her employer loyally for many years, building a reputation as someone who cares deeply for her students and their well-being. She is a joy to be around.

Her family life is also interesting, and her story about her husband's illness and his amazing recovery is a lesson for all of us regarding faith and seeking the best treatment. She places a high priority on family both here in the states as well as in Ireland.

Her story about the process of immigrating to the U.S. and her thoughts about it today are interesting, because they differ from what you hear in the press or from others who have never experienced the process to become a U.S. citizen. Clearly, in the years that she went through the process, the U.S. did not make it easy to become a citizen, but I will leave that to others to decide if that is a bad thing or a good one!

Her perspectives on the differences between the U.S. and Ireland are fascinating, and helps us all put into perspective many of the blessings we have in the country that we sometimes take for granted or do not even think about.

I especially liked that Cathy shared with me a note that a friend sent to her after a girls' happy hour:

"By the way – adjectives to describe my dear friend, Cathy!

Kind, Generous, Warm, The MOST organized person I know

Lively, Genuine, Supportive, Dedicated to whatever she does

Has a beautiful Americanized Irish accent, has a heart of gold

Someone who can be counted on, follow through is better than most

Fun, A beautiful soul, Loyal"

I could not have said it better myself! Thank you, Cathy, for making our country a better place by coming here, and for your contributions to society!

CHAPTER 10:
Jeff:
The Executive Who 'Changed Collars'

BACKGROUND

I first met Jeff through the game of golf. Jeff was a solid golfer and later, we served on a board together. He actually lives in our same community, and I always notice how neat and well-kept his yard and home are. You will learn that he takes a lot of pride in his home, community, career, and family.

Jeff is friendly to all, and is very good at telling 'tribal stories' to get a point across to those younger or with less experience. He has a distinctive habit of pausing in the middle of a story or tale, that accentuates the point he is about to make.

We share a similar background in terms of family and transitioning from a blue-collar family to a white-collar career, and I can relate personally to many of his experiences and lessons in life. I hope you will enjoy hearing his story, because it is perhaps a classic Boomer tale.

EARLY LIFE

Jeff was born in 1957, and grew up the youngest of 4 siblings in a lower-middle-class family in western Pennsylvania. His father was a coal-miner with a 7th grade education, his mother worked in a local department store, having a high school education.

His father was the second eldest in his family with 8 siblings, and had to go to work in his youth to support the family, since his father died at a very young age. Early on, his father was an underground coal miner. Later on, he operated a large coal shovel, but the job was very demanding physically and after a time, his legs would not allow him to operate the shovel anymore. After that, he worked to maintain the mining equipment, which was also demanding physically, being out in the cold or heat. Jeff recalled that the family suffered from labor strikes from time to time, which caused its own challenges financially.

Jeff lived with his parents, a grandmother, an older sister and brother, as well as his twin sister. "We were not a wealthy family by any means and all of us lived in a three-bedroom, one bathroom home. While we had very little, my parents worked very hard to provide for the family, and all the necessities of food, clothing and shelter were always available. There was a big age gap between my older brother and sister and "the twins". I remember one Christmas; they gave up their presents so that my sister and I could have a big Christmas. Everyone sacrificed to help ends meet. Jeans with patches were a fashion statement in our house. Having said that, it was a secure childhood. Our hometown was a small rural community, a safe place to grow up."

Jeff recalls that with his parents so focused upon hard work, they had little time for raising the children. "My Grandmother was the matriarch of the family and was essentially our nanny when we were young." His father was a staunch Catholic, and the children were raised to be honest and ethical, but in Jeff's words, not necessarily religious. "We were expected to be good children and there was little tolerance for bad behavior. As a lower-middle-class family, it became very clear early in our lives that you worked for what you had. I credit Mom and Dad for instilling a good work ethic in all their children."

Upon reflection, how does Jeff view his parents' opinions and views at that time?

"My parents had a very restricted view of the world. I think living their life in small rural community and not attending college limited their ability to look beyond the daily struggles of life and making ends meet. We never went on vacation, and a two-hour car ride was a big deal. They had a very pragmatic view of life, which was to handle that which is directly in front of your face. Today, we are bombarded with global news, but back then the local papers and few news programs were all they had to understand the world. They read and watched religiously, but there was not much in the way of diverse content."

Jeff recalls that his parents most significant concern was the Vietnam War. With two sons, they were very concerned about when the war would end. He remembers them watching the death totals every night on the news. "Fortunately, my brother had a college deferment and had a low eligibility status due to his eyesight, and my age group was the first group of males that were not required to register for the draft."

Were his parents disciplinarians? "I can only think of one time I was spanked, and I remember spanking one of my boys once. I would say physical punishment was very judiciously used by both my parents and me. Their discipline was more reflected in their actions and expectations of us. I'm grateful for what they taught me. They instilled ethics, responsibility, and the value of hard work in all their children, these are lifelong values. They were tough but very loving. I don't know if our views on life were ever in disagreement, it was just that I knew there was much more to experience outside of our little burg."

Jeff recalls that his first job was delivering newspapers, and that it taught him interpersonal skills in interacting with his customers as well as the responsibility to do a job well. "I also worked in a peanut butter factory and brick factory while in college, and that reinforced my thinking, beyond watching the effect on my father, that manual labor was not for me. I also worked as a draftsman one summer. My job was to correct the staff draftsmen's errors after review by the head draftsman. I quickly became aware of office politics. Each draftsman reacted differently to some inexperienced college kid modifying their work. Some took it well, some not so well. I had to walk a thin line and learned dealing with the sensitivities of others."

Jeff wishes that his parents would have been more involved in his life, but on the upside, he appreciates the independence that parenting style created. "I did a lot on my own while growing up. During the transition from high school to college, I made sure I took all the college entrance exams, applied to college, obtained student loans, etc. They never really pushed me, but they never dissuaded either."

Jeff and his twin sister have more of an older brother / younger sister relationship. "She became very sick when we were in first grade. She missed much of the school year and needed to repeat her grade. My parents made the decision not to hold me back and consequently we had different circles of friends as we grew up." His sister's husband was a career Navy man and they lived in many locations inside and outside the U.S. They eventually parted and went separate ways. She works as a sales rep for a retailer. "She had a hard life and has done a wonderful job raising her family and providing for them. I know I can't relate to all the challenges she had in life, and I am sure she has no idea of mine."

In high school, Jeff chose classes within the 'college prep' path. Why college prep? "My older brother and sister both attended college, and my dad basically told me to make my own decision to either go to college, enlist, get a job, etc. It was not that he was not supportive of going to college, he just didn't suggest one path or the other. My mother was very encouraging however, of me attending college."

Jeff described himself then as an above-average student and a member of the National Honor Society. He recalls that he found the academic side of high school easy. He played varsity basketball, and sports were always a big part of his life, but sports did not come easily for him. "I would say I was blessed with limited ability and always had to work hard to compete. I was a little chubby kid. I didn't even play much basketball in the 7th and 8th grade, but worked hard, got in shape, honed my skills and slowly passed those ahead of me. I won the only award our coach gave out, the Hustler Award, given to the person that gives over 100% every day. It reinforced the lessons from my parents that you only can achieve what you work for."

What about his friends and his social circles in high school? "I was not the most popular kid in high school and would say I never fit into any of the classic niches. I had friends that were the best students, the academically challenged, jocks, band kids, a diverse lot."

How did you choose your path after high school? "I remember being very upset on graduation day. I think it was more the thought of the unknown that bothered me. It was really the first time I experienced that big move from the familiar to the unfamiliar, the first time I was forced to make that major life decision that shapes your life forever."

ON TO COLLEGE

Jeff chose to attend a small private college in western Pennsylvania and graduated with a degree in Mechanical Engineering. He feels as though his college experience was similar to high school.

"I don't feel it was better or worse than high school. It was different, in that it was the first time I was on my own and completely independent. I realized that my failure or success was completely dependent on my commitment to education. I had a great time, maybe too great. I made a lot of lifetime friends, and I met my wife at college."

Any regrets? "If I have one regret, I would have hit the books a lot harder than I did. I don't think I took maximum advantage of my educational opportunity."

ON TO A CAREER

Jeff had several job offers, but chose to pursue a career with a Fortune 500 company in Ohio, thinking that there might be more opportunities with a larger company. Jeff worked there for 38 years and rose to a position as a senior executive before retiring at age 59. "My first full time job was as a product design engineer. I learned the value of not only understanding what to do, but why it's done the way it is. I learned a great deal throughout my career. When you go from staff to executive, each level taught me something new.

What was a key role that he is most proud of? "I led a project to integrate systems simulation technology into product design, and this was enabled by supercomputing technology that had become available at this time. This was a huge challenge since the product design function was well-established and many engineers had adopted a process which worked well. Using this technology required that the design process had to be changed, and the change required huge investments in computing technology, software, process changes, testing, etc."

Throughout his career, Jeff recalls that he seemed to be asked to do the projects that were never done before, which he took as a compliment. He was also asked later in his career to revamp the global purchasing processes, which he thought was very successful, and he reflects on this experience and is very proud of the results and the savings the team achieved.

Near the end of his career, he admits to being disappointed that after contributing for so long, his retirement was not under ideal circumstances, but he recalls that in mentoring others, he suggested they get a written agreement when they are assigned to a new location.

As Jeff neared the end of his career, did he notice anything significantly different between the generations of employees?

"I grew up in a generation that saw companies change from being paternal to strictly results-oriented. I went from working with lifetime employees to younger employees whose mindset was sometime 'what's in it for me?' They wanted success, responsibility, and progression quickly. I still am of the school that one needs to do the time to develop the skills and the decision-making processes required. I noticed that experience is now somewhat under-valued."

What about recent college graduates? "When recruiting new graduates, we had pretty high standards, such as GPA minimums, for those graduates to even be considered for employment. I am concerned that standards are being lowered at some institutions. If this continues, I worry that student preparedness will decline and consequently, our global competitiveness will also decline."

Jeff takes pride in his involvement in mentoring younger employees also. "I always had a paternalistic approach to dealing with employees, I mentored a lot of engineers that went on to be very successful. One piece of advice I always had was for them to decide what they wanted to do and to develop a roadmap to get there. We would discuss other executives and their career paths as a way for them to consider different ways to achieve their career goals. I also tried to stress the importance of building relationships with others and how to be a team player. I also discussed with them the process of change, and that is a natural part of change for human beings to resist, but that eventually things work out. I always told them that once they worked for me, I would always be there for them if needed no matter where they ended up. That attitude served them and me very well. I would like to believe that helping them find their way has been a big benefit for the community and for them."

Given that his parents had a blue-collar background, did they understand his work life and job responsibilities? "While I think my parents were very proud of me, I don't think they were able to understand the challenges I faced during my college days and those I faced in my 38-year professional career. I think that was due simply to them being blue-collar parents, and I was a white-collar professional. I knew their world, but they did not understand mine."

COMMUNITY INVOLVEMENT

After retirement, Jeff served on the board of his local country club. "I'm very proud of how, as a team, we moved the club from being on the verge of going out of business, to the current status of the club being vibrant, growing, making investments, being the hot club in the area." Jeff observes that many members have no idea of the transition and the tough decisions that were made during the past five years, but that they do not need to, they just ought to enjoy the club and its assets. "It took years for the transition to take place, basically due to the efforts and contributions of a string of qualified board members and a string of excellent employees and management leaders."

FAMILY LIFE

Jeff met his wife at college, but they did not begin dating at that time. How did they meet? "She was an accounting major, and her sorority threw a party at my fraternity house, and the next day, the girls came over to clean up after the party. My future wife walked by, and I looked at her, blonde, blue eyes, beautiful, and I said to my friend sitting there, who turned out to be my best man at our wedding, 'I am going to marry that girl!'

When he needed a date for a dance later, he went over to the sorority which had a roster of girls living there, and he recognized her name, and asked her to go to the dance with him.

After renewing their relationship once out of college, they were married, and started a family, having two sons. "I wrote her a letter after college, when she was living with her parents, and suggested that maybe we meet up again."

"I have been married for 39 years to a loving wife, and we raised two wonderful boys. They are on a great track, real gentlemen, and well-educated. They are two solid people, and my wife gets most of the credit for that. I'm very proud of my family and the multitude of career accomplishments that my wife and I achieved together as a team. I think we experienced the typical ups and downs of married life. We love each other very much and there is no doubt we are committed as they say, "to death do us part". We have been blessed and are grateful for what God has given."

Jeff reflects on his various assignments and how they were tough on his wife, as they were assigned for three years in Europe, and lived in Oklahoma out in the middle of nowhere, and how he put in tremendous hours at his job, leaving her more-or-less alone quite a bit.

"I wish there would have been a way that my wife would have had the chance to pursue a career, and regret all she had to give up personally, but I am comfortable with the decision we made as a team for her to be home with our sons."

POLLING FOR OPINIONS

If forced to list only three of the most important lessons in life you have learned, which might benefit others, what would they be?

Live your life with integrity and never compromise it. Your word is your reputation.

Set goals for yourself in all aspects of your life and work toward them. Don't be afraid to change them as your situation changes. I firmly believe if you don't set goals, wherever you end up, good or bad, is purely an accident.

Make the most out of every opportunity your given, don't fear change. Windows open and close in life and you need to take advantage of them when they are offered.

If a Millennial or Gen X or Gen Z person was sitting next to you on your death bed, and they asked you "What is the meaning of life?" What do you think your answer would be?

Life is short, so live it to the maximum. Try to leave this world with minimal regrets. You don't want to lie in your death bed saying 'I wonder if....'. Be happy in being responsible to yourself, your family, and your friends.

How about the relationship with your sons?

I think they respect what I've accomplished. I also think as they got older, they started to appreciate the values they were taught. My wife was very involved with their education and extra curriculars as they grew up. I know I could have been more involved and at times did not do a good job of managing the work/life balance.

How would you compare the values of yourself to your children?

I think our values align very well. They do differ from me in that their priorities in life are different. I believe they value their free time much more than I did. Work-life balance is more critical to them than professional careers. I also see a sense of entitlement at times that I never had. Maybe that is the result of the childhood my wife and I provided for them. They wanted for very little.

How would you compare the relationship you have with your children, vs the relationship between your parents and you when you were their age?

We are much more involved in their lives compared to my parents. I don't blame my parents, it's simply a matter of being able to relate to what they are experiencing.

Were your parents stricter than you were as a parent?

I don't think we were any stricter. My sons both say I was tough and demanding.

Do you still help your children financially even if they are adults?

Yes, we help our boys out financially when required. We spend a good bit of time with our boys. If they need or want our help, we are there for them. They are both independent and we are learning that when they have a problem, an ear, not advice is what they want. When I was their age, I had left the hometown, so it was a little different situation. My parents could not offer financial support. I think my parents also had that "sink or swim" mentality.

Do you think you worry too much about your children?

I hope I worry the right amount. It's a tough world out there for young adults today, given the challenges of social media and how aware others are of everything they do. I only worry that they are happy and never lonely. I want them to meet their definition of success in whatever they do.

As for my parents, it depended on the child. They worried a lot about my older brother and twin sister, not so much about my older sister and me. It was situational. The biggest compliment my father ever gave me was telling me he never had to worry about me.

Do you think that society does or does not value enough a parent who stays home with children?

In this world of dual income families, yes staying home is under-appreciated. I don't think most young parents understand the impact of having a parent at home can have on developing their children. I also think the sacrifice of the parent that stays home, in lieu of their career objectives and self-actualization is under-appreciated.

Is there anything you would do differently in parenting in looking back?

I think I needed to be a better listener.

Do you believe that the generations following ours will be, in general, better off, or worse financially when they get to our age?

Generally worse. I believe some are victims of their parents' success. In some ways, their lives were too easy. Some have a big safety net. However, anyone with the drive to be successful and financially secure can achieve those goals.

Do you believe those generations will live in a better country and world in the coming decades?

Worse. The nuclear family is undervalued, and winning as opposed to simply participating, is less emphasized than when I grew up. This tends to degrade the value system, breeds a lack of competitive drive, and leads to a sense of entitlement. This ties into my comments above with some children being victims of their parents' success.

Tell me about your parents and your involvement in their care as they aged.

My parents were comfortable in their senior years and lived a modest, but comfortable life. My one regret was missing my mother's symptoms of heart disease. One time we were all home for Thanksgiving, and she just did not look right, or seem right, and later she had a massive coronary and we lost her. She passed earlier than she should have.

Were you a caregiver for your father?

It was a shared responsibility among the siblings. He was always well-cared for. However, I worried about loneliness as he aged. It is tough to see the slow loss of independence of a parent. That experience was a bit of a view to my future life, and I just hope that I can be gracious to my sons if they are involved in my care, as I lose my independence.

What are you planning to have happen with any funds or possessions after you die?

It will be shared among our boys. I ponder doing some more philanthropy, but have not decided with what organization. Growing up relatively poor, providing a better life for my family compared to what I experienced was always a priority. I am confident that my boys will be very secure in their later years.

Do you remember your parents or older relatives talking about the great depression? Could we have another one?

My parents and grandparents never talked about it. They were very much Great Depression babies though. Nothing was purchased unless paid. No food was wasted. When things broke, they were fixed, not replaced. They always had cash hidden around the house. I remember when my dad passed, he had a safe in the bedroom with over $80k in it! We had to go through the whole house to see if he hid any money anywhere else. We have found cash in coats, hidden in the piano and dining room table, behind pictures. I can only attribute that to how the great depression affected them. They saved what they could and always taught us saving for a rainy day was important. Consequently, my wife and I always paid ourselves first and have been avid savers. I think when one considers the inflation we are currently experiencing, the climbing national debt, and the push for increased federal spending, yes, I think it's possible for us to have another Great Depression.

How did music impact you growing up?

I listened to all kinds of music growing up. I remember watching the Beatles on the Ed Sullivan show. I can't honestly say that music had much of an effect on me. I was too young to appreciate the music of the civil rights era or the Vietnam war. To me, disco was a fad. Rock and Roll was party music. Music was for relaxing.

Boomers have, and had, a reputation for drinking beer/wine/alcohol. What about you?

We did do some drinking while we were growing up. I think like most, drinking was part of the college experience. I did do marijuana in college, never experimented beyond that. I always believed that regarding drugs and alcohol, you must draw a line for yourself and never cross it. I told the same thing to my boys. My partying got out of control my sophomore year in college and it cost me dearly. If I went back, I would handle that year completely differently. I put myself in a hole and had to work hard to dig myself out of it my last two years at college. Like most things in life, moderation is wise. I'm not against legalization of marijuana, but it needs to be strictly controlled. I do have concerns about it being a gateway drug. On the other hand, I do believe legalization could aid in reducing black market drugs. Regulations need to be reasonable from a financial perspective, or growers and processors will not be able to compete with illegal supply lines.

How would you describe your adult friendships?

I'd describe most of my adult friendships as casual. I do have several close friends and many who would be there to help me with anything I needed. Life gets busy and my advice to all is you get out of your friendships what you put into them. Family is very important to me, and as I get older, I find myself connecting more with my siblings and boys. I love my time with my friends too. I think my relationships are in balance. But I do wish I'd kept in better contact with some of my college friends.

In what ways have you changed as a result of losing someone close?

I have a very pragmatic view of life. Death is simply a phase of life. I grieve and move on. I did lose a good friend to cancer. As a result, I try to take good care of myself and don't ignore symptoms. I think about the time when my wife and I will part. I'm sure it will impact me greatly; she has been my best friend for many, many years.

What about global events or new technologies and how they impacted your life?

I'm a technologist. I expect my life to be changed as technology advances. I look forward to the next advancement. Technology advancements will keep our country competitive in the global market. As far as world events go, I believe I've been lucky to live in the best of times and my life hasn't been affected to a great extent. I'm sure if I would have lived through the great depression, a world war, etc. my opinion would change. I do worry about the rise in crime. I find myself more on guard when I travel now. It's a growing trend that needs to change.

How has the press and media changed in your lifetime?

I think the press has changed over time. The news used to be about the facts. Now, it's more about the political ideology the paper or news channel supports. Social media has also changed the landscape for the worse. I think I went from believing what was written or presented to finding I must do more research for myself. I'm lucky, I have the time to do that. Most Americans don't have that luxury, so I understand why some take the positions they do. My trust in the press has declined. I find the spinning and omissions tiring. All must be taken with a grain of salt and the source's perspective must be taken into consideration.

What about 9/11? How did that affect how you think about our country and about terrorism?

9/11 taught me not to take our safety for granted. I was aware of the conflict in the Middle East, but I think like most, it was limited to the conflict in Israel. I never really realized how hated the West had become. I do not think our current leaders are doing enough to protect the Country from those who wish to overtake us as a superpower. This extends beyond physical harm, but also economic harm.

Any thoughts about minority / women's / men's rights and equality today vs. in your youth?

I believe the inequality issue has become politicized. I have had the opportunity to travel all over the world. Most Americans have no idea how lucky they are to live in the U.S. We're not perfect, but I do believe we strive to be better. History has proven that. I am very concerned about the education of our youth. I do believe there is an indoctrination occurring around the 'supposed' oppressed and elite. Politics today, particularly Leftist policy, is dividing us into classes based on race and economic status.

How do you feel about U.S. immigration, the border wall, and our illegal alien policies?

I believe in legal immigration. I believe in secure borders and consequently the border wall. Immigration policies particularly, in processing those who want to legally become citizens needs to be improved. I believe we should do something for the "dreamers" as they are essentially 2nd generation Americans. I do believe in immigration quotas. Not to preclude anyone wishing to immigrate to the U.S., but to make sure our infrastructure can adequately absorb the influx. I believe we have moved away from a process that assimilates immigrants into our society to one that simply facilitates numbers for political reasons.

What would you say about the younger generations vs. Boomers?

I've commented previously that particularly the Millennials feel entitled to some degree. Their attitude is much different from when I grew up. We have bred a generation of children that were taught participation as opposed to winning is more important. Most have had easier lives due to the success of the Boomers. I believe the Boomers must take some responsibility for that. When I graduated from college and started interviewing for jobs, I was concerned how I could contribute to the company. The Millennials want to know what the company will do for them. They tend to want to be given responsibility quickly and expect the company to reward them quickly either monetarily or through promotion. On the other hand, most are much more concerned about their work life-balance as compared to the boomers. They tend to be better prepared to enter the workforce than the Boomers and are technically well-prepared. I have found them to be very bright and innovative. They have no fear of failure and are very self-confident. They are very transient and expect to often move from job to job or location to location. They see this as the best way to accomplish their career and financial aspirations. Very few will be lifetime employees of one company.

There is a segment of Millennials who made choices toward degrees that do not yield the financial rewards which keep them in the lifestyle afforded them by their parents as they were growing up. Millennials tend to be "spend as you go". They aren't big savers.

My advice to them would be to find a vocation they love. Don't be in a rush; be realistic. Learn well their field of expertise. Understanding and experience will serve them well as their careers develop. Find a good mentor to help guide them through the learning process.

What about Boomers do you think is negative and what ways could they be better?

Boomers tend to be risk-averse and resistant to change. They tend to find their comfort zone and stay there. Having said that, they tend to be dedicated and loyal. Boomers were savers and built economic security for their families. They have an excellent work ethic and are very family oriented. Boomers set their children up for success and most will leave a financial windfall for them when they pass.

Surveys show that non-Boomers are much more positive about socialism than Boomers. Thoughts?

They are a product of an education system that is very liberal in nature. As I said before, they grew up in an environment where everyone participates, winning was not necessarily the goal. Everyone shares the wealth. Socialism doesn't work, it leads to government control of everything. Throughout history, socialism has led to failed economies and countries. If it was good, our borders wouldn't be overrun with people trying to get into the U.S.

China on the other hand is a growing superpower. I believe they have exploited the capitalism of the West, particularly the U.S., to their advantage. However, it is a country of wide economic divide between the working class and the elites. Eventually, this will lead to unrest.

Are we as a society too hard or too easy on convicted felons?

Too easy. Crime is rising. The result of liberal DA's and no cash bail has given criminals the green light to commit crimes. Where's the risk? I do believe there are non-violent offenders who can be rehabilitated and can become good members of society. They should be given a second chance. The problem today is we have used a 'peanut butter' approach where violent and non-violent offenders get the same treatment. I do believe in the death penalty in the case of murder.

How do you feel about the second amendment and gun rights?

There are not too many "legal" guns in America. No gun has ever gone off without a person pulling the trigger. People misunderstand the premise of the 2nd Amendment. It was for the people to protect themselves against a tyrannical Government. It also allows people to defend themselves in life-threatening situations. I grew up in a hunting family. Gun safety was taught and strictly adhered to. I believe there should be stricter gun education and proficiency requirements for anyone trying to legally purchase a gun.

How do you feel about the US role as being 'watchman of the world'?

I think we should play that role. I do believe NATO Allies should pay their fair share and we need to hold them accountable for that financial support. A strong NATO keeps China and Russia in check. I have no problem with humanitarian aid, but that should be limited to just food, shelter, schools and defense. With all the homeless we have in our Country, more money needs directed to those causes. There are some funding programs that need to be better scrutinized. Just this week I saw a report, that the federal budget includes $30 million for, of all things, crack pipes!

What are your feelings about green initiatives and the state of our planet?

There is conflicting data on global warming and there are many fear-mongers describing exaggerated imminent danger. In my lifetime, I believe global warming should have destroyed the planet 2 or 3 times by now. Clean energy and protection of the environment is important. I don't understand why our political leaders can't accept the coexistence of two competing thoughts. Energy policy is just one example. We should invest in clean energy alternatives and technologies, while using fossil fuels to keep our economy strong. An energy independent U.S. makes for a safer overall world. The U.S. is the leader in reducing carbon emissions and should focus more on pushing countries like China and India to step up or the battle the environmentalists are fighting is a lost cause. I believe I read that if the U.S. had zero carbon emissions, the overall global impact would be minimal. The saber-ratting needs to stop and real progress from other countries needs to be made.

Do you feel that we are taxed too much or too little?

Tax revenues are not the problem, out of control spending is the issue. It would be nice to see meaningful legislation proposed that does not have millions and millions of pork added to each bill. I am in favor of the line-item veto for this very reason. Someone must hold Congress accountable for all the frivolous and special-interest spending. What we pay in taxes is something that needs to be studied in detail. From a fairness perspective, a flat tax across the board makes sense. The more you make, the more you pay. There should be a cutoff point though for low-income families. No doubt staying within the budget is a problem. We can't continue to increase the national debt. Balancing a budget is quite simple. The decisions you must make to do it is the hard part. It requires sacrifice and compromise. We should spend only what we take in. Seems a hard concept for our political leaders to understand. I must do this at home and did it for years for the organizations I led.

How do you feel about the compensation of our political representatives?

I am not familiar with what our politicians make, but why would anyone in government make more than the President? I know some do. I think many politicians and administrators make more than their constituents. It would be interesting to see exactly how many are in the top one percent. I'm in favor of term limits and requiring Congress to put their money in a blind trust while serving. I feel there is a lot of insider trading going on in Washington D.C. No politician should be allowed to use their position to gain personal wealth.

Should we have more or fewer governmental programs to help the underprivileged?

There is enough money in the budget for the underprivileged, it is however mismanaged. Welfare programs need to be better monitored for abuse. Those receiving assistance should have to meet requirements to qualify. We have a tremendous number of job openings in the U.S. and I'm confident there are many able-bodied who should be working but choose the free ride. I would be in favor of more dollars for program enforcement within the current funds available.

What about the growing national debt?

Instinct tells us it's a problem, however, it doesn't seem to have impacted much up to now. If our economy stays strong, I'm not convinced it has much of an effect. Should the economy turn, a weakened dollar will exacerbate the issue. I am concerned about the portion of debt held by foreign countries. My understanding is it's $7 trillion of the $31 trillion total. If they choose to call in that debt, we will have to take immediate action to cover the cost. Not sure how that refinancing would be done but depending on how drastic the action taken would be, it could have a very negative impact on our standing around the globe.

Why are politicians so divided? Has it really changed, or has it been like this for a long time?

It's a difference in ideology between the two parties. I think the Right are constitutionalists and believers in capitalism. The Left, over a long period of time, have slowly moved way to the left of center to a more Marxist view and are socialists. This has happened over time, and I am quite concerned that its roots are in our educational institutions. You see this in our younger congressional representatives.

Do you consider yourself to be a conservative or liberal or somewhere in between?

I'm a conservative, been one all my life. I believe in capitalism, the Constitution, and smaller government. Our freedom as citizens and the rights we have in the U.S. cannot be matched by any other country. Today we see indications that our rights are being attacked. It's frightening.

The press talks a lot about the growing disparity in income – is that a big problem in your opinion?

It is somewhat of a problem, but the wages gap was being closed under the previous Administration. It is a symptom of bigger issues. Free money is not the answer. Our educational system, the decline of the nuclear family, and job migration out of the U.S. all needs to be addressed. I think some politicians are hyping this to be a bigger problem than it really is. Wealth, race, and disparities are being weaponized for political gain. I do believe our value system needs re-evaluation. For example, salaries of entertainers, sports figures, and corporate executives do seem to be out of balance.

Are you more worried about the environment now vs. when you were in your teens or in the middle of life?

More worried now. The litter that pollutes our land and oceans is growing exponentially. This needs to be addressed.

Do you believe the US should be more focused upon our country mainly, or more focused globally, in terms of how our tax dollars are used?

I'm a believer in sweeping your own front step first, but as the leader in the free world I do think we have an obligation to help those less fortunate. We do need to control frivolous spending abroad. When you see the homeless situation in this country one would say our standard of living is declining. It needs to be addressed.

Do you think the country is headed in the wrong or right direction?

Wrong direction. I believe capitalism and our Constitution is under attack. Historically we know socialism eventually fails every time and that's a direction a faction in our Country is heading. I have never seen our fundamental principles this Country was founded upon, being questioned like they are today. On the upside, I think these past two years have created an awakening.

Do you have more 'stuff' now than when you were younger?

Yes, but that depends on your definition of "stuff". The Boomers were financially responsible and for most, our means improved, and we could afford stuff we wanted. I'm concerned our younger generations may not. I think some have taken for granted the lifestyle they grew up in. I don't think they understand the sacrifice their parents made to achieve it. We are getting rid of some of our stuff now, as I find that having all these things is stressful.

Many Boomers believe that education is very important for the younger generations. Is advanced education more or less important than it was when you were growing up? Why or why not?

I believe advanced education is more important if we are going to continue to be competitive in the world economy. It is also a matter of national defense. However, I also believe the trades are important. It's the blending of technology with the ability to manufacture the products it creates that will make us successful.

Tell me about your health care coverage and its value?

My health care coverage is excellent, but expensive. I do believe we need some cost controls on the medical industry. The family practices are being gobbled up by the big hospitals to stay in business and prescription prices are out of control. I am not a believer in socialized medicine, but treatment is too expensive. No one could afford it without insurance.

Relative to other concerns you have, where does your health and your family's health rank?

Number 1. It's hard to have a good life when your health is bad.

What are your views about social security and funding for it?

I am collecting social security, but we are blessed that we could still live a very comfortable life without it. Saying that, it's an indication that one can fund their retirement years on their own, but some type of transition needs to occur. Too many people count on social security to make ends meet. I understand the surplus social security taxes collected are invested in Treasury Bonds. I believe there are better vehicles to increase the ROI. Unfortunately, given the funding situation, actions will need to be taken to keep the program solvent. It's a complex problem. I tell my boys not to count on it. They both started saving and investing as soon as they got their jobs out of college.

IN SUMMARY

As I finished writing Jeff's story, and re-read it several times, I smiled because I could see so many parallels to my own life, especially his blue-collar background and his successful transition into the white-collar professional world, and his dedication to mentoring younger professionals.

As a Boomer who:

1 - grew up in a family of seven people in a house with one bathroom and three bedrooms

2 - lived in a household focused upon making ends meet

3 - never took a family vacation while growing up

4 - worked several jobs as a youngster to help make ends meet, and

5 - had little if any guidance on attending college or pursuing a professional career, it is no surprise now that he values hard work and sees life as a 'you get what you work for' journey.

Jeff grew up like many Boomers with a fear of what the Vietnam War might bring to him and his family. He had to develop the skills to become independent and to learn new things quickly. He saw the business world change from being paternalistic to employees, to one where financial results were the overriding goal, with employees perhaps becoming a means to an end. He and his wife made some tough decisions to end her career progress, in exchange for the stability of the children being taken care of by Mom. He takes a lot of pride in his family and his giving back to younger professionals he mentored. He sees a clear difference in the generations and expectations, perhaps due to the success of Boomers who provided much more for, and demanded less from, their children.

Jeff reflects back on, and is thankful for, what he learned from his parents and grandmother, including the value of hard work, saving, and preparing for the future vs. living for today.

If anyone can be critical of Boomers, it would be tough to imagine someone finding a lot of faults with Jeff and his story, and his contributions to society. His story is one of those 'American dream' stories that many Boomers heard about in their youth. Through his life's work and dedication to family and friends, I cannot help but admire what he has done and how this world is a better place because of him. Thanks Jeff! Thanks Boomer!

CHAPTER 11:
Jamie Martin:
The Boarding School Boomer

BACKGROUND

I first met Jamie at an industry event while I was still working. Later, our paths crossed due to my company merging with the company that employed Jamie.

The cultures of our companies differed in some ways, while in other ways they were similar. Large company mergers are always challenging, and finding ways to cross cultural divides is sometimes the most difficult part.

As I got know Jamie, I was impressed that he wanted to see our combined companies succeed, and he was an outspoken advocate for the customer and for customer service. In this respect, we were absolutely aligned! Jamie was a valuable leader in that he understood his company's products, services, and customers very well. We seemed to get along well in those early days, although it was clear that Jamie was not going to lead the process of finding common ground between differing opinions, rather, he was steadfast in his beliefs and ideas about how things should be done to grow the business.

Jamie and I were both management leaders of our newly merged division. One day, our human resource director came in to tell me that he was concerned about how Jamie and I may or may not get along. When I asked why, he said that he had reviewed some of the personality tests of the leaders that came into our company via the merger, and that he just reviewed the personality test results of Jamie. He said that he had NEVER seen anyone with a personality 100% OPPOSITE of mine, and that he thought, per the test, that we would always have a lot of friction. I just laughed and said that we were fine and that I could assure him that we would NOT going to kill one another! (I was not a huge fan of these tests to start with!)

I only share that background because in learning so much more about his background via writing this book, I realize now that our differences in personality were probably not a company culture issue, but rather, just a result of Jamie's extremely interesting upbringing and experiences early in life. In learning about his story, it amazes me how very different our upbringing was, and now I can see why Jamie's opinions were often different than some others in our group.

Interestingly enough, after he and I both retired, he reached out via email to check on me, as I then did with him, and we stay in touch much more frequently than many of my co-worker friends with decades of history. If you ever meet Jamie, he is someone you never forget, and I appreciate him and admire his story.

EARLY LIFE

Jamie was born in May of 1946, one of the first 'Boomers', and grew up in Massachusetts. He grew up as an only child of parents who had no college back ground, nor did any of their relatives.

His father started working in a factory on second shift on the day he graduated from high school. His father's goal was to improve his lot in life and make sure that Jamie had the opportunities he never had. "Everything I remember was about improvement, whether school, little league or building stuff. My father became a licensed electrician just in case he lost his job, as an insurance policy against a crisis."

His parents were no-nonsense, and an occasional spanking was not out of the ordinary. "But that was the common parenting style back then."

In Jamie's words, they lived a fairly modest lifestyle until around 1955. About then, his father was promoted from the factory into the office. "His goal was for me to have the tools and opportunities to go to college, something nobody had ever done in my family."

Jamie was active in boy scouts, and worked his way up to Life Scout, three badges short of an Eagle Scout.

At 11 years old, in the summer of 1957, his family took him to Europe on the Queen Mary for 5 weeks. Prior to the trip, he got into a fist fight with his best friend, who lived across the street. It seemed that his friend, a devout Catholic, was upset because Jamie's family was not going to visit the Pope while in Europe.

The next spring, his mother received a call from one of her friends, asking her about the sign-up for college prep classes at the junior high school, and his mother asked Jamie about it. He knew nothing about it. So, his mother called the principal asking about the sign-up, and she was told that Jamie was not college material, and that he was going the route of 'manual training' in 7th grade. Clearly, that answer was not acceptable to Jamie's mother and father.

"The following Saturday, I was at an interview at an Episcopalian boarding school for boys a couple of towns away. It was quite an experience." The uniform at the school was a coat and tie, school was twelve hours per day, 6 days per week, including church and chapel time every day. Jamie commuted to that school for four years, then in his final three years of high school, he boarded there with most of the others. Can you imagine Jamie as a 7th grader, having to take a cab from his house to a local doctor's office parking lot, then waiting for the bus to take him the rest of the way to school?

How did Jamie feel about being forced to switch schools and to attend a new environment? "I can't say that I fully understood the significance of the change, and I did not fight it, but in hindsight, it was the best change for me and my future career. That boarding school set the tone for my life. *'Non Ministrari sed Ministrare', or translated* 'Not to be served, but to serve'.

I got a good education, learned discipline, and understood the family objective of me being the first in the family to attend to college."

The commitment to boarding school took time away from scouting, and his progress towards becoming an Eagle Scout stopped.

Jamie believes that this school was absolutely pivotal in transitioning his life. "The motto, the discipline, the teaching, the coaching, the individual attention, the teamwork, the church; all provided a culture I liked, and one which I enjoyed carrying on. Give more than you get. And we had zero free time, the school focused us upon the classroom, sports, and religion, and there was little time for anything else."

As a sidelight, the school closed in 1970, as did most single-sex private schools that had no endowments. "The coat and tie, short hair, and discipline did not sell well in the late 1960's. Ex-students now have a reunion every fall, which I attend every year and most of my classmates do as well."

It is interesting to me that later in life, Jamie and his wife also sent all three sons to private schools. First, a local private junior co-ed school named Mooreland Hill School from grades 6-9, and then Avon Old Farms School (an endowed school) from grades 10-12, as day students. Avon Old Farms was an all-boys school. "Our sons all turned out great, and we feel that they developed the right mindset and discipline which helped them to be successful in different fields. It was a significant commitment of time and funds, but an excellent investment." That experience, it seems, along with guidance and support from Jamie and Lindy, led to their success in their occupations and as responsible adults.

The childhood friend from the Catholic church moved away, as did Jamie, so they were no longer living close together. "We reconnected in the early 1970's, 15 years later or so, and would get together for beers at his house during the holidays and enjoy ourselves. A few months after our last get-together, he committed suicide running his car in his parents' garage. I drove three hours to attend the service. This had a significant impact on me."

ON TO COLLEGE

Jamie applied to several universities, and finally enrolled at the University of Denver, far from home, but close to skiing, which he loved to do. "It had all the things I did not have in high school, including more freedom and girls attending the university. I lived a life with very upscale people, and we skied every weekend, but I did not have the allowance that enabled me to go to bars, go out on dates, and even ski, so I landed a job in a factory as a carpenter from noon to 4:30 five days per week." He attended night class from 5:45 – 8:00 p.m. to maintain a full-time course-load. "That routine put pressure on me to be more disciplined, but the pressure did not always work. I paid the price, and in looking back, I got the most out of a party school." Jamie graduated in 1969 with a degree in economics.

So, how well did Jamie do academically in college? "I flunked out twice, but was able to talk my way back in. It probably was a turning point in my life, I learned that I had a skill of getting people to do things they would not do normally. Thus, I pursued a career in sales."

VOLUNTEERING

After college, Jamie was determined to join the Peace Corps, as he had worked one summer on an Indian reservation in North Dakota while in prep school, and enjoyed it. Once he joined the Peace Corps, he was flown to Hawaii to receive language training to prepare him and others for an assignment in Western Samoa. He, along with about 20 others, were sent there. Most of the group was assigned to a project to make water-sealed toilets and to install them. Jamie was assigned to be a research economist for the government, an office job at the capitol building. "I hated that job, and after a few months, and only four months before my 26th birthday, I quit. I didn't realize it at the time, but almost 40% of the volunteers bailed out early." Being in the Peace Corps provided an exemption from being drafted into the service, so when he left the Peace Corps, he knew he had to make a decision.

Upon arriving home in early 1970, the draft board letter came to him, he was number 175. "The last thing I wanted to do just before my 26th birthday was to go to Vietnam. I joined the National Guard, and that summer went to boot camp in Fort Dix, New Jersey, and was trained in advanced infantry. That lasted six months, then I started weekend service one time per month, and two weeks per summer on active duty. That commitment lasted for six years." Jamie observes that the National Guard was not a great experience, as he was not a military guy in any way. "I was paying the price for being a chicken and just sucked it up, and did everything I had to do to complete my service."

ON TO A CAREER

Jamie had worked part-time jobs early in life, in factories, on a farm, dishwashing in restaurants, etc. "They were all meaningful experiences with a lot of memories."

But his first professional job after college was at a large company in the Boston area. In his first week on the job, he attended a wedding, and a college friend introduced him to someone who lived very close to his friend. Her name was Lindy, and they began dating in December of 1971.

He attended a training program to be a salesman in the appliance group. After training, he was on the road fulltime, working there more than two years, and while there, got married to Lindy in October of 1973.

So, what role did Lindy plan in your career and in taking care of your family?

"During my entire career, Lindy has supported me both in my professional career and in our personal life. When the boys were in school, she continued to work as a private consultant in education for private, public, and parochial schools, but her (our) focus was always on family and our boys. We supported and focused on our family in all aspects of our lives and have now been married for almost 50 years, due to patience on my wife's part!"

"In 1973, we were living the good life. But one day I was brought into the office of my boss's boss, and was fired with no explanation, which really blind-sided me, as I had done nothing wrong. About that same time, I met a guy at a party at my in-laws' house who was the VP of sales at a manufacturing company in New Britain, Connecticut. He suggested I should come to work for him, which I later did."

The job loss stuck with Jamie for many years and was troubling, as he could not understand how he could not have succeeded in his first job in that company. "It took 20 years or more for me to figure it out. But I suspect now that I had uncovered some improper activities within the company, and I had shared my thoughts with someone in upper management about it, and they wanted to get rid of me."

When Jamie first considered going to work for his new company, there were openings in Chicago and Dallas, but with his love of skiing and sailing and only being married a few months, those jobs were out of the question for him. Eventually, an opening came up in Philadelphia, and Jamie interviewed in New Britain, Connecticut. The management team indicated they needed to infuse some new talent into the organization, so Jamie accepted and attended a four-month training program. Then, he was off in his new sales role, on the road four days per week. "This assignment was a great learning experience, the leadership, coaching, and development was excellent, and I learned a lot about different industries calling on original equipment manufacturers and distributors." He and Lindy moved to Philadelphia per his new job, which was a sacrifice for her as she had to leave her family and job behind.

During their time in Philadelphia, Lindy earned her Master of Education degree from Lehigh, and landed a job in special education as a supervisor. After over three years in this job, Jamie was promoted to assistant manager of distributor sales, and they moved to Kensington, Connecticut in 1978. Later that year, they had their first son Nathaniel. In 1980, Thatcher was born, and in 1986 Alexander was born.

Later, the parent company decided to sell off the Jamie's division to another company, and they were merged with the new company's division which produced the same kind of product. "The new company was most focused upon the automotive business and heavy industry, while my division had a stronger focus upon the aftermarket / replacement business which was serviced via distributors. Many of the management of my division took over key roles in the aftermarket business, while the new company management took over many of the key roles within the Original Equipment Manufacturing business. We were good at what we did, and we grew and improved many functions within the aftermarket division."

Shortly thereafter, the company had developed a computer system for managing order processing. Jamie championed the need to measure 'hit rates', or the number of times a customer requested a part and it was in stock, versus being out of stock and thus a lost sale. "I wrote a letter to the VP of information technology about this need and how important it was to be fixed."

One morning, the president was walking in the door and saw a big truck unloading paper to the IT center loading dock, just under his office. He asked what he was doing there, and the truck driver said that his boss had indicated that due to a new computer system, this company was going to be one of their best customers! The president confronted the VP of IT about this, and the VP mentioned that Jamie wanted more reports and that would require more paper.

The next thing he knew, Jamie was in the board room face-to-face with the president (who was a tall, intimidating character) of the company, debating what was most important to measure, bookings or hit rates. "I stressed that not only hit rates were important, but also how we performed on handling the order such as accuracy of shipment, pricing, packaging, and forecasting."

The president called in the VP of sales to join the discussion, and it went on until 7:00 p.m. that evening. After the meeting, the VP told Jamie to get on a plane in the morning and go make sales calls, even though Jamie had nothing planned with customers that next day. "Our VP was trying to cover my ass, he was afraid that if I came into the office that next day, the president would fire me. He knew that if I was not there, he couldn't do that. Out of sight, out of mind, I suppose." But things worked out well.

"I learned a valuable lesson that day; to stand up for what you believe in and fight for what is right. From that day forward, the president and I had a wonderful relationship, and shortly after the meeting, I received the largest raise in my life."

Jamie related that the president implemented some changes that he believed changed the culture for the better. He pushed everyone to be trained in total quality management (TQM) and he shared a story that convinced him of the positive change.

"One day I was in the credit department asking a clerk for some invoice data for a delinquent bill of a customer. She asked what I was going to use the information for. Before I could say 'just give me the damned information!", she then said "If this is a recurring problem, I could arrange to have this for you every Friday." That proved to Jamie that the culture had changed for the better.

"Our office was full of Baby Boomers, and it was the best work environment. They adapted better than any other generation, and most of the people I worked with, or hired and managed, agreed that the environment was the best of their career."

Throughout his career, Jamie always played important roles in sales and marketing.

Later in his career, after spending a great deal of his professional career working with and servicing industrial distributors, he was awarded the Bearing Specialists Association (BSA) 'Lifetime Achievement Award', and he was the first person from a manufacturer ever given this award. (BSA was primarily a distributor organization, and manufacturers were invited as guests to some of their annual meetings)

IN RETIREMENT

Today, Jamie is retired and usually spends his winters in South Carolina. He continues to serve others and has many hobbies. "I coordinate a few programs at our club, stay in touch with many friends, enjoy my family, and am very happy and satisfied." Just two examples of what Jamie spends time on are (1) he builds, maintains, and inspects 65 bluebird houses weekly from April to November at his country club, and (2) he captains the senior inter-club golf team.

POLLING FOR OPINIONS

What are the most important lessons he has learned in his life?

The goal is not to be served, but to serve others. Also, never give up, and be as tenacious as you need to be to accomplish your goals. If you have setbacks, you can overcome them.

How will he and Lindy share their assets upon death?

We have made a priority to donate to 529 accounts for our grandchildren's education. We will donate a portion to local charities and foundations, but the majority will go to fund the ongoing family, and we have confidence that the money will not be spent on Porsches or airplanes and used wisely.

Would you do anything differently in raising your children if you could?

Not really.

Do you think the Great Depression could happen again?

My parents shared a lot about that time, but I do not believe that with all the news and TV coverage and communications, it would ever happen again.

What about alcohol usage and drugs?

I drank a lot of beer and stuff, it was a regular part of my life, but no drugs. A lot of friends smoked pot, and I would be in favor of making it legal, since it is legal in some states already.

What about the younger generations and their apparent affection for socialism over capitalism?

I do not agree that is true. I think the newer generations also realize that you only get what you work for.

How do you feel about the news media today?

To say that I am a news junkie would be a mistake, but without a certain conservative news channel, the story would be biased in the other direction to an extreme. I try to watch a balance of news channels so that I can hear both sides to any story.

What about crime and law enforcement?

We need harder enforcement and stricter penalties.

What about the second amendment and guns?

I got my first gun at age 11, and currently own four shotguns. I was an active hunter and sport shooter. I am a strict supporter of the second amendment.

How do you feel about the U.S. being 'watchman of the world' and investing so much outside of the U.S.?

I think our role in the world is the right strategy, to help and foster freedom. I do think that Vietnam was an example of us overplaying our hand.

Should we have more or fewer government programs to support the underprivileged?

We need fewer programs and a much higher level of enforcement to reduce people taking advantage of the programs we have.

Should our priorities for our tax dollars be more focused upon global issues or more upon country issues?

Our country should be first.

How do you feel about two-income families versus families where one parent stays at home with the children?

All our daughters-in-law have fulltime jobs and their kids are watched by nannies.

Why are our politicians so divided today versus the past?

I think our last president created or increased the division.

Do you consider yourself a conservative or liberal or somewhere in between?

I have always been a conservative; you work for what you get.

Is education today more or less important than when you were growing up?

It is much more important today. Look at the people who have advanced degrees, they are what you need to climb up the food chain. All of my kids have advanced degrees to enable them to survive and prosper.

What about social security and its funding problems?

Social security is a necessary evil, as a lot of people survive with it. Pensions do not exist anymore for many, so the inflow and outflow to the social security fund should be balanced.

Are you more concerned about the environment now vs. earlier in life?

It is clear that the damage to the environment has created serious problems with global warming and it is going to get worse. The rest of the world is way behind us in terms of doing what is right with the environment. I think we are on the right track doing more. It is a sensitive issue because not everyone is aware of the seriousness of the issue or the true causes.

Do you believe that the next generations will live in a better country and world in the coming decades, versus the world and country as we aged?

I think worse off, due to the communication spiral and the liberal voice being prominent.

Do you have more 'stuff' now than earlier in life? Do you want to get rid of it or get more stuff?

We have too much stuff, and should be getting rid of it. The kids are never going to want it.

What about tax rates? Are we taxed too much or too little?

The very rich should pay more, and everyone should pay some level of tax, just like social security. When you are working, you pay into it. Taxes should be the same.

How do you feel about compensation for politicians?

All you have to do is look at our president and all he has earned in his life from multiple political jobs. It is criminal, and there should be term limits.

SUMMARY

Jamie's story and background is quite different than other Boomer stories. In particular, in his youth, his parents cared so much about his future that they pulled him out of his school and sent him to a private boarding school fairly distant from their home. That says a lot about their love for him. That decision had to be a tough one for his parents to make, and clearly that decision had a significant impact on Jamie and his philosophy of life.

I liked his response about the most important lessons he has learned in life. He cited (1) serving others, (2) being tenacious in achieving your goals, and (3) that you can overcome setbacks, no matter what they may be.

His answers in the 'polling for opinions' section were direct and brief, and it is clear that he has thought through many of these issues and knows where he stands and what his beliefs are. Likewise, his conversational style is also direct and brief, which I think his friends enjoy and admire. I also appreciate how he will stand up for what he believes, no matter the repercussions. He exemplified that in his career many times, as is described in his story.

I am happy to see that Jamie, in retirement, is enjoying the good things in life, and still serving others and enjoying his friends and family. For those of us who know him, he is someone we will never forget!

CHAPTER 12:
Gregg:
The Insurance Agent & Golf Enthusiast

BACKGROUND

I first met Gregg at a junior golf tournament I played in at Hartville, Ohio in 1971. I finished second in my 13-15 age division, and remember posing with him and his mother, the sponsors, after the round for the local newspaper. I remember that he seemed to be a nice guy and worked for a large insurance company, but after that, I forgot about him. About 10 years later when I needed auto insurance, I had no idea where to go or who to call, so I looked for his name in the phone book. I have been a customer of his and his company for 40+ years since. Later in life, I came to learn that we had a few other things in common, in that we both played on the golf team at Kent State University, and were both huge golf fans. Throughout my life, when life situations changed, I found myself in his office or on the phone making policy changes for house insurance, and car insurance for my wife, and for my children. He was always a good friend, although we were never close in terms of hanging out together. But he always struck me as professional, entertaining, and someone you could trust.

A few years ago, when my golf coach at Kent State was retiring, they invited past players, and I ran into Gregg again and renewed our friendship.

HIS STORY

Gregg was born in Canton, Ohio in 1947, an early Boomer baby. He attended city schools from kindergarten through high school, graduating from Canton Lehman high school in 1965. Growing up in the 1950's and 1960's, he describes his childhood as 'a very good life'. He lived in a baby boomer neighborhood that had young families who had similar if not the same values. He had two brothers, Bruce and Daryl.

"Our home was right next to the park, and all the kids congregated there. I was never without friends as the park brought us all together. There was baseball, basketball, football, tennis, sled riding and even supervision by the city recreation department."

His parents grew up in the depression years, and their early adulthood took place during the years of World War II. "They were married before the war, and my dad served in the Army Corps of Engineers in Europe, while my mom worked at a large manufacturing company. They had purchased their first home even before the war began, but I think that once I was born, they decided to relocate to a new neighborhood as a better place to raise children."

Gregg also grew up in a musical family. "Music was always in our home growing up. I played the piano, my brother played the guitar and had a rock band during the late 60's, and my other brother played the drums in the high school band. The Beatles, Beach Boys, Temptations, Supremes, and others were always being played at our home. Hard rock never made it in our house when it became popular. My mother had some piano training and both my parents loved the big band era and danced to the music. Come to think of it, most of my friends, and us, had a piano at that time. Nowadays, it seems as though nobody has a piano at home. But I still play, and somehow, the music and notes come back to me, sort of like typing once you learn to type."

Gregg describes how his parents arranged for piano lessons for him when he was young, and how he is very happy now that they asked him to do that, as he enjoys the piano greatly.

How did he and his siblings develop their values growing up? "As far as my parents, their values that they instilled in us were to 'work hard and play hard', which to us was a philosophy of prioritizing your work and taking responsibility to get it done, before you took the time to enjoy hobbies, sports, interests, etc. My parents were active socially, and danced a lot at the Meyers Lake Ballroom as well as other ballrooms around northeast Ohio. They made a lot of friends that way, and that social activity rubbed off on the kids. Our values were also shaped in part by family TV shows, such as 'Ozzie and Harriet', 'Lassie', 'My Three Sons', and Disney Movies such as 'Davey Crockett'. Our loving Mother was always home, and made sure that she knew all the kids we played with."

"My Dad was employed at a large manufacturing company as a machinist and then as a part time insurance agent starting in 1947, working first at home to grow his insurance business. He did both until 1966. He was able to begin receiving a small pension after 30 years as a machinist. He then focused on his insurance business to be his full-time work, as he operated it out of our house until his death in 1969."

His dad was a hunter as a hobby, and they had guns that were used only for hunting. They hunted on their aunt's property primarily. "Our rec room had the guns hanging on the wall. In thinking about it now, those guns should have been put away."

How does he think about guns now? "It is just an awful situation now. There needs to be more mental evaluations at schools or at home. It seems the discipline at home is not there anymore. The ability to own a gun that can shoot X rounds very quickly seems wrong in the wrong hands."

His school years, especially in high school, he rates as a '10'. "The high school had very good teachers and a great school spirit. I was elected senior class president and was very active in extra-curricular activities. Also, I was on the varsity golf team for all four years. All those high school years were wonderful except the first term of my freshman year when I was very intimidated by the culture compared to the grade school experience."

Gregg describes that the city schools at that time were divided by ethnic heritage and nationality. One school was mainly Greek and Italian, another was very diverse. His high school was centered within the northwest part of the city with most residents living in both upscale homes and middle-class homes. There was also a vocational school for those students not focused upon college. "I was the first in my family to focus upon college. But most of my friends intended to go to college also."

ON TO COLLEGE

After graduation, Gregg enrolled into nearby Kent State University in 1965, and in 1969, received a Bachelor of Business Administration degree. Again, his freshman year at Kent State was intimidating but in his sophomore year he pledged the Sigma Phi Epsilon fraternity. "This was a very good experience to bond with fellow brothers and participate in all the social activities. I was on the varsity golf team as well."

During summers while not attending college, Gregg held several different jobs, including being a test car driver, a counselor at church camp, serving on the maintenance crew for a natural gas supplier, and his final two summers he attended ROTC boot camp.

Why did he choose to become an ROTC student at Kent State? "The draft was always a reason to stay as an active student. If you failed as a student and dropped out of school, the draft would activate you immediately and more likely than not, you would be sent to the Vietnam war. This was the greatest motivation to go to class and have passing grades. If the war was still going upon graduation, I thought that I would rather be an officer than a private. That was my logic, and my primary incentive to be a successful student."

Gregg enjoyed his experience in college, still gathering with many of his fraternity brothers and alumni golf team members.

His first three years, he did not play on the varsity team that often, but going into his senior year, he decided to really work on his game and got in shape the summer before. That fall, he contended for a varsity spot, and through the season battled another golfer for the final spot on the varsity golf team. "I saw my coach several years later and told him that I was probably the only senior 'walk-on' that he kept on the team. He agreed with me."

STARTING A CAREER

Upon graduation, he also earned an ROTC commission as a 2nd Lieutenant in the U.S. Army, in the artillery branch. At that time, ROTC graduates had no idea where they would be assigned. In his class, he had a lot of West Point grads, and he was expecting super recruits with engineering backgrounds. "We were training how to be forward scouts, and were learning the math behind artillery shooting. As it turned out, the West Point grads were party animals, and most had new Corvettes which they purchased right after graduation. They were NOT what I was expecting!"

While training in the Army at Fort Sill, Oklahoma, he received terrible news. "My father, Walter Schorsten, died unexpectantly due to an aorta aneurism at the age of 53. With help from our local Congressman, Frank T. Bow, I was released from active duty to return home to take over the family business as an agent for the insurance company. My younger brother was still in college, and my other brother Bruce was in training for the Reserves. When he came out, he joined me as an agent. We worked together for a time to take over the business. But eventually Bruce became interested in real estate and moved to California. Eventually Bruce and his wife moved back to the area to pursue their careers. So, it was up to me to continue the business that my dad had started. I had some great training from my company to help me transition into the job and business, and some great advice from my manager. The company was always supportive and it was a good environment among the agents and managers."

Gregg fulfilled his military obligation in the Army Reserves for the next 4 years when the Vietnam war ended for the United States.

He spent his career helping and supporting clients in the area, developing a reputation as a helpful and responsive agent as well as a pillar in the community.

FAMILY LIFE

One evening, earlier in his career, Gregg met a friend at a local bar to have a few drinks at 'the hot spot' in town. After a drink or two, Gregg suggested that they go grab a sandwich at 11:00 p.m. at the local restaurant, as he was getting hungry. The friend wasn't all that interested, but agreed. At the restaurant, they ordered and had dinner. At the end of the meal, his friend suggested that he ought to be paying attention to the waitress instead of trying to meet girls at a bar. "To be honest, I wasn't really paying attention to her, but once he suggested this, I started to talk to her and we started dating. She claimed that I only left a 25-cent tip! Her name was Sharon. She was 21, and I was 27. The timing was perfect, I was ready for marriage, she was too. It turned out she was a military brat, attended Jackson high school, and her dad was a retired pilot from the Air Force, who retired in Jackson Township. She enrolled at the local nursing school." They were married in 1974, and they celebrated their 48th anniversary recently. "Sharon has been a wonderful mother and a wonderful grandmother, and today works at a veterinary clinic, a job she loves. She is a pretty good golfer too!" Gregg describes that she is really focused now on hosta gardening. Gregg describes that he had some retired friends over and they said that she should rent the backyard for weddings it is so impressive.

"We have two sons, Christopher who has been a high school Math teacher for the last 20 years, graduating from Miami University, and Brian who is a PGA golf professional at Colonial Country Club in Fort Worth, Texas, who graduated from the University of Akron. Chris is married to Julie and they have 3 children, and Brian is married to Kristin and they have 2 daughters.

"The good fortune of my family is what I am most proud of. My life has been blessed and I have been very grateful."

What is he most proud of during his 42-year career?

"I was proud that my employer was a well-managed company in many ways. As an agent, I was part of the sales team and service team to the policyholder. I have always tried to service the customer as I would like to be treated. I retired from there at age 66."

Before retirement, Gregg got very involved to establish the first local First Tee organization. "I drank the Kool-Aid; it was such a great cause. It was originally focused on inner city youth, although he says that today, fewer inner-city kids participate versus suburban youth. The site today is 15 acres, and today's renovated clubhouse was an old pole building, and the golf course used to be a garbage dump. "We bought that land at a very good price. Most First Tee facilities have a driving range and three holes of golf to play, but we had the goal to have a full 9 holes of golf! So that is what we did. This local First Tee is celebrating its 20th anniversary this year."

It is difficult to assess the positive impact on the youth who participated in the First Tee program over the years, but there is no doubt that his efforts have had a very positive impact in many ways for youth and our community.

POLLING FOR OPINIONS

What are the most important lessons you have learned in life?

Gregg discusses various 'creeds' that have influenced him in many ways throughout life. He lists nine creeds or guidelines that he believes are important, which are below. (All are easily found on the internet if you are interested.) Why creeds instead of specific lessons of life? "In 2021, I heard a sermon at a church in Canton, where the topic was the importance of creeds. What stuck with me was that people are to be faithful to our creeds, they are important, they give power, and they determine who we are and how we behave. If we lack creeds to live by, others do our thinking and shape our beliefs. That sermon stirred me to list the creeds that affected me throughout my life:

1) The Scout Oath

2) The Apostles Creed

3) The Sigma Phi Epsilon Fraternity Creed

4) The ROTC Commission Officer Creed
5) The Jaycee Creed
6) The Rotary Creed
7) The First Tee Core Values
8) Deacon and Elder Pledge to the church
9) The Habitat for Humanity Mission

Although I confess that I have fallen short many times relative to these values, I have tried and prayed to uphold them. I consider them as my foundations in life."

Can you briefly describe the meaning of life for someone from other generations?

The meaning of life is to love your God and to serve your fellow man....to me so much has been given and it requires so much to give back in return.

How would you rate your relationship with your children?

They were successful students, active in sports, music, and golf. Golf was our common interest and it was important for all of us, even today as they have their own families.

How would you compare the values of yourself to your children?

Our values are very close to the same.

Can you describe your relationship with your grandchildren?

All 5 of them are growing fast and maturing well. We attend their activities in sports, music, ballet, and we use Facetime to stay-up-to date with the out-of-town kids.

How would you compare the relationship you have with your children, vs the relationship between your parents and you when you were their age?

About the same.

Do you help your children financially even as adults?

So far, we help when we are asked and support them in all they do.

Do you still worry about your children even as adults?

I am very proud of our kids' success as they raise their children. I believe they have successful 20+ year marriages and are raising the grandchildren extremely well.

How did you manage the care of your mother as she aged?

There was always concern about her health and safety since she was living alone, but in general she did a great job managing living by herself.

What are you planning to have happen with any funds or possessions after you die?

We are in retirement years and will be living on investments and social security until the second surviving spouse dies, and any remaining assets will be divided between our sons.

Do you believe we could experience another Great Depression, as described by your parents and others?

I do remember grandparents and my parents referring to the hardships of the depression. I'm not sure if a depression can occur again due to safe-guards we have today. I have lived through recessions with high interest rates, real estate collapses, pandemics, etc. Anything worse is always possible.

How does he feel about alcoholic beverages as a Boomer?

"I never tried beer or alcohol until freshman year in college (beer only 3.2 proof). Since then, drinking has always been a part of social life. I am not sure that I ever went overboard.

How are your friendships at this stage of life?

Friends have always been a part of my life. Most were also customers and/or golfing friends. Many friends were with me on different boards and committees on volunteer organizations. I have no regrets about having great friends with common purposes and interests in these organizations.

What are your thoughts about the press today?

The role of the press and its impacts today are much different than when I was younger. I have mixed feelings. Back then, we would get maybe 30 minutes of news on just 3 networks. Now, there are many networks and 24x7 news reported. The more we seem to know, the more it appears that the world we live in is very depressing. Maybe that was true in the 50's and 60's but we didn't know it. Truth and conspiracies have divided us and I see this as a very bad time.

Surveys show that non-Boomers are much more positive about socialism than Boomers. In fact, one study showed that Millennials and Gen Z think slightly more positively about socialism than capitalism. Why do you think that may be?

Capitalism is our way, but the fallen in our society for whatever reason, need a system to lift them up. Maybe they believe socialism is the way.

Should we reduce our global influence, or expand it?

I am not sure we as a country can ever walk away from foreign aid.

What are your feelings about 'green initiatives' and the state of our planet?

We are doing a lot, but not sure about other countries.

How do you feel about our politicians today?

Term limits certainly make sense; however, it seems very unlikely that term limits will ever be implemented when the House of Representatives and Senate members can never agree. In fact, in today's circumstance, they cannot agree on anything. The guideline of "what is the truth" doesn't exist between the parties. The checks and balances that the Constitution set up are working but could be better.

What about the growing national debt of around $31 Trillion?

The national debt is so high and continues to grow no matter who is in office. It doesn't seem to be serious enough for government to change. When the government spends in the trillions, I don't think the congress people even know how many zeros are in those numbers. It is hard to relate to big national issues such as this, whereas most of our lives are more involved in the local community, and we have lived in a great area to raise a family, and a great community where people care about one another, and where giving back is just accepted as a way of life.

Why are politicians so divided? Has it really changed, or has it been like this for a long time?

If they have been divided in the past, we didn't have cable TV 24 x7 to know. It is awful how they conduct themselves when dealing with each other.

Do you consider yourself to be a conservative or liberal or somewhere in between?

Somewhere in between. I used to be a republican, and vote that way. When a party nominates a candidate that behaves like our past president, I will be independent and vote democratic.

The press talks a lot about the growing disparity in income – is that a big problem in your opinion?

If income inflates the payroll, the price of products and services will inflate. A vicious cycle will continue.

Are you more worried about the environment now vs. when you were in your teens or in the middle of life?

Yes, the environment is vitally important and more controls must be put in place.

Do you think the country is headed in the wrong or right direction?

Our country has changed since our youth. Our example to the world was strong because of military might. We must now lead by example of our character, not our might.

Many Boomers believe that education is very important for the younger generations. Is advanced education more or less important than it was when you were growing up?

It was important in our youth and its important now.

Tell me about your health care coverage and your thoughts about the benefits you get vs. what it costs.

Health care expense is one of the fastest growing expenses. As I participate in the Medicare program, the cost is reasonable compared to times when I was raising a family.

How about problem of social security funds running out by 2035? What should we do to fix this?

I have been collecting since age 66, and had paid into the system since age 22. I am not sure if anything should be different.

IN SUMMARY

So here is a guy who had life by the horns in his early adult years, had early successes, was in the military, and then gets a terrible call about his dad passing away unexpectedly. NEVER have I heard him complain that he had other plans in life, that he had to sacrifice everything to take over his dad's business, or that he had to give up his dreams for the benefit of his family. He seems to be a Boomer who has made the most out of any situation in his life.

When Gregg and I met to discuss his chapter in this book, we found that we had so much in common, and talked for a long time about golf and various golf clubs and courses we have played, and how our families benefitted from golf via learning the sport, making good friends, and making memories. "You know, in looking back on golf, the tournaments and scores and rounds of golf are fine, but it is really about friendships and memories that we developed through golf. Nothing else really matters." As I get older, I agree completely!

When talking to Gregg, I find that his energy and positiveness are contagious. It is such a treat to share a coffee with him and talk about what is going on in life. He is one of those rare individuals that can find nothing negative to say about others, and can always find a positive comment to say about any situation or issue, or can find some insight that anyone else might not even consider.

That is so refreshing in today's world. He represents Boomers in a way that puts all of us Boomers in a positive light!

CHAPTER 13:
Jake:
The Engineer, IT Geek, and Barbershop Singer

BACKGROUND

I first met Jake a few years into my first professional job as a programmer. He was a project leader and systems analyst, and knew a lot about our company's manufacturing plants and processes. I recall a vivid memory of Jake when we were jointly working on a project to implement a new computer system and new computer hardware at a new manufacturing plant in North Carolina. At that time, after a long day of work, four of us met up in his hotel room and our project leader made us some martinis. It was a first for me, and I did NOT like martinis after tasting one. Later, we became friends and he and his wife invited my wife and I to join them at their cottage at Lake Erie to swim on the beach.

Jake has always been very modest and never wanted to take much credit for anything. I found out a few years later that he sang barbershop and had an excellent singing voice, yet he never bragged about his singing.

Jake was one of those people who quietly did his job well, was never one to grab the spotlight or headlines, and was a model citizen and example for others to follow. Like many Boomers, he has served society and his country well, and will leave behind a legacy of goodwill and family along with a stellar reputation of character.

EARLY LIFE

Jake was born as the sole child in his family in Springfield, Ohio in the 1940's, and graduated from Springfield High School in a class of 600. While growing up, his parents always told him that he was going to be the first college graduate in the family. As a result, his primary goal during high school was to earn grades good enough to enable attending college.

While growing up, his parents were staunch Democrats. "I recall that my mother was worried about John Kennedy running for president. She was fearful because he was Catholic and would have to tell all the country's secrets to the Pope. My father had been a Catholic before marrying my mother, and he changed to the Lutheran church. My mother told me that she thought that was a premature decision, and she wasn't very happy he did that, because she hadn't even considered marriage to him at that point."

Jake's father was an Italian, growing up in a family of 8 children. He was born in Colorado in a tent city of coal mine workers. He and two brothers changed religion when they were married. "My father was on the church council and treasurer of the church. My mother played the piano for Sunday School and taught the Adult Ladies Class. I suppose that's how I ended up in the Lutheran church, where I have served as treasurer for over 30 years."

Jake's first 'job' was delivering television guides on a route. Then he began delivering newspapers on a paper route. Both required him to make collections and pay the costs, with the 'profits' staying with him.

Jake recalls his parents talking about the Great Depression, and how they considered themselves lucky that both of them stayed employed during the depression. Those sentiments still reflect with Jake, as he talks about how fortunate he was to stay employed with the same company for 37 years, even though the low economic times weren't nearly as deep as the Great Depression. "During my MBA program, I minored in finance, which developed within me the confidence that a depression like that one would never happen again. In retirement, I still have that belief, but drops in the stock market give me pause now."

In high school, Jake recalls having a lot of fun. "I had a lot of friends in high school, and was first trumpet in the band of 110 students. I had my first steady girlfriend then who played flute in the band. I also had a car, a 1930 Model A Coupe, which I still have and restored mostly on my own." Jake remembers that his mother repeated one piece of advice to him over and over. "I had better not ever hear of you forcing yourself onto a girl!"

What about his high school experience, would he go back and do it again?

"I always said I wouldn't want to go back, but think I would now. I used to feel like I didn't belong to the group whose parents were "rich" in my opinion. Having gone back to my 50th reunion, I see that I misjudged people by my feelings of not belonging."

Much later in life, Jake lost his father at age 76 and his mother at age 95.

COLLEGE LIFE / SERVICE

He was accepted at the University of Cincinnati, which was then (and is now) rated one of the best engineering schools. He spent a year and a half there and quit because he knew he couldn't make the necessary grades to graduate. He transferred to Ohio State, and found out later that his father always wanted him to go there.

"After 6 quarters in pre-engineering I declared electrical engineering as my major and started a whole new grade point average. I flunked my first two electrical classes and changed to mechanical engineering. I was thrown out after two more quarters because my grades couldn't pull up what electrical engineering grades had pulled down."

Jake then joined the National Guard in Springfield, Ohio, to avoid the draft and Vietnam. "I was in a National Guard Infantry Company for 6 years. I really enjoyed that experience and it gave me more self-confidence than I had when I joined. I joined in Springfield, Ohio because when I was out of school between changing majors, the draft board came after me. While the Vietnam "conflict" was going on, we got called up to quell a riot at the Columbus Penitentiary twice, and Central State College in Ohio when race riots were becoming common. Even then I lucked out. After taking the tests to join, they told me to choose whatever job I wanted because I had just scored higher than anyone else in their history. I picked the motor pool. The officers told me I should be a clerk in battalion headquarters. They were right. I always worked in that headquarters until transferring to Canton and 'had it made' working with the officers. At summer camp every year I always had a starched uniform with three stripes on the sleeve, put my rifle in a deep freeze of my office so that I wouldn't have to clean it and during the tactical phases where you had to be up all night, the officers sent a messenger to the officer's club bar to get booze for the evening. I was included and they always brought back a bottle of scotch for me."

As a member of the National Guard, Jake does not recall ever being looked down upon by others his age who did not serve, unlike some of the Vietnam veterans who returned to a negative response by many who were anti-war.

"When strangers today find out that you're a veteran, it's always 'thank you for your service' without questioning what you did in the service. Since I've got some knee problems now, I really like the parking spot reserved for 'veterans only' at certain stores."

He then went back to Ohio State and transferred to the Business College majoring in production management because he decided that he wanted to work for a manufacturing company. Clearly the change in majors was the right move for him, as he made the dean's list! "I was invited to the Dean's office, and after that visit, I vowed never to return there again because the dean looked up my grades, and gave me flack for flunking out of my earlier majors."

Jake was married during the last year while his wife worked as a high school teacher. "We met at a Chi Omega event; I was there with another date. At that time, I worked keeping the books for a civil engineering firm. It was an ideal job, I could come into the office when I could, and I could work the summer full-time for an hourly rate the same as the drafting supervisor there."

During college, Jake also had a repeating job each summer at a large bakery loading truck trailers with goods that were delivered to a variety of grocery stores throughout the state of Ohio. Any complaints about the accuracy of the order shipped came directly to the truck loader. "As the youngest person on that dock, I took a lot of ribbing about everything, but each fall when I went back to school, they all wished me luck and said to return next summer…even the boss."

CAREER

While at OSU, he interviewed with several manufacturing companies with the hopes of landing a job in shop floor management. He chose to go to work for large manufacturing company in northeast Ohio, and his first role was in a Columbus, Ohio, manufacturing plant. He was told he would probably retire in that plant if he did well. He worked in industrial engineering as a beginning role, with the expectation that he would start his training to be a shop supervisor within six months.

"One of my first projects, I used my FORTRAN (programming language used by engineers) skills. In that project, I had to send computer cards back and forth to the headquarters office. The headquarters was God to the people in our plant." As it turned out, Jake was transferred to the Systems Department 18 months after starting with the Company. "I asked for an extension to be transferred as we had just had a daughter 2 weeks prior. No deal…. come now or forget it. We were renting a ranch home in Columbus and had to get out of that and move in 2 weeks to a duplex in our new location."

Later on, he decided to take advantage of a program where the company would pay for his advanced education, and he began pursuing his MBA. It took over 5 years attending school in the evenings after a full day's work.

Jake was married for 20 years before divorcing. They had two children. "My wife did most of the child-rearing until our daughter was in her last year of high school. She had gotten my daughter into the Canton Ballet in the first grade and she was in it for 12 years. She tried to get my son into group sports, which he hated, and I finally rescued him from that. Then she filed for divorce. That was something new to me because I didn't even know of anyone that had gone through a divorce. It was absolutely the worst time of my life. I had my daughter headed off to college, a son who was a junior in high school, and I got custody of the kids. I really needed my mother during that time, she really helped me."

During that time, Jake was working on a project where he was working out of a trailer at a new steel mill. He would get calls from the school that one of them was sick, or some other problem, and have to leave to get them since there was nobody else at home. "One day my boss, who was the head of metallurgy at the mill, appeared at my trailer after everyone had gone home. He had heard of my problems and just stopped to tell me that anytime I needed to go for my kids that I should just go. He said his approval was all I needed to do that and that I should not only keep him informed but to ask for help if I needed it. I always respected him for that."

Jake met his second wife in a hospital psychiatric unit, where she was working as the managing nurse. "I had brought in some supplies to a friend who was living there who used to babysit the kids, and this very nice nurse handed me a card and offered to have a drink or coffee with me sometime if I wanted to talk. I think we are both on the same intelligence level, which is good; we have some great 'discussions'. We have been married 27 years now."

RETIREMENT

Jake spent 37 years at the same company before retiring in 2004. "I thoroughly enjoyed most of the first 30. I still think that the company took good care of me during that time. In my final years, I was sort of 'shoved under the rug' doing small project work within the business."

"I turned 62 in November of 2004, and my wife convinced me to get out, so I was gone December 31, 2004. But that decision to go to work for my company was a good one, and my career opportunities provided me a good life."

Jake still stays in touch with high school friends and friends from his career. "We keep track with most using Facebook, but the use of email in our lives made a significant improvement in our relationships to this day."

POLLING FOR OPINIONS

If forced to list only three of the most important lessons in life you have learned, which might benefit others, what would they be?

Enjoy life more in all phases of it. It goes by fast. Always have your eyes on something new to learn about or experience. Trust in your God to see you through the tough parts. I've done that more since retiring.

If a Millennial or Gen X or Gen Z person was sitting next to you on your death bed, and they asked you about the true meaning of life, what would you say?

Take more time to enjoy life in general. If you become a parent, take the time to enjoy your kids. You can't repeat those times, but you can change the rest of your life any day you choose.

How does his relationship with his children differ from the relationship he had with his parents?

I worry a lot about my kids, mainly because one of them divorced and I know how difficult that can be. But I think I have a great relationship with my son and daughter.

What is Jake most proud of from the years raising his children?

I don't know how my parents paid for my college, so I was determined that my kids would get out of college free of all educational expenses, but they worked jobs at school also to help with the expenses. I am proud of both my kids!

Does he believe that the generations following his will be, in general, better off or worse financially when they get to his age?

Based on what I see with both my kids and my wife's kids, I think they will be better off. Just looking at their incomes and how they manage expenses makes me feel this way. They are smart and can take care of themselves.

What is Jake most proud of from his career?

I am most proud of the fact that I always seemed to be part of projects that had not been done before. I was also always proud that I could walk through any part of the steel mill and hourly people would holler, wave and even motion me over to talk or answer questions. I had a reputation with the rolling mill people for walking on the line above them when I was upset with something. The billet stamper would always yell up 'Who are you pissed at today?'

How did music impact him growing up?

I took private piano lessons for 12 years. I hated them for the last nine years but by then I was the feature pianist for the recitals. I also took trumpet lessons from the high school band director and was a first trumpet for 3 years in the band. I wish I had kept up with both, but it's only recently that I wish I could sit down and play piano comfortably in front of others. My music tastes were into the 50's music and the crooners of old tunes. I now have some music on my iPhone to connect to the car, so I can selectively play what my mood at the moment is. By far the biggest section is the 50's with the Platters and Dion and the Belmont's on top. Next on the list are the more recent biggies like Sinatra, Willie Nelson, Nat King Cole, Johnny Cash, etc. What a mixture huh? I've been singing barbershop for 46 years now, but I can't do that anymore because of the cancer radiation on my vocal cords, but I still belong.

Boomers have, and had, a reputation for drinking beer/wine/alcohol. Did you drink growing up? Has that changed as you aged, and if so, how?

I turned 18 while in the dorm at University of Cincinnati on the same floor as the football team. The offensive line took me up the street to Art's Tavern that night and bought my first beer. My roommate at Ohio State was a fellow engineering student at Wittenberg when we met in the college bar in Springfield. When we both discovered that we were transferring to OSU, we became roommates for the next 5 years. The corner neighborhood old folks bar was down the street from our rooming house. John and I took each other there for our 21st birthdays. I remember ordering scotch on the rocks. When the waitress asked me if I wanted green or black label, I was stunned and said black. It was a long time when I figured out why she asked, and that I had picked the most expensive one. I have a bottle of Blue Label almost gone from my ex-son-in-law who could buy it cheaply at the Naval PX. After retiring, I've created a habit of having a Manhattan or Scotch every night before supper, unless my wife gets an itch for me to make Old Fashions. I got back into wine making several years ago. My ex and I took winemaking classes in Akron for 5 years to learn how to make the different wines. It's been a year since I've made any because the rack is full. I like pinot noir and my wife drinks chardonnay.

Were there any times when you felt you got a bad deal and it affected you a lot?

I had just finished up as a project manager for a large steel project, and during the project I was asked to take over the development of a section which was behind schedule. I found out that the outside software development firm had laid down their pencils until they got some answers from our engineering partners. I had the outsiders removed from the project and we got back on schedule. We processed the first heat perfectly and on time.

Shortly after that, I moved back to another office. The new performance rating system for people that used grades 1 – 5 (5 being the highest) had been started. I received a '5' rating and my GM congratulated me, then asked what I had been doing of late, and showed me three letters from mill management and the contractors that he and his boss had received about my performance at the mill.

The next year they changed to a 1-4 grading system and I had just been transferred to work for a different manager. When we sat down, he handed me a small paper note that had a '1' on it. When I looked at it, he apologized and said that he wanted me to know that three other managers had gone in to protest that grade and whoever wouldn't change it. That was a crushing blow to me and from then on, I was never given above a '3' rating even after being commended for my work. That was when I decided that I had to get out of there and retired at the end of the year. It left me with a bad taste in my mouth, since that was not the Company that I knew.

What about his friendships in retirement?

I think I have many, many friends between the things I've been associated with, both from my career, and outside interests that I've acquired. I recall after the divorce was final that my son told me that he and his sister talked a lot during the year of settling, that they were staying with me and one reason was that I had so many friends that had helped the three of us during that time. I was kind of proud that they had recognized that.

We have all lost loved ones. In what ways have you changed as a result of losing someone close?

There's morbidity in watching friends from all over dying and you realize that maybe you didn't pay enough attention to them as you should have. The biggest loss in my life was my dad. We were never really close as we had different interests. After his death, I keep having a recurring feeling that I missed a lot of him and his side of the family. I've been trying to catch up with that. But I don't think I hurt him. We were just different and knew and understood that. I used to tell people, jokingly, that I didn't like my own kids until they could drive and we could talk more. Since then, I've tried to change that. In the summer, my son and I spend a lot of time together out on Lake Erie, and are now working on the house up there, and he shows me how to do things. Even fishing, I've asked things like 'Why do you raise your rod so high in the air when you think you have a nibble?'. His response was 'That's the way you taught me to fish'. The tables are turned now, and he teaches me, especially on the computer. My daughter always tells me that I'm her favorite person.

Consider for a moment all of the history of the time you were growing up. What do you remember most and how did those historical events affect you?

I followed the news of the Cuban missile crisis, moon landings, assassinations etc. out of interest in how our country was involved. I just missed being at the Kent State shootings because our unit was called but had loaned out vehicles to another unit. I did not support the shooting of live ammo, but also did not approve of the actions of the students in defiance of legal authority and responsibility. I didn't pay much attention to the others except for Laugh-In, a favorite TV show of mine then. I used to deliver bread door-to-door on Saturdays to give my uncle a day off from his six-day-per-week job. That kind of job keeps you aimed at college.

I did buy an Apple IIe for my son when he was in 7th grade. I wrote some programs, such as printing mailing labels, in Apple soft which was much like Basic. My son really took to it and eventually in college he dumped his original major and switched to Information Technology. Money-wise he has done much better at it than me, and now does the same kind of work that I did in my career.

What do you recall about the press (TV and newspapers mainly) when you were a teenager and in your twenties? How does that compare to now?

I trust the press more now than I trust the politicians, government and elected officials. The press could be sued for false information but politicos are experts at spreading the partial truths and downright lies. But I think people respected the national reporters on TV more than they do local reporters now.

What about 9/11? How did that affect how you think about our country and about terrorism? Were you very aware of what was going on in the Middle East or terrorism before 9/11?

I will never forget sitting at my window at work on the 5th floor, and seeing the news on my computer monitor. The fact that someone would even consider doing something like that caused me to shake. My fear was that we were now involved in the Middle East whether we wanted to be or not.

Regardless of your race or gender, is there anything you would offer in terms of your thoughts about minority / women's / men's rights and equality?

I guess I lived a sheltered life as a child. I knew of racial problems but women's and minority rights were something I ignored. That is probably because my parents were very much against racial biases.

How do you feel about U.S. immigration, the border wall, and our illegal alien policies?

The border was a big splash in the news. I believe the president had the right idea about the immigration policy but made decisions and issued orders without any consideration of how to enforce them with thought-out measures over time. It seemed his actions were for show and with no forethought of future outcomes. And that's the best you'll hear from me about anything positive about him.

What would you say about differences between the generations?

I didn't pay enough attention to the GenX's or any of those classifications. Only from my own kids and step-kids did I notice a difference between them and my generation. They either didn't take their employment as seriously as I did, or their companies were run much differently than I knew. They had much more interest in their kid's sports and school programs than I did or even do now. The younger generation seems to spend more time on kids' sports and other activities, and less time at work. I couldn't have done that, my job required much more time and dedication.

Are we as a society too hard or too easy on convicted felons? Should we, or should we not, outlaw the death penalty?

I would keep the death penalty only for particularly heinous or despicable crimes. I would also quit giving prison sentences for initial stage drug abuse, and less vicious crimes.

How do you feel about the second amendment and gun rights? Are there too many guns in America? Or is this a constitutional right that you highly support?

I think the gun issue is not so much about beliefs as it is political stubbornness. One party takes a stance so the other one argues against it. My opinion is that the constitution provides the right to bear arms, period. It doesn't say what kind of arms or the rules of owning one. Thus, I see no reason why banning the sale to the general public of machine guns or other military or police weapons are against the constitution. And, per usual, the first objections to that point are that it may be the first step of taking guns away for all of us. True, some countries have done that but it is against our constitution. I don't believe that current rules of selling weapons have any teeth and needs redone quickly.

How do you feel about the US role as being 'watchman of the world'? Should we reduce our global influence, or expand it? We spend billions on foreign aid. How do you feel about your tax dollars being used for non-US aid, versus it being spent here?

After several trips touring Europe, my wife and I feel comfortable being around people and their countries than before. Why would we want to disconnect ourselves from the world? China already tried that. We need more people to travel to foreign lands to gain a new perspective on home.

What are your feelings about 'green initiatives' and the state of our planet?

I don't understand how some people can say they don't believe in global warming. The only people in the world that don't believe that seem to be the far right in the U.S. The Amazon rainforest is disappearing also, this is a big problem. I know that other countries aren't doing nearly as much as the U.S. is to reduce emissions, but I am not sure what we can do about that.

How do you feel about the compensation of our political representatives at the state or national level, including benefits and pension?

I am a strong supporter of term limits. It's too easy for people to keep long term politicians in office but complain about it. They're wealthier because they are mostly lawyers and approve their own pay amounts. As to outside fees (speaking fees or consulting fees), I'd let them charge what they want because someone must be interested enough to pay those fees. It's like professional football players. I love football, especially on the college level, but I think the players are all over-paid and I don't attend any pro sports. I didn't like the fact that they can pay collegiate players now.

What about the growing national debt?

When I was in my first MBA class, our professor was teaching economics. The professor told the class that the national debt was not a problem because the government could just wipe it off the books whenever it wanted. My classmates and I talked about this on the way home that night, but never did figure out how you could do this. Maybe the problem is in the definition of the contents of the debt. I still haven't heard of a good argument for paying off that debt as opposed to just stopping financing it any further.

Why are politicians so divided? Has it really changed, or has it been like this for a long time?

Yes, after the 2016 elections, the whole political picture in the U.S. changed and that change is noticed by the rest of the world. Several years ago, we were touring the Vatican with an Italian guide and someone in our traveling group asked him what Italians thought of Americans. His answer was 'We love Americans. We just don't like your government.' To which one in our group said 'Well, neither do we.' I don't remember who was President then but I wonder what that response would be now.

Do you consider yourself to be a conservative or liberal or somewhere in between?

Definitely in between but don't know and don't care. We make up our minds on the candidates and not the party they are representing this time around. I've voted both ways since leaving college.

The press talks a lot about the growing disparity in income – is that a big problem in your opinion?

It seems to be. But I think that where you think you fall on the income range explains how you feel about it. I think that the disparity is spread out more now as compared to the 1920's through the 1950's. There are more people in the income ranges of the very rich families of the 1950's."

Are you more worried about the environment now vs. when you were in your teens or in the middle of life?

Absolutely. That is, of what I can remember in those years, but the environmental changes now are disturbing to me and I'm not going to be around to suffer from the changes as long as my grandkids.

Should the US be more focused upon our country mainly, or more focused globally, in terms of how our tax dollars are used?

I think it should be global. This country cannot survive on its own anymore. But the list of whom we are giving it to, and for what, should be revised.

Do you have more 'stuff' now than when you were younger? Are you going to start to get rid of your 'stuff'?

My kids and step-kids don't have those large accumulations of things to begin with. They can borrow things that we have when they need them, like my tools that I'm not using. We're trying to get rid of stuff already and the kids don't want it, such as collections and tools that I can't use anymore, memoirs of the past, etc. I hold on to the antique glass that I have accumulated because I don't want to see any of it sold at local auctions. Except for that kind of stuff, space is becoming more important than what is in it. Since I will probably pass on first, I'm not going to have to decide what happens to my things. I just take comfort in the fact that I don't have to make that decision. My will says that my Model A that I've had since I was 16 and restored myself goes to my son. I'm not sure that he's that interested in it and I've told him that he can sell it with much less sadness than I could. I saved to be able to afford some antiques, and now it is hard to part with those items because it is not worth what I paid at some time, and I still like these things.

Many Boomers believe that education is very important for the younger generations. Is advanced education more or less important than it was when you were growing up? Why or why not?

Not more important for all careers. I think it's just that more people have obtained a higher level of education so our kids need more just to stay equal in the job markets. The trades are turning around now and they now get more respect and income.

What about health care coverage and your thoughts about the benefits you get vs. what it costs?

I have had surgeries on both shoulders which cost me nothing or next to nothing compared to the actual costs on the billings from insurance. Now I'm about to have knee replacements. I had arthroscopic which did next to nothing and still, the costs were very little to me. But the aftermath rehab was $45 per trip to me compared to the $10 per week with 2 sessions per week that I had years ago with my shoulders. I've overheard some people at the rehab counter that still pay $10 that's costing me $45. Overall, the current plan was alright and completely free to me but I intend to change next year from the current retiree plan offered by the company. I think I can do better on my own after talking to other retirees.

Relative to other concerns, where does health and your family's health rank?

In the last two years my health has gone downhill but I've escaped pretty well. Two years ago, I had a biopsy on my vocal cords and 28 radiation treatments for cancer, bisecting of my thyroid for cancer testing (was negative) and of last month I was clear of cancer for 2 years. The latest arthroscopic surgery on my right knee has led to the appointment that I am getting this week for knee replacement, eventually on both knees. Compared to my father who died from his first heart attack at age 76, I feel I've done well with health to date. My wife has had knee surgery. She had Covid before the vaccines were available. I just had it but wouldn't have known if I had not tested again.

How do you feel about the upcoming social security funding shortfall, and what would you recommend to address it?

If I had to choose one solution, I would increase the tax rate of those working. I don't think people drawing their benefits now should have to take the brunt of the fix. But also, we have had Presidents of both parties 'borrow' from the social security pile of money to use for other things. That should have been illegal. That probably will not happen again given our political climate.

SUMMARY

Jake to me is a very interesting Boomer, in that he has lived to date a fairly typical 'Boomer' life (getting a college education, staying loyal to one company for his entire career, having a family, retiring at a reasonable age, living comfortably in retirement, etc.) yet his views do not match the typical reputation that Boomers have.

In nearly all cases, when I asked about his views, he seemed to reach his beliefs and views independently, based upon what he saw in his life. You might call his views conservative and right-wing when it comes to guns, the KSU shootings, and politicians and term limits, yet his views definitely lean left when he talks about the environment and global warming, Trump, the danger of the growing disparity of income, and his views about the importance of the country remaining a global leader versus having an 'America First' opinion. He confirms that when he describes himself as neither left or right wing, or liberal or conservative, as he says he doesn't care about labels, he just votes for the best candidate regardless of party.

I suppose like many Boomers, he defies categorization, because he is an individual with his own story and his own experiences. He has a strong belief about future generations doing better than his own, and is optimistic about their lives going forward. And he shed a lot of light on an issue I have struggled with, namely that most Boomers realize that they have too much stuff and belongings, yet are not, in the main, focused upon getting rid of excess things. I think he put this into perspective for me when he said 'I love my restored Model A, and I would sell it as I don't need it anymore, but after I am gone, my son can sell it with a lot less emotion that I ever could!"

Perhaps Boomers, as the 'saving generation', sacrificed a lot to acquire assets that they liked and enjoyed, and they don't want to feel bad about parting with things that they sacrificed so much to acquire. That makes sense to me, although that does place some burden on the next generation and/or heirs to dispose of so much after death.

Either way, Jake is a unique character who is a joy to talk to, who loves family, friends, and faith. Hard to find any fault with a Boomer like that!

CHAPTER 14:
Jim:
The Techie / Scout / Philanthropist

BACKGROUND

I have known Jim since I was 22 years old, as we began our careers in the same profession.

As you will read, Jim has been a Boomer who did a lot of things right in his life, and quietly made contributions to make the world a better place, in his own way, and in a focused way. Jim will likely not grab newspaper headlines for his contributions to scouting and youth, or for his being a good citizen who has done all the right things that we ask citizens to do (obey the laws, pay their taxes, help your neighbors, etc.)

Jim had the advantage of growing up in a solid family, with parents who were strict, and siblings who set a good example for him. But we all know that there are many who have not taken advantage of getting a solid start in life. Jim did!

EARLY LIFE

Jim is a core Boomer age-wise, born in 1957 in northeast Ohio, near the place he lives today. He was born into a larger family, with 5 siblings, with ages spread widely, with the oldest and youngest being 20 years apart. He had solid parents, with each having specific interests and skills.

"My parents were notable in their own way: my dad was very smart, making a solid living in hardware/sporting goods. He was president of his senior class. My mother was a classically trained soprano, with singing engagements starting when she was 12 and continuing into her 40s."

Jim views his parents and their parenting style as 'most decidedly strict'. They determined bedtimes, what TV shows to watch, what curfews were in effect, etc. Like many Boomers, Jim was raised in a time when 'paddling' for punishment was common, and Jim carried that practice forward as a parent also. "The key is to paddle when you are calm, not when you are angry. Then it remains discipline and does not escalate into beating. My guess is I was paddled until I was about 8 or 10. After that, I just received some good talking-to's."

Did Jim feel loved by his parents even though they were strict?

"In looking back, my parents showed love to their kids by how they treated them. There was not a lot of hugging and kissing and statements of 'I love you'."

Like Jim, his siblings were also very intelligent, as his older sister was the class valedictorian and National Merit finalist, and his older brother scored an 800 on his math SAT. His three sisters all play piano, and all siblings sang in the choir or select choir, with two being leads in musicals.

"Shortly after I was born, my parents built a new house in town on some property they had purchased a few years before. I was child #4, so more space was needed for a growing family. We were then close to the center of town, so schools, banks, grocery store, the YMCA, etc. were all within walking distance."

During high school, Jim did well and ran track and was in choir, and began to plan for college. But unlike some Boomers who revel in the memories of high school, Jim does not. "Looking back, I was book smart, but I was not a good friend to anyone, nor did I learn how to socialize well with others. Even though I was active outside of the classroom, I never built a strong friendship in any of those activities. In some sense, I was very self-centered in what I did or why I did it." What were his priorities at that time in his life?

"Clearly, academic success was my number one priority given how my siblings did so well. I did not want to disappoint or be the one that might shame the family!"

Interestingly, Jim also participated in Boy Scouts, mainly because his older brothers did so. Little did he know that later in life, Scouts would become a major focus for him.

Although his parents did not experience the Great Depression as adults (they were in school), Jim could tell that they heard many stories that affected how they behaved and how they managed money. "In our household, we saved bread bags, we burned our dinner scraps in the incinerator, we had meals that I never ate as an adult, such as liver and potato pancakes made from the prior evening's crummy mashed potatoes. We carefully unwrapped Christmas gifts so we could save the wrapping paper for next year. My mom washed towels once a week, I didn't get a fresh bath towel every day. Worn church shoes became school shoes. Worn school shoes became play shoes. Our parents wanted to send all of us to college, and they could not do that without being very frugal, given six children."

Did Jim's childhood experience impact his behavior today? "To be fair, today I buy store brand breakfast cereal, wash and reuse plastic zip bags, save the calendars and notepads mailed to us by charities, drive an 11-year-old car, etc. When we reach 30% unemployment and inflation is in double digits and we put folded newspaper in our shoes because the soles are nearly gone... then that will be another repeat of the Great Depression. Even though there were difficult times in 2008 (the Great _Recession_), people still had good clothes and cell phones and things to do."

Did his parents attend his sporting events or take him to practice?

"When I played little league, as an 11-year-old, I rode my bike to practice and to games, my parents didn't run me around, it was up to me to get there if I wanted to play."

If Jim could go back, what would he do differently?

"I would slap my 15-year-old self and say: 'Make a friend... by inviting them over to do something. Anything. Keep in touch with them. Do fun stuff together. Don't let time or distance get in the way of maintaining a friendship.'"

How did music from the 60's and 70's affect him?

"Growing up, most of the music I listened to was classical, or current pop or oldies since my mom tuned in to the local radio station for many years. To wake us up Sunday mornings, my mom would put classical music on the stereo for all to hear. My three sisters all took many years of piano, so I was familiar with traditional practice pieces as well as some more difficult works. I heard rock or current music only occasionally through my teens. I still like classical orchestral and piano music. College introduced me to rock and pop music, which continues today. I get a kick out of introducing my wife to music from The Doors, ELO, Queen, The Eagles, Bread, Styx, ZZ Top, and so on. She has heard many of their songs, but never knew the artists. My siblings and I certainly sang in the school choir group, but also in church choir. So, there are many religious songs that stir me. When my wife and I got married, there was one couple who came to the wedding. They were from the church, but we did not invite them. They came because they KNEW that we would have wonderful music for the service. It was!"

Jim reflects back on how it was growing up in the 60's and 70's. "Those times were tough on parents and their kids. Boys wanted longer hair. Girls wanted shorter skirts or to wear make-up. Parents wanted control back to their conservative views. For me, I ended up with a conservative viewpoint, partly due to my parents and partly to me working at a conservative company. My siblings, especially those who went into teaching, were more liberal in their views."

What about alcohol or drug use during this time of his life? "I drank beer and some hard liquor during college because that seemed the thing to do. But no drugs or marijuana, ever. I did have too much hard liquor to drink at a party during my last year in college, and have not consumed any since. I drink wine and beer, but not too much. And I sometimes go weeks between alcoholic drinks." Hmm, certainly dispels the Boomer rep as heavy alcohol users!

Just after high school graduation, Jim took on his first real job, as a busboy at a local restaurant. He remembers staying busy, and always moving or doing something. "I was surprised that there were some employees who did just the minimum. I could tell because when I showed up for work, I saw the lack of progress from the prior shift. I also took on tasks that most busboys do not normally do, such as driving to a bakery for bread rolls, or washing, drying and folding the cloth napkins and tablecloths. Or taking a ride with the owner to help carry liquor."

Jim enrolled at Mount Union College in the fall. After a year there, where he was on the track team as a pole-vaulter, his financial aid was cut due to his dad getting a bonus. He then transferred to, and graduated from, Kent State University with a degree in Mathematics. "I was in Honors College at KSU, which afforded me the opportunity to earn college course credit teaching a few classes. But I realized that I was not cut out to be an instructor."

Jim enjoyed the college experience, but would not want to re-live it. "At college, I verified that I was able to be on my own, study to keep pace with the instruction, and score well on subjects I disliked as well as the ones I liked. But re-living college would be exhausting. Looking back, I'm not sure how I found the time for studies, intramural sports, parties, hanging out, etc.

My first dorm roommate at KSU was not a serious student, so I paid a little more and got a dorm room of my own so I could focus on studying. And once I was done, I could not be convinced to work on a master's degree."

What about military service? Was that an option Jim considered?

"At KSU when money was tight, I considered joining ROTC as that would pay for much of my remaining schooling. In 1977, with the Vietnam conflict just ending and the Cold War still continuing, my dad was very emphatic that I should not go that route as it would require a 6-year commitment after graduation. In his view, he was looking out for me. Dad even served for 18 months in the South Pacific during WWII, and I just found out from my brother last year that Dad told him, given his early draft number, that if he wanted to move to Canada to avoid the draft, he would support him in that. I was flabbergasted that Dad told him that, given how conservative he was and how he served in the military himself."

During his senior year in college, the KSU Career Center had businesses come onto campus for 15-minute interviews, and he was offered a second interview with a large manufacturing company locally. His on-site interview went well, and he was offered a fulltime position as a computer programmer. "In my view, they were paying me buckets of money to do things I would like to do! I accepted the offer, and cancelled my Spring quarter KSU classes, since I already had enough credits to graduate. I began work in April 1979."

Jim did well in his career working for this large company in their corporate headquarters, and he invested 36 years of his life there before retiring. His main focus was in information technology and computer systems. He held roles as a programmer, supervisor, did application support and development, was a process analyst, served in information security, and also database support.

What are some of the best memories during his career, in terms of pride he has today?

"For the employees in IT, I was able to simplify their jobs with some of the development tools that we created. In the late 1980s, I was part of a small team to work on an effort to connect our company notes/email system to all global teletype machines. Remember, this was pre-Internet. Once done, our project was submitted to a publication which named it one of their 8 finalists for innovation, and requested that we write up the details of our efforts."

"I was part of a small group that studied and implemented a common user interface after studying a draft copy of an IBM manual. IBM saw it and was impressed at what we produced. We were featured in an IBM video on how we implemented it at our company. We continued creating these applications using a code generator, and we ended up with dozens of computer applications that our employees found easier to use because they all operated in a consistent manner."

"I was also able to change employee behavior. When I first started on the information security team, I was invited along to watch a consultant do an after-hours audit of computer workstations, looking for poor practices that could jeopardize information security. While the consultant found many sensitive or confidential items, there was no feedback to the employees involved. I resolved to educate employees in all future information security audits. Employees, now aware of where they personally fell short, changed their behavior."

Jim also began the plan for all the computer work required to transition from the year 1999 to the year 2000. Although many of today's youth may not know anything about this, at the time, some predicted that the 'world might end' because many computer systems would stop working because programs would think that a two-digit year '00' was less than '99' and ignore current data for important calculations and reports. Up until the 1980s, computer cards were the default method of collecting data and creating files, and the cards only had 80 columns on them. That created a strong incentive to conserve space on file layouts and to reduce space, and most companies and organizations used two-digits only to record the year in date fields. "We started efforts to plan for needed computer program changes for the year 2000 in 1995. I was the lone corporate person working on that effort until 1999. We ended up with a good outcome with negligible problems, and were largely on budget, based upon our company size and our computing environment. When 5 other employees were added to assist in 1999 for the final push, I became junior on the project. During their first few weeks on the project, they would find that we should address some specific items. In almost every case, I had already addressed or created what was needed!"

So, what about his relationships and current family?

"I was married in 1981, but that ended in divorce in 1992."

What happened?

"I realize now that I still had to mature, and my emotional maturity was not where it needed to be. My patience especially was not good. My daughter was born in 1987, and ended up splitting time between our two households, which was a difficult situation for a kid in terms of continuity. My second marriage in 1995 has been a good one, going on 27 years now. Karen has been a good influence to help me with some of my weak points, and she has taught me about unconditional love. A good marriage makes everything else in life so much better. We are able to have arguments and still resolve them without making it a big deal."

How is the relationship with his daughter now?

"After being "Bad Dad" for 6-8 year during teens and college, my daughter figured out that I am kind, funny, and a good source of information. She calls to check on me if I let too many days pass without contacting her. We both do things that drive each other bonkers, but today it is a great relationship in my view."

Is there anything he would do differently in parenting, reflecting back?

"I would seek guidance on how to handle rebellious teens."

As a Boomer, does he think that the Millennial generation has it better than the Boomer generation at the same age?

"I did the math - my starting yearly salary was on par with the total cost of my college tuition/room/board. For my daughter, her first job's salary is only about 30% to 40% of her education cost. I lived at home for about a year after starting my career, and that enabled me to live on my own since. We were able, through savings, to pay for her college without incurring student debt. She is thankful now for that. I supported her after graduation to help her for a few years. Her career is now doing well, and she is doing well financially. Looking back, part of the difference is that I scored a career in a growing field that paid lots of money to smart young talent. My daughter started in a well-established field that is competitive for job seekers."

What makes Jim most proud of his daughter and his involvement in her growing up?

"I was able to watch, then assist, her as she played softball, and attend most of her choir concerts. Some of the proudest moments have come more recently when I realized she WAS paying attention back then. (Hey Dad! You wanna have a catch?)"

SCOUTING

Jim was in Boy Scouts as a youth and enjoyed it.

After college, he started helping out with his scout troop again, attending meetings and campouts. He served in leadership roles like committee chair and Scoutmaster. He also trained other scout leaders in his district, and was asked to serve on council committees.

"I guided many youths to earn Eagle Scout rank." He was awarded district, council, and national awards for his leadership.

Among the highlights of his time investment in Scouting included:

- taking 2 groups to Philmont Scout Reservation in New Mexico for 11 days on a backpacking trek
- taking 1 group to a Florida Sea Base for a high adventure in the ocean
- taking 2 groups on canoe treks of 5 days or more
- racking up around 700 nights camping in tents or rustic cabins.

Jim led a committee to suggest changes that would accommodate girls in the Scouting program at summer camp.

Jim served as a Scoutmaster for 18 years, and a rough estimate of time volunteered is 1000 hours per year consumed in campouts and outings, meetings, planning and preparation, adult training, etc. Jim estimates that he also used about 40 weeks of _personal vacation time_ for scout camp and high adventure treks during his career.

Why the focus on scouting? What drove you to invest so much of your free time?

"I observed as a youth that some of the adult men remained involved even when their sons became too old to participate, and they did so because they saw a lot of value for youth, and that stuck with me. So, I had to learn, as an adult, the coaching side of scouting so that I could help the youth coming into scouting. Most people don't understand the appeal of sleeping on hard ground, winter camping in tents, carrying all your food and water, hiking 10-15 miles a day with full packs…for FUN!"

Tell me about some key memories of scouting?

"A measure of a memorable campout is when something goes wrong. Nobody remembers the campout in perfect weather when no one got hurt, all the meals were done correctly, etc. But they do remember the campout where the scout brings cheddar cheese for the spaghetti! Or when Calvin loses a tooth, pukes, and has a bloody nose! Or when Chris breaks through the ice and is up to his thighs in water! Or when Nathan becomes afraid of the owl perched on their patrol table! (It's a plastic owl, mind you!) Or when Mrs. Smith leaves her purse on top of her car and its contents are now scattered on Cleveland Avenue!"

Jim shared a lot about the changes required in scouting, such as female requests to be involved in Boy Scouts. He also describes how lawsuits became more commonplace and how the scouting organization stepped up to provide mandatory training for adults. They also implemented new rules to ensure that adults are never solo with a scout group, versus having several adults with scouts at all times. "It is very rewarding, especially when a single mother or father thanks us for providing an opportunity on a weekly basis for their child or children to be exposed to activities with good male role models."

PHILANTHROPY

Jim began participating in the North Canton's Alumni Association around 2009, and he has been president of that organization for the past 5-6 years. "Each year we award a few scholarships to graduating seniors. We also honor graduates and others in the area who have excelled in their field or made an impact in their community. During my time as president, we have created a website for mostly static information, established an email account, created a Facebook page for current happenings, began sending our newsletter (or link) via email, added a new scholarship, improved our Hall of Distinction selection process, and created an endowment fund through the Stark Community Foundation."

After his daughter graduated in 2006, he realized that there would be no more from his family attending his high school, so he thought it timely to begin a scholarship to be awarded to a graduating vocal music student, since all of his siblings and their children excelled in the vocal music program. "My siblings also contribute funds to this scholarship. To date we have awarded fourteen $500 scholarships and two $750 scholarships."

POLLING FOR OPINIONS

If forced to list only three of the most important lessons in life you have learned, which might benefit others, what would they be?

1 - Plan ahead. At least think of what you need to do TODAY to be able to do the things you want to do next year.
2 - A plan not written down is just a dream. I'm a list maker from way back. Both work and home saw lists that contained items to be accomplished and then checked off.
3 - Be kind always! We don't know the difficult paths walked by others. Show them patience and kindness.

Do you believe that the generations following ours will be, in general, better off or worse off both financially as well as overall when they get to our age?

I think that delayed gratification is becoming scarce in today's society. There seems to be a desire to want things NOW, and lots of things, too. Make coffee? NO! To the coffee shop! Want a meal? Have it delivered! Buy new clothes? Click here for Free Shipping! It also shows in the lack of planning on the part of the younger set. 'What do you mean I have to wait 12 weeks for a passport? I have to thaw the Thanksgiving turkey HOW MANY days before Thanksgiving?

Tell me about your parents as they aged, and your relationship at that time.

My first warning was my dad calling to ask for advice on a letter he received. I drove over and saw that it was a gas aggregation notice with an option to opt out. At no time during the phone conversation did my dad say 'utility' or 'gas' or anything that would give me a hint. This was the start for him with Alzheimer's. After that, it was a growing concern for driving, paying bills (my sister handled that), and my parents feeding themselves. We later found that my mom largely lost the ability to cook a meal; 75% of their meals were cold cereal. They came from a generation that hid these things. So, they never asked for help. We had to pay attention and figure out that they needed help in some things. When we moved them to assisted living, their quality of life greatly improved, and it was a godsend for us. They passed away in their 90's.

What are you planning to have happen with any funds or possessions after you die?

My grandma always said 'Do your givin' while you're livin', so you're knowin' where it's goin'.

I will try to convince my wife that we should be able to do some large charitable donations in the coming years. I do suspect that my daughter will receive a good sum when we both pass.

Tell me about your thoughts of social media and friendships at this age.

Social media is great for acquaintances to keep up with each other. Classmates or others who live far away now share their experiences and we can enjoy that. As for friends, true friends, I think that you have to do it the old-fashioned way: do things face to face. Cultivate the friendship, share thoughts, ask questions, laugh at jokes.

One friend lives in another state, and we keep up through texts and emails and a rare phone call. Another friend lives about 45 minutes away, and we meet about once per month for dinner with our spouses.

What are your thoughts about the press today, both newspapers and TV?

I do not watch TV "news" shows. Many times, I end up researching what I hear on the radio or read about in the newspaper or social media. I try to find the source. I am disappointed that at times what I hear or read is twisted out of context with the actual documents or events. I think the "press" is more in the entertainment business than the information business. People watch what is sensational. If it is boring, people don't watch and ratings and money plummet.

What about the state of equal rights and/or discrimination in our country?

My best friend, who is a white woman, is married to a black man. Their feedback on what is racism and what is not has confirmed much of what I already thought about race relations in the U.S. Just one example: Her husband is a college basketball coach. For one job early in his career, they held a social function for the prospective coaches and spouses, presumably to gauge social skills. She realized that she was not the "right look" for them, and her husband did not get the job. She now declines these parties so that her husband can be evaluated on his merits, not her looks/color. Also, her husband, during recruiting trips, has been stopped on a few occasions because he was a black man driving an out-of-state licensed rental car and just "looked wrong". He was taught, and also taught his children, to remain calm and compliant and all will be okay. Yes, he had to have "the talk" with his kids.

How do you feel about U.S. immigration, the border wall, and our illegal alien policies?

We should be able to limit the number of new immigrants coming into this country. And guarding our borders is not an unreasonable expectation.

Surveys show that non-Boomers are much more positive about socialism than Boomers. In fact, one study showed that Millennials and Gen Z think slightly more positively about socialism than capitalism. How do you feel about socialism vs capitalism?

Perhaps their inexperience in life tends to lead them toward easier or "fairer" solutions. They will certainly cite that rich people have better health care than others, but, quite frankly, they always will. If I'm rich and need surgery, I'll pay the extra to hire my own doctor or go out of the country, rather than wait weeks or months for heart surgery or a transplant. Non-Boomers will think that it is unfair, but, frankly, life is unfair in many respects.

How do you feel about the second amendment and gun rights?

My opinion is that bad people with bad intent will do bad things no matter what tool they use. Sadly, a number of people were killed and injured by a bad person with bad intent this past weekend in Waukesha while he was driving an SUV. A firearm is a tool, just like the SUV.

How do you feel about the U.S. role as being 'watchman of the world'? Should we reduce our global influence, or expand it?

If your neighbor's home is in need of repair or yard work, and he is incapable of caring for it himself, what should you do? If you ignore it, your property value suffers. If you help, both properties look better and you may have gained a friend. If you can help but don't, what does that say about you as a neighbor? We can help. We should help.

What are your feelings about 'green initiatives' and the state of our planet?

While the US is a big consumer of many things, there is still plenty of clean drinking water, reduced smog, monitored landfills, sewage treatment, and more. From what I read, China, Vietnam, India, Thailand, and some South American nations LEAD the world in ocean pollution. I have no doubt that they also are crummy caretakers of their air and land. I think enacting more legislation in just the US for this is just going to negatively impact our economy without significantly impacting the global environment.

How do you feel about the compensation of our political representatives at the state or national level, including benefits and pension?

It is appalling to read of so many multi-millionaires in the peoples' house, the House of Representatives, especially those who became that after being elected. As for insurance and pension, it should be consistent with time in office. Should it be OK to give speeches for compensation? Yes. Serve on boards? Not until you are done serving your constituents.

Do you consider yourself to be a conservative or liberal or somewhere in between?

Conservative. I may be a bit more liberal than my parents in some ways, but pretty much along the same lines in fiscal matters.

The press talks a lot about the growing disparity in income – is that a big problem in your opinion?

I think we are also seeing a disparity of effort. Some people want top dollar for little effort.

Do you think the country is headed in the wrong or right direction? What alarms you?

I see a few signs that personal responsibility is not what it used to be. College loans and students who say that they cannot repay them is one.

Many Boomers believe that education is very important for the younger generations. Is advanced education more or less important than it was when you were growing up?

Education is a great equalizer and remains important. But we still need to encourage a career in the trades. I don't want a world where there is no one to repair my furnace/water/sewer lines/electricity.

Some would argue that we cannot afford the social security program that exists, and that we will be unable to pay the full amount to beneficiaries within 15 years or so. Experts predict that the Social Security surplus will run out in 2034, and at that time, benefits paid must match the social security taxes paid in by individuals and employers. Thus, current payment levels will have to be reduced unless action will be taken. How do you feel about social security?

We seem to have molded Social Security into a government pension program, instead of the aid for those unable to work, or surviving spouses, or children in need, etc. My thoughts are that the program should be for those without a company pension and those truly in need. I will accept what the program gives me, but I was taught long ago to ignore Social Security when planning for my retirement.

SUMMARY

Jim's story is one of a Boomer who had a good life growing up with solid, but strict, parents who were there for him and his siblings. He has shown a consistency in being responsible and in helping others, in his job, in the Scouts, and in the community. He is proud of the contributions he made in his career and to his company and co-workers. He has a wonderful track record of being a good teammate in whatever activity he was involved.

The hours he invested into Scouting and other community interests is nothing short of remarkable.

He clearly has spent a lot of time examining his own life along with strengths and weaknesses, and admits today that part of the reason for his divorce was due to his immaturity. Not many would admit to that, looking back over their life.

If there were ever a Boomer life story that fell into the category of 'an everyday Boomer who did not grab headlines or undeserved attention', Jim's story would fall right into the middle of that category.

In hearing his story, and in knowing Jim personally throughout his career, I can attest that he made solid contributions to society, to his employer, and to youth involved in Scouting. He is someone that we can all respect and admire for his dedication, spirit of volunteerism, and focus upon making life better for others. Thanks Jim!

SEX, DRUGS, ROCK and WAR: The Boomer Generation

ANALYSIS

Hopefully you have learned a bit about these Boomers and the environment they came from, as well as their views and beliefs in their later years.

In conducting analysis of each question that I asked them in the 'POLLING FOR OPINIONS' section of each life story, I found some interesting conclusions. Recall that each question was optional, and many of the Boomers in this book answered less than 2/3 of the questions for a variety of reasons. So, the analysis here is of the answers I received, as told to me, even if there were few answers.

Let me say, from a personal standpoint, that I am fairly opinionated about most important issues, and when I wrote the life story responses especially in the POLLING FOR OPINIONS section, I found it difficult to report objectively their views, especially when they might have differed so much from my own views. But I kept telling myself – "Be a true reporter, report the facts, do not bias anything based upon your views or disagreements!" I believe that I accomplished that.

STATISTICAL VALIDITY

I will not claim that based upon fourteen Boomer stories, these analyses are valid statistically to make any claims about the broader Boomer generation values or opinions. I will just say 'it is what it is', and I appreciate that there may be some differing conclusions each reader may make based upon the analyses.

KEY GENERATIONAL CONFLICTS

So, let's revisit some of those Boomer complaints from Gen Y and Gen Z, especially those outlined in the FOREWORD section, and explore each issue relative to the Boomer life stories you have read about.

Boomers Have Polluted the Planet and Caused Global Warming

I asked each Boomer the question – "What are your feelings about 'green initiatives' and the state of our planet? How do you feel about how serious global warming is? Should we be doing more or doing less? Do you think other countries take this as seriously as we do? Or are they ahead of the U.S. on this?"

Nearly all 14 Boomers acknowledged that this is a serious problem and that more needs to be done. The group was split between those who (a) believe the U.S. needs to take the lead (or continue to take the lead) on what actions are needed and to demonstrate to the rest of the world that it can be done, and (b) those who believe that the U.S. is doing enough, and that other countries are not pulling their weight. In particular, China and India were cited as two countries that complain about the U.S. needing to do more, yet they would appear to be viewed by some of these Boomers as the worst caretakers of their environments.

Several Boomers commented that the U.S. cannot seem to understand that green energy and fossil fuels can coexist, at least until green energy is more mature. Another observed that as much progress has been made on various technologies in all areas, we still rely upon the combustion engine that was invented in the late 1800's. Another claimed that they had read that even if the U.S. had zero emissions, the impact to the entire world would be minimal.

My conclusion, after reading all the comments, was that I was pleasantly surprised that this group of Boomers *all* agreed that action is required to address the global warming concerns, and nobody denied that this is a serious problem. This is in contrast to what we may read about Boomers denying all the climate change concerns.

Boomers Got Us in Debt (via the national deficit of over $31.6 trillion) and We Will Have to Pay It Back!

I asked each Boomer the question – "What about the growing national debt? Is this becoming a very serious issue for our country, or is it just one of many issues that we need to monitor?"

The interesting observation on this question is that only half of the 14 answered the question. The ones who did, recognized the seriousness of the problem, but seemed to have gotten so used to this being an ongoing issue, they may have become numb to the problem and solutions. One said that our lives are more impacted by what goes on locally, not nationally, and that it is hard to even understand how much money this is. Another said it is so ridiculous and that our politicians will continue to 'kick the can down the road' regardless of who we elect. Three however, expressed deep concern that this will just bury our kids and grandkids, that it could force us into socialism, that it will lower our standard of living, and that this is a national security risk.

On the flip side, one commented that the younger generations probably benefitted in some way with all that deficit spending on things such as roads, infrastructure, services, etc., and that at times, especially during recessions, government spending in excess of the budget is a useful tool to get the economy going again. Two even wondered what would happen if we just said we were not going to pay back the national debt!

My reaction about this issue is that I was surprised that this was not perceived more seriously by more of the Boomers I interviewed. It seemed as though since the issue gets very little media coverage, that some of the Boomers here were less informed about it and thus, had less of a concern vs. other issues we discussed. Or, it could be that this has been a problem for so long that some may have concluded that nothing will be done about the national debt.

According to 'usdebtclock.org', our national debt will grow by about *1.4 trillion dollars* this year. If you take the national debt of about 31.6 trillion dollars, and divide by the 127 million taxpayers, the national debt per taxpayer calculates to about $250,000. That is, if for some reason, all the lenders to the U.S. government demanded their money back tomorrow, Uncle Sam could come to all the taxpayers and demand $250,000 from each of us!

This issue is not going away, and in fact, is beginning to gain more coverage as Gen X, Y and Z begin to understand the burden this debt will create for them going forward, and they are beginning to rightly make some noise about this topic. According to an article by Josh Boak of the Associated Press, the national deficit is once again in the headlines. He quoted Kent Smetters, a professor at the University of Pennsylvania and director of the Penn Wharton Budget Model, who claims that to just stabilize the debt at near current levels, the federal government would need to slash all spending by 30%, raise tax revenues by 40%, or some combination of both! And those actions would not *reduce* the current federal deficit of over $31 trillion, they would just stabilize it where it is at currently. If we somehow stop or slow the rapidly growing national deficit, which sooner or later we must, all generations still living will be forced to accept fewer services, yet pay much higher taxes. It is not a wonder that politicians who bring this topic up during campaigns get bombarded with negative press. As a result, they ignore the topic, at least while campaigning, and if they start to discuss it after being elected, the opposing party makes sure that citizens know that Senator X or Congressperson Y is going to raise taxes and cut programs that citizens enjoy today. In my simple way of thinking, citizens *should demand* that those running for office present their plans to how to corral the growing deficit and to begin reducing it.

I interject here that there is an emerging theory called 'Modern Monetary Theory' (MMT), which is being espoused by some as an entirely new way to think about the national deficit. MMT would say that balancing the budget, and reducing the national debt, is unnecessary, since the government can create (print) all the money and currency it needs to pay for a variety of national needs. I have studied this new theory in some detail, and all I can say is that I would encourage everyone to read about this, since more of our administrators and elected officials in the federal government are buying into this theory, which is scary to me. It may just my naïve point of view, but my take on MMT is that it is one of those new concepts that many would like to believe because it rationalizes what is happening and encourages us not to worry about the rapidly growing national debt. Why should we not be concerned? Per MMT, at any time, our government can just create more currency to pay down the debt, or pay for any other program that will help stimulate the economy or provide whatever relief we may need at the time. MMT would suggest that the only reason to be careful about over-spending by the government, is because it could cause inflation to spiral out of control. But the suggested remedy to that inflation is to tax all of us more to reduce demand. In effect, that course of action would take dollars away from taxpayers, and put more dollars in the hands of government to spend freely. Not exactly a great solution for us taxpayers! Plus, it sounds a bit like centralized planning, as if the government can better decide what to do with our dollars than private enterprise can.

Not to bash this emerging MMT, but here is my take on all of this, from someone who has been around the block a few times, and has listened to so many 'too good to be true' stories that turn out to be wrong in the long run. (Like many, I have lived through Enron, Bernie Madoff, that cigarettes were healthy, etc.)

First, per the Congressional Budget Office (CBO), the annual interest costs on the national debt in 2022 was about $400 billion. The CBO also projects that these interest costs over the next ten years will grow, and will be about *$1.2 trillion* dollars per year by 2032! These numbers will actually be higher if we do not get inflation under control, resulting in the Fed continuing to raise interest rates, which means that those loaning the money to the government will require higher payback amounts, meaning they will demand higher interest payouts.

Second, today, of all the federal income taxes paid by individuals, taxes on profits paid by companies, and use fee taxes (gasoline taxes, cigarette and liquor taxes, etc.), about 10% is used JUST to pay the interest on the national debt. In 10 years, per the CBO, *the interest payment will consume 25% of all taxes paid!* Just think what could be done with all that money, we could fund much-needed programs, solve our social security funding issue, provide better job training, etc. But no, we will continue to consume larger and larger percentages of all tax revenue just to pay interest on this debt!

Third, this new theory is based upon the belief that government drives the economy, and that by printing money and using it for government spending, they are investing in things that we need, such as pollution control, new jobs, additional support programs, etc. MMT says that because the government creates taxes and tax laws, individuals seek out employment just so that they can pay their taxes! (MMT also explains that the government monitors the tax revenue to see if the tax rates need to be higher, especially if inflation is increasing, because higher taxes are the best tool to reduce inflation and to redistribute wealth!) Strange, I always thought that individuals seek out employment so that they can pay for food, clothing, shelter, health care, education, etc., with the hope that they will have enough money left to pay their taxes. The MMT does not appear to recognize that!

Again, I would encourage all of you to read more about this. If nothing else, please do a Google search on 'modern monetary theory'. In my opinion, this is a very dangerous concept, and we all need to be aware of what some are espousing as fact, when in fact, it is a theory, and to me, one that is illogical. Of course, I am not an economist!

Boomers Have Created a Country Where Gun Violence is Out of Control

The question I asked related to this issue was "How do you feel about the second amendment and the right to bear arms? Are there too many guns in America? Or is this a constitutional right that you highly support?"

Ten of fourteen answered this question. All were in support of our right to bear arms to defend ourselves. Most mentioned that we need better background checks, better education, or limited-to-zero use of automatic weapons. One mentioned that the original thought behind the second amendment was to help citizens defend themselves from a tyrannical government. One also mentioned that the right to guns is even more important now that there is a movement to defund the police and decriminalize crimes.

I was not at all surprised by the responses, they seemed in line with what I expected to hear. Clearly, these Boomers want the right to bear arms! Most, by a small percentage, are OK discussing the idea of more thorough background checks and limiting or stopping the use of semi-automatic weapons.

<u>Capitalism might have been fine for Boomers, but it is not working for younger generations. The rich keep getting richer, the poor just keep getting poorer. Socialism would provide a much fairer and improved lifestyle for most.</u>

I presented this question to the Boomers related to this issue: "Surveys show that non-Boomers are more positive about socialism than Boomers are. In fact, one study showed that Millennials and Gen Z think slightly more positively about socialism than capitalism. Why do you think that may be? How do you feel about socialism vs capitalism?"

I was surprised that quite a few of the Boomers recognized that indeed, the younger generations felt they needed more government help, and that they did see socialism as an appealing form of government. But nearly all Boomers interviewed rejected that socialism would truly be a better way, as evidenced by these comments: 'All that happens with socialism is that those at the top of the pyramid get even MORE money.' 'Younger generations want a system that they think is fairer, but life is not fair!' 'People who truly have needs should be helped, but things are getting out of hand today.' 'The younger generations are a product of the liberal college system, the things they cram down their throats are disgusting.' 'If socialism was so great, we would not have millions crossing the border illegally to get here.'

My assessment here is that I believe the Boomers have this pegged correctly. I have studied what has happened in other countries that 'went socialist', and the outcome was never good, at least in the long run. I guess I am a typical Boomer! I am hopeful that Gen Y and Z will do more studying about socialism and its history in other countries before concluding that it is an answer to our problems. In particular, it would be worthwhile for all to read about what happened in Venezuela once they decided to become a socialist government, as well as understanding Cuba, North Korea, and Sweden. Some say that Sweden is a socialism success, yet most economic experts would say that Sweden is more a capitalist economy than a socialist one.

Boomers created a society that discriminates against minorities, women, and others.

The question I asked related to this issue was "Regardless of your race or gender, what are your thoughts about minority or women's rights and equality? How would you compare our gender and race equality status now vs. your years growing up?"

The general consensus is that we have come a long way in the past 50 years, but that there is still a way to go. Most agreed that there is still some bias, but that some in our society are using this as an excuse as to why they cannot make progress. The specific comments, however, did show some sharp difference of opinion.

There were those who defended where we are as a society. For example – 'Racism was about dead until the democrats realized they could use it for political advantage.' 'Most have no idea how lucky they are to live in the U.S. We are not perfect but we always strive to be better.' 'Those who feel entitled are a problem, they believe they should get things or rewards because of who they are.'

Then there were those who commented that things are still a bit of a mess. 'Systemic racism is alive.' 'I have a friend who is black, they tell me things that just prove how racist we still are.' 'Gender was a handicap in my career, I could not get accepted into an engineering program because I was a woman, and I saw fewer promotions, lower pay, and less tenure for females.' 'Anyone who thinks that there is not systemic racism is not paying attention.'

All I can surmise from these answers is that even this Boomer group is divided, so I can safely assume the millions of Boomers are not at all aligned on this issue, perhaps because of what they have seen in their lives, and what they are noticing now.

OTHER QUESTIONS AND CONCLUSIONS

Besides the complaints I heard from younger generations about Boomers, there were many other questions I asked these Boomers, and most of the questions deal with major issues going on in our country or the world today. I share here the questions I asked, along with a summary of responses.

What are the most important lessons of life you would want to share with younger generations?

The answers here were extremely interesting. When you think about it, this is a very difficult question to answer. These Boomers had to assess their entire lives and choose the very best lessons to share. There was no unanimous 'lesson' that emerged. But there were a few mentioned several times:

#1 – Be ethical and honest in all you do (4 mentions)

#2 – Do the best you can (3 mentions)

#3 – Many ties with 2 mentions each – Kindness matters, treat others as you want to be treated, serve others, enjoy life, always strive to learn new things, plan ahead, failure is OK as long as you learn something from it.

There were many '1 mention' items, and the list is long. Some of the more interesting ones were:

'Always drive a convertible!', 'Never give up', 'Trust in God', 'Family and friends are a treasure, never forget that', 'Know all the little facts so you can see the big picture', and 'To rue is destructive'.

If a Millennial or Gen X or Gen Z person was sitting next to you on your death bed, and they asked you "What is the meaning of life? What is it all about?" What do you think your answer would be?

Another very deep question for our Boomers. The answers again were varied, with some overlap with the prior question and answers.

#1 response – (Tie of three answers) Serve others, be kind, and take more time to enjoy life.

#2 response – (Tie of seven answers) Do the best you can, live the Golden Rule, learn so your next life will be better, don't leave with any regrets, grab the bull by the horns since life is not pre-determined it is consequential, love God, and 'read Desiderata!'

Boomers have, and had, a reputation for drinking beer/wine/alcohol. Did you drink growing up? Has that changed as you aged, and if so, how? Did you have any drug experiences? Were they overall good or bad? How do you feel about legalizing marijuana and other drugs?

Most of the Boomers said that they have enjoyed beer or wine or alcohol throughout their lives, only a few indicated they ever had any drinking problems as a result. A few said they don't really drink now. Regarding marijuana, most had tried it at one time or another, but most also quit using it after experimenting with it. Surprisingly, they were in favor of legalizing marijuana by a 4-to-1 ratio. A few had never tried it but were in favor of legalizing it, which I found interesting. Why would they be in favor of legalizing a drug they had never tried? The general answer was that they had read enough about it that they did not believe there were any long-term health effects. A few felt very strongly that it was a gateway drug and that it should not be legalized.

If you have children, you chose to either stay home with them or hire a sitter / daycare to take care of them. Do you think that society does or does not value enough a parent who stays home with children?

By a ratio of 4-to-1, these Boomers said that society does not appreciate or value enough a parent who stays home with children. Those who did make that choice do not regret it, even given the sacrifices financially and to their career. A few commented that more parents should choose to stay at home, and that most do not appreciate the impact a parent can have on their children by being there most of the time. One the other hand, one said that most parents today cannot afford to give up one income, nor should they, and another saw nothing wrong with both parents working even if they could afford to live on only one income. Perhaps when Boomers grew up, the affordability of life was greater than now, allowing some the choice to only have one income. I suspect many from Gen Y or Z would say that for many, this is no longer a choice they can make given how expensive things may be.

Were your parents stricter than you were as a parent?

By a ratio of 4-to-1, these Boomers said that their parents were stricter than they were with their children. This has implications for Gen X or Gen Y, because if this is true for the broader population of Boomers, it is likely that Boomers experienced a much stricter upbringing than their children did. If so, this could have implications for the behavior and discipline of these younger generations, although it is difficult to say if those implications are mostly positive or mostly negative.

It was also interesting that several mentioned that their children, as parents, were even less strict than they were as parents. Could it be that we have a series of generations that have successively become more lenient in raising their children? If so, I will leave it to the reader to assess the effect of that trend.

Do you still help your children financially even if they are adults?

I asked this question because I have the sense, just talking to fellow Boomers, that 'gifting' to Boomer children is happening regularly, yet I also got the sense that this did NOT happen with Boomer parents after Boomers were grown and on their own.

It turns out that these Boomers, in the main, *were* gifting to their grown children even though the children were on their own and independent and doing well. By a greater than 2-to-1 margin, the Boomers made regular or occasional financial gifts, either directly to children in cash, or to grandchildren via cash or 529 accounts. Those who do not, indicated that gifting is not a goal, and that they sacrificed a lot for their children when they were younger, but that they see no reason now to do so.

So why might this habit have changed between generations? I suspect it has to do with the improved financial situation that some Boomers find themselves in, relative to their parents at the same age. Some Boomers indicated that their financial advisors told them that if they can afford to do it, gifting regularly is much more tax efficient than waiting until death to disburse financial assets.

Do you believe that the generations following ours will be, in general, better or worse financially when they get to our age? Do you believe those generations will live in a better country and world in the coming decades, versus what our generation experienced as we aged?

This question drew a lot of detailed responses and strong opinions. Ten Boomers thought that future generations will be worse off when they get to their age, and also said that the country and world will also be in a worse state. Only two thought the opposite. Of the majority opinions, here were some comments:

"Some of these young adults are victims of their parents' success, their lives were perhaps too easy, with big safety nets. Too many have a sense of entitlement."

"The world is not better, it is more isolated, selfish and there is no sense of the common good."

"Younger generations' work ethic is different; they want things in life but are not willing to work as hard to get them. Good luck to them in trying to change the world."

"Younger generations assume they are entitled to things; they spend more even if it means more debt. They confuse *needing* something with *wanting* something."

"I think delayed gratification is becoming scarce today. Make coffee? No! To the coffee shop! Want a meal? Have it delivered! Buy new clothes? Click here for free shipping."

"A future hellscape is coming. Media is pushing the creation of anger between classes."

"The liberal voice is more prominent today due to media, and the communication spiral is out of control."

"I am unsure, but no doubt we are declining relative to China and Russia."

There was only one positive opinion, with that Boomer saying that future generations will be better off due to the foundation we have built for them.

Of all the answers I collected on all questions, this set of responses alarms me the most, and it might alarm the younger generations. At best, these Boomers seem to see a different work ethic and spending/debt pattern with Gen Y and Z, and at worst, they may have resigned themselves to not being able to do anything to reverse what they see coming in the years ahead. I hope they are wrong.

Do you remember your parents or older relatives talking about the Great Depression? Did you believe growing up that a Great Depression could occur again, and as a result, did you tend to save more than if your parents had not shared those stories about the Great Depression? Do you think a Great Depression could occur again?

By a 3-to-1 margin, these Boomers do *not* believe a Great Depression could occur again. Clearly, however, some believed that what their parents or grandparents experienced in the Great Depression had an effect on their upbringing and their resulting saving / spending habits. So, it does appear that in some way, *Boomer habits and behaviors have been affected by the Great Depression*, even though Boomers did not live through that period.

How would you describe your adult friendships? How important are your friends vs family? Has your time spent with friends changed as you have aged?

Nine Boomers described satisfaction with the friends and friendships they have at their stage of life, although two said that there are fewer friends due to deaths. Two Boomers said that as they have aged, they have shifted their focus away from friends and towards family much more. It seems clear that as these Boomers age, family becomes a bit more important vs. spending time with friends, even though their friendships seem to still be dear.

How did music impact you growing up? What sort of music do you listen to now, and how does it differ, or not, to what you liked growing up?

This question got an enthusiastic response, as it would seem music is such a big part of the lives of Boomers today, as it was in their earlier years. Some said that their best memories of their earlier years are linked to specific songs, and when they hear those songs now, those memories come flowing back. Two Boomers said that music was 'huge' and 'a great impact' on their lives, and another said that their piano at home was a big part of their lives which steered him into singing Barbershop. Two said that music was NOT a big part of their lives, saying that they never let music affect how they lived. Most said that the music they listen to now is from their time growing up, from the 70's and 80's mainly. Music seems to be one of those hobbies that Boomers have enjoyed their entire lives, and they continue to enjoy music today. None of the Boomers mentioned that they enjoy *current* popular music today.

What do you recall about the press (TV and newspapers mainly) when you were a teenager and in your twenties? How does that compare to now? Do you feel the press does a better, or worse, job than they did when you were much younger? How has your level of trust in the press changed as you aged?

Our Boomers responded, in the main, very emotionally to this question, and not in a good way. Most comments were that they have little-to-no trust in the press, the lies and spinning of stories is terrible, that it is all about ratings therefore the truth is not important to them, and that 24-hour news has changed the news for the worse. Other comments were that there is no real journalism anymore, 'they are liars', that most news is bad, and there are rarely any positive stories. One person said that if it were not for Fox, all the news would be liberal and completely for the Democrats. One other comment that is interesting, that I can relate to, is that when the Boomers were younger, they were just not that aware of all the news just because there was not enough time in the day to stay informed, given job, family, chores, etc.

How did 9/11 affect how you think about our country and about terrorism? Were you very aware of what was going on in the Middle East or terrorism before 9/11?

The responses were as you may suspect, that the day instilled fear that has not gone away, that it was terribly upsetting, that even though America rallied together, the realization that radical factions in the world hated Americans was a shocking change. Another said that that there is no cure for terrorism, and that they feel that our leaders are not doing enough to protect us from future terrorism.

How do you feel about U.S. immigration, the border wall, and our illegal alien policies?

The Boomers clearly thought a lot about this issue, as their responses were measured and included some areas of gray. The majority agreed this was a complex issue, and that our current policies are not working. Most expressed amazement that we do not focus upon secure borders, when in contrast, as one said "We are donating billions to Ukraine to protect *their* border." Most agreed that we need a better process than what we have now. Some said that with so many jobs going unfilled, that a larger number of immigrants may be a solution for the U.S., but that the situation today is out of control. "Illegals are ruining it for immigrants who want to enter our country legally in the right way." "We should not blame the immigrants and illegals; they are just doing what is in their best interests." "Who is going to pay for all the housing, food, medical care, clothing, etc. for the millions of illegal immigrants who will never strive to become citizens?"

What would you say about Gen X (born 1965-1979), Millennials (born 1980-1994), or Gen Z (born 1995-2015)? Does anything stand out to you as significantly different than Boomers in how they think/act/behave?

Only half of the fourteen answered this question. I thought one response was interesting and fairly balanced: "Most have easier lives than we did due to Boomer success. We are responsible for that, and perhaps that has created some problems for them. They are much more focused upon work-life balance than we were, and tend to spend as they go and not save. They are bright and innovative." Other comments focused upon the younger generations' focus upon non-work activities, that our education system and/or parents are not apparently teaching respect or a work ethic, and that they do not respect authority or themselves. Another said that the time they consume on using their smartphones is causing problems and lack of focus on what is important.

I find it a positive if the younger generations truly are more focused upon work-life balance. I know that many times in my life, I invested too much time on career and not enough time on family, although I do believe that the key word is 'balance'. Time demands cannot always be prioritized for family over work.

This issue of smartphone usage is one that I have done a bit of research on, and on one extreme, there are those who claim that it is an addiction of younger generations that stops them from experiencing the important things in life, whereas others say that the smartphone has changed the world, and anyone using it for a lot of time is likely leveraging this new tool to get tasks and work done, improving their productivity greatly.

Do you believe we should have term limits for our politicians?

All but one of the Boomers agreed that we should have term limits. The lone dissenter said that it takes time and experience to learn the job of being a representative or senator, and that it is not an easy job at all. The rest made various comments about how their pensions and health care should not be for life after serving just one term, that lifetime politicians lose perspective in not knowing what the average American is dealing with, and that the opportunities and temptations to take lobbying money, donations, or favors is too great over a longer period of time. One person observed that too many career politicians have entire families that are extremely wealthy without them ever holding down a job in the private sector.

What about Boomers do you think is negative or could be better? What are you most proud of about Boomers? In looking back, as a group, how well did Boomers position younger generations for success, freedom, prosperity, etc.?

These questions generated little in responses. On the 'Boomer negatives' question, the comments ranged from 'we didn't leave the next generation in a great position, but who would have guessed that the media would collapse?', to 'we started this mess, just think about the music, Woodstock, demonstrations, how we treated veterans on return from Vietnam. We are the parents who raised our children, who then raised *their* children that we see now with a lot of problems'. Another said that Boomers are very risk averse and resistant to change. On the positive side, the comments were aligned around the observation that Boomers are dedicated, loyal, savers, have a good work ethic, built economic security for their families, and are family-focused.

Are we as a society too hard or too easy on convicted felons? Should we, or should we not, outlaw the death penalty? Do you feel the penalties should be significantly different for first-time offenders vs repeat offenders for non-capital crimes?

I wanted to ask this because generally, I have a theory that the elderly become very intolerant of crime and want maximum penalties, while youth seem to have a more 'live and let live' philosophy. Our Boomers fell in line with this hypothesis, but they created a dividing line between first time offenders and repeat offenders. They were very aligned that we are too easy on repeat offenders, but they all mentioned that we need a different process for first-time offenders. "Our criminal justice system is totally broken. Criminals face minimal punishment, and we are seeing the escalation of crime as a result. Defund the police and no cash bail? You have got to be kidding!" "Crime is rising due to liberal DA's and no cash bail. Non-violent first-time offenders should be given a second chance." Another said that it is difficult for felons to go straight, as it is difficult for them to get jobs and they cannot vote.

How do you feel about the U.S. role as being 'watchman of the world'? Should we reduce our global influence, or expand it? We spend billions on foreign aid. How do you feel about your tax dollars being used for non-U.S. aid, versus it being spent here?

Nine of eleven comments were in support of maintaining the U.S. role, with some limitations. Two stated that we need to keep doing what we are doing, even though they are not comfortable with our position. "NATO needs to pay more, and our homeless deserve some attention vs. giving so much away to other countries." "If we reduce our aid, China and Russia will fill the void." "Vietnam was a case where we overplayed our hand."

Do you feel that we are taxed too much or too little? Do you believe that the rich need to pay more or fewer taxes? Do you believe that the poor need to pay more or fewer taxes? (Just for reference, the Tax Policy Center reported that in 2020, 61% of Americans paid 0 federal income taxes. In 2021, that number is expected to be 57%, then fall to 42% in 2022 due to expiring child tax credits. In 2019 it was 44%, and in 1986, it was only 18%.)

As I researched this issue, I was shocked at what I learned, thus I included some of the facts in the question. To understand that over 60% of wage-earners paid ZERO federal taxes in 2020 was something I had not understood before, whereas in 1986 the number was 18%. I suspected that the way I posed the question would result in more responses about the lower wage-earners, and that they should at least pay *something*, but only one Boomer indicated that we should change the lower income brackets so that everyone would pay something, as we do for social security taxes.

One said that taxes were too high for all Americans (but they cannot get any lower for those paying nothing). Four indicated that the rich should pay more. Three indicated that tax rates were not as much the issue as inefficient and excessive government spending. '$30M for crack pipes? Are you kidding?' 'How can we pledge $20 billion to Indonesia to move them away from coal? If he had directed that to the social security fund, it might have helped solve a real problem. That $20B no doubt will be wasted or go into pockets of bureaucrats.' 'It is a travesty – how can billionaires pay a lower tax rate than me?' 'Individuals and businesses must balance their budgets, but the federal government does not?'

Should we have more or fewer governmental programs to help the underprivileged? Which programs are a good use of your tax dollars? Which are not? To what extent do we have a national problem of some taking advantage of programs by cheating? If so, do we need more focus on enforcement? Would you be willing to have your tax dollars be used for higher levels of program enforcement?

I suspect the Boomer responses here are very different than the responses of the younger generations, if we had asked them the same question.

Most indicated that programs for those truly needy are fine. Three said that we needed fewer programs, one stated that we need more. However, the hot button seemed to be that nearly all who commented said that we need more focus on enforcement, and that a percentage of every program for the underprivileged needs a percentage allocated for better enforcement. The specific comments were telling: 'Make them work for a check, even if minor volunteer work. Anything is better than handing out money for doing nothing!' 'We need to root out the bullshit claims and make those lazy asses work.' 'Forgiving student loans is insane.' 'Cheating is a big issue, and we need more enforcement.' 'Cheaters need to pay back what they stole.'

I thought about why this group of Boomers would be so focused upon the cheating aspect of governmental programs, and I remembered that so many of this group worked as children helping out the family when times were tough, or who worked hard for below-minimum wages just to support their families. Quite a few held down multiple jobs, not just one, at different points of their lives. I am sure that for them, the thought that someone could falsify information and sit home collecting funds, while others were working hard and paying their taxes, must be revolting and unfair.

Why are politicians so divided? Has it really changed, or has it been like this for a long time?

One said that it has always been this way. Five said it is much worse than when they grew up. One blamed the democrats; one blamed the republicans. Of more interest were the comments as to the root cause of this. 'The two-party system needs to be changed. Nobody wants to compromise anymore.' 'Rudeness is acceptable now; it is all about slamming the opposing party.' 'The causes are 24-hour news, social media, and gerrymandering.' 'We have migrated to two parties, one that believes in capitalism and the constitution, and one that is socialist and Marxist. The roots are in our education system.'

Are you a conservate, liberal, moderate, or something else?

I was expecting that a group of Boomers I interviewed would mostly be conservative, because many claim that most of us gradually migrate our views from more liberal to more conservative throughout life. However, this group does not conform to that theory. Five said that they were moderate or independent, four said conservative, and three said liberal or leaning left. So much for my expectations!

Do you think the country is headed in the wrong or right direction? What alarms you? What makes you feel positive? Are the changes in our country just 'normal' and in line with changes we saw earlier in our lives?

Well, this was surprising. There were three who did not state 'wrong' or 'right', but they commented on related issues. *All* the rest said that our country is headed in the *wrong* direction. For such a cross-section of Boomers who spanned the spectrum from conservative to moderate to liberal, I was expecting a few 'right direction' responses, but there were none. Some of the comments – 'Our politicians have made our country way too toxic.' 'Personal responsibility is not there anymore, such as some saying that they cannot pay for their college loans. But they were the ones *asking* for the loans, right?' 'Capitalism and the constitution are under attack.' 'We need to always guard our freedoms.'

Do you have more 'stuff' now than when you were younger? Do you want to get RID of stuff, or GET more stuff? If you want to get rid of stuff, are you actually doing it?

This may not seem like a big issue in our world or country today, but it is one that I find a bit mystifying, and one I wanted to explore. Boomers, and even the generation of their parents, are known for having collected a lot of 'stuff' that sits in garages, closets, basements or storage units. You have probably seen the TV show that just focuses on storage units being auctioned off because the owner stops paying for renting the unit and apparently does not want the contents. My siblings and I are going through the process of selling my father's house and contents (he passed away at age 94), and there are so many items in storage, it is just amazing and overwhelming.

I have talked to others who have gone through the same process, and they are just overwhelmed with the workload, as well as the guilt of having to throw away or sell things that they know meant something to their parents. It is emotional, draining, and time-consuming. I know that I don't want my children to have to go through the same process if I can at all help it. So, I wanted to explore this issue a bit with these Boomers to try to figure out the phenomenon.

Exactly half of the Boomers indicated that they are <u>*not trying*</u> to get rid of their stuff, and half said that <u>*they are*</u> working on it. (Good for that half!) Of those not working to get rid of their stuff, some remarked that they know they should downsize and get rid of things, but that they are having trouble actually doing it. I thought one comment was insightful – 'I sacrificed so much, and saved for so long, to afford some of these things that I have stored here. I know I <u>*should*</u> get rid of them, but it would be too painful to part with something now that is likely not worth much, given the sacrifice I made. I know my kids won't have as much pain parting with my stuff after I am gone. I'll just let them deal with it.'

I get that sentiment completely, and understand the emotion involved. But what I do not get is that if you love your children, or whoever you want to have your things, after you depart this earth, why would you want to put them through the emotion and turmoil of doing so when they have their own lives to live, problems to resolve, their own families, etc.? Perhaps the issue is that as we age, we run out of energy to tackle such a large project of downsizing and getting rid of things. Or, perhaps for those who have children, forcing them to go through all your things after your death is one way to try to get your children to spend more time together and to remember your life. Anyway, I encourage Boomers to really think about this going forward, and for younger generations, perhaps you want to discuss this with your Boomer parents or grandparents!

<u>The trustees of Social Security now predict that the Social Security funds surplus will run out in about 2033, and at that time, benefits paid must match the social security taxes paid by individuals and employers. Thus, current payment levels to beneficiaries will have to be reduced to around 77% of the current benefit payments, unless action will be taken. What should the country do to avoid having to cut social security benefits in 2034 and beyond? Or are benefit cuts OK with you?</u>

The Boomers responded with a myriad of solutions, with nobody agreeing on one specific plan. Here were just some of the suggestions: (1) Grandfather in all existing beneficiaries at current payments, have cuts for those going on social security in the future. (2) Just give social security to the poor, stop payments to the wealthy. (3) Increase taxes to those who are working, and keep your mitts off of the funds for beneficiaries, we paid into social security all our lives. (4) Social Security should not be a pension program, change it to provide for those unable to work or really in need. (5) A complex problem, but funds need to be better invested. (6) Nothing needs to change, let it alone.

I understand that there are no easy solutions to the problem, but it is concerning that any current politician who steps forward with a proposal to begin to address the funding issue, just get annihilated by the press and the opposing party. As a result, this can keeps getting 'kicked down the road' until at some point, this issue will become a major problem for those beneficiaries who depend upon Social Security payments to survive. It is interesting to note that the same problem has emerged for Medicare benefits, and just recently, the trustees of the Medicare administration stated that benefits will have to be cut by 2031, two years *before* Social Security funding is depleted!

SUMMARY

From what I discussed with these Boomers, and from the research I conducted preparing to write this book, I found that, as one example, Gen Y and Gen Z seem to care a lot about the environment and about equity / inclusion, and have significant concerns about the expensive cost of living relative to the income they have. Many seem willing to invest the time to get involved in illuminating these issues in social media, if not being active politically in various ways.

Recall that the Boomers also were known for demonstrations and protests, and sometimes the protests were less than completely peaceful. Back in the Boomer years, the Vietnam war and Korean war were not universally supported by the younger generation at that time, and to many Boomers, the goals of each war were not worth the loss of thousands of lives of their friends and relatives of their generation.

The Boomer stories here convinced me that, as much as these Boomers were very aware of these wars, their main priorities were more focused upon a combination of issues. These included completing their educations, finding and holding good-paying jobs, saving so that they could purchase their first home or car, and then raising and/or sustaining their families.

What I heard from most of the Boomers I interviewed was that, during their early years growing up and starting a career and/or family, it just seemed that they were ***so busy*** working at their job(s), taking care of chores, paying bills, doing maintenance on cars, homes, etc., that there was little if any time to focus upon fixing larger problems with their country or the world, or even to stay current on the news. The lone exception seemed to be during their college years, for those who attended college, that there may have been time for a few to focus upon the 'big problems' of the day.

Think back to what history says about the 60's and 70's, as well as the personal productivity of the Boomer generation, compared to the productivity of the younger generations today.

There were few if any 'work from home' policies, so Boomers spent sometimes substantial amounts of time in their cars and public transportation commuting to and from work.

There were no smart phones during their early decades of life, so coordinating issues, problems, meals, etc. with their spouses and friends was much more difficult than today, where today we can send a few texts or get something organized using a social media group. (I still remember trying to organize a baseball game with some friends when I was 12 years old, and it took a half day for me to ride my bike, knocking on doors of friends throughout our town, finding a common time to meet, and finding enough players who had nothing better to do that day.) Home phones were not always useful, as many of us had 'party lines' where our phone line was shared with neighbors, and if those neighbors were on the phone, you could not call anyone.

The internet and computers were not yet invented at the time most Boomers were growing up, and clearly there was not yet an Amazon, or online banking, or online anything, therefore it became much more time-consuming to get in the car, fill the car with gas, comparison shop going store to store, contact others, resolve problems, or handle banking tasks.

There were only a few items that they may have been able to have delivered to their home, and that was usually a newspaper, or perhaps bread and milk from the milkman, if you were lucky enough to *have* a milkman!

In the 1960's and 1970's, when Boomers did go shopping for food, clothing, maintenance items, medical supplies, etc., there were no barcodes, therefore waiting in line at stores and checking out took enormous amounts of time as cashiers had to locate the price tag, enter the price into the cash register, and if the price tag was missing, call for assistance to get a price on an item. I still cringe when I remember the cashier announcing on the intercom 'Price check on register 7!' It meant waiting for what seemed like hours to have someone come to the cash register and get the item, then take it back to the store aisle to see what the price should be.

Bank credit cards were not available in the 1970's, and the few credit cards that were available were issued by specific retail stores. Boomers had to make trips to their bank to get cash so they could pay for the next week's expenses at the grocery store or restaurant or retail store. Some would ask their employer to pay them in cash to avoid having to run to the bank. Since there were no ATM's, if a Boomer did need to go to the bank, they had to wait in line for a teller, then request assistance. Personal checks were available, but who wanted to hold up the line in a store while you pulled out your checkbook, write out a check, sign it, and record the amount in your checkbook?

Something as complex as doing their taxes each year, was significantly more complex as Boomers had to fill out paper forms, read each form in detail, along with form instructions, trying to understand what to fill in for each space, using a calculator and organizing reams of paper documents. Today someone can buy an inexpensive tax package to use on their computer, which automates many of the calculations and ensures accuracy by asking the taxpayer all relevant questions.

The idea of NOT having a car was just out of the question for most Boomers not living in major cities. In cities, public transport may have been readily available, but not in suburban or rural areas. Uber and competing transport companies did not exist. Taxis were much too expensive to use regularly.

Because of the lack of internet, smartphone, and technology availability, driving place-to-place doing chores took up a large percentage of Boomers' spare time. Since having a car to enable all these trips to complete chores was a must, saving for a car, and maintaining a car once you could afford one, consumed additional valuable time. Most Boomers recall that automobiles were *not* as reliable as they are today, and maintenance tasks were critical to keeping their cars running. It was not uncommon to have your car break down on the road, stranding the driver and passengers without a way to call for assistance. Today you might call a towing company or text a friend to come get you, but back then, you had to wait for a policeman to drive by, or perhaps one of you might hitchhike or walk to the nearest town to get help.

I recall after college, and landing my first professional job, it was more or less expected that since I was making my own way, I would leave my parents' home and stop eating their food and taking advantage of free water, electricity, heat, and shelter. I had to obtain a car, rent an apartment, and put deposits down on the apartment plus electricity and water. I had to buy a bed, plus basic furniture, cookware, dishes and utensils, and other supplies, which consumed all the funds that I had saved to that point in time. Bank loans were not available for someone just beginning a job with no collateral or assets. There was nothing left in the budget to pay someone to change my oil (there were no quick-change oil shops back then), grease the bearings, change the spark plugs, replace windshield wipers, rotate the tires, etc., let alone pay someone to wash the car.

I recall on Saturday, if I did not have to work that day, it was always 'chore day'. I would go the grocery store, buy supplies for the week, and put them away. Then I would do my disliked chores such as cleaning the bathroom, doing laundry at the laundromat, ironing shirts, doing dishes (by hand in the early years), sometimes change my own oil in the car, wash the car, or perform other car chores. I had no equipment to do any of these chores, so they consumed lengthy periods of time. To grease the bearings or change the oil or rotate the tires, I used the car jack (not a safe way to do that work) that came with the car, and maybe a jack stand, and used manual tools to get things done. I used Saturday afternoon to pay the bills that had arrived in the mail during the prior week. These tasks just took forever, or so it seemed.

Costs of certain things were outrageous given pay rates at that time. The price of a 19" color TV was around $400-$600, back in the 1970's! A stereo receiver and turntable, with two speakers, also cost anywhere from $400 - $1000. Given pay rates back then, the newly employed often went without a TV or stereo until they could save enough to purchase one on their own. Some were lucky enough to have parents help with these. These prices were in 1970's dollars, not current dollars!

The point of relating this, is that *personal productivity in the Boomer years was terrible relative to today*. That is, the amount of time required to get chores completed was quite long, relative to today and the technology available. There was little time left over to read the newspapers in detail, watch the news, or get involved in country political issues or rallies. The lack of social media and 24-hour news created a bit of a void in allowing Boomers to understand what was going on globally. The consciousness of most Boomers to external events was just not there, unless they happened to come from very wealthy families, who had the wherewithal to pay others to do personal chores for them.

Boomers, and their parents, seemed to have a much higher focus upon survival, meaning getting food into their refrigerators, working long hours that were expected by employers, earning enough to afford the basics of food, shelter, health care and a car, and to possibly save a few dollars.

Not one of the Boomers I interviewed talked about their awareness of the rising national debt during their youth. Nobody said that pollution was a major concern of theirs in their teens, twenties or thirties, as compared to their focus upon their livelihood (even though the smog problem was definitely in the news in larger cities). Nobody mentioned that the income gap was a worry of theirs, and I would be willing to bet that in the 60's and 70's, most Boomers would not even know what an income gap was.

Many of the Boomers in this book served in the military, and none of them complained about their lost time while in the military, or bad experiences, or sacrifices they made for their country. Some talked positively about the discipline that the military instilled in them, which they said helped them later in life.

Their lives, and their livelihood, seemed to be number one on their agenda. Their focus upon their jobs and families and the tasks of everyday living were nearly absolute. Only later in their lives, once they became more comfortable financially, and once they became more productive through investments or new technology, could they begin to focus their time in other activities, such as community involvement, hobbies, or becoming more aware of the news.

So, when some from younger generations criticize Boomers for the country or world they have created which is a 'mess', they may not realize that most Boomers did not have the time to focus upon some of the major issues of today, just because surviving was paramount, and surviving meant getting things done given poor productivity and less personal time available than what our youth may have today. Did the national debt grow during the 1970's and 1980's? Yes. Did college costs escalate? Yes. Did global pollution and climate change worsen during these years? Yes. But for Boomers, none of these issues seemed to elevate above the day-to-day responsibilities of living their lives.

But aren't these just excuses that Boomers use to avoid the blame that is coming their way? Clearly, there is a responsibility every generation has to collectively monitor what is going on in the world and to 'step up' to rectify major issues if possible. It is easy to argue that Boomers could have done better. But I hope that understanding this small slice of Boomer history has shed light on the challenges Boomers had to 'do better'!

HOW HAS THE MEDIA IMPACTED THE GENERATIONAL WARS?

As I interviewed the Boomers in this book, we occasionally talked about some of the more impactful TV shows that they watched during their youth.

There were quite a few sitcoms on TV which were focused upon the day-to-day challenges of families. Ozzie and Harriet, Leave It to Beaver, All in the Family, The Andy Griffith Show, and My Three Sons, were just a few.

In the main, these shows had parents who were working in a 'normal' job earning 'normal' wages. These parents had a variety of different jobs and professions. Usually, each show had a lesson for the children in the show (and of course the viewer), and most lessons had to do with developing character, valuing honesty, accepting others who were 'different', and the importance of family, friends and community.

The families were generally not wealthy. Their stories dealt with a variety of issues besides teaching a lesson. Some that I recall involved families managing their financial resources as best they could, children that wanted more than the family could afford, parents teaching their children that honesty, hard work, saving, taking care of what they had, helping around the home, etc. were values and habits that would serve them well in later life.

I don't recall any of these programs ending with someone in the family winning the lottery or winning a game show and becoming a millionaire. Nor do I recall any shows or stories then about becoming a realtor in large cities selling multi-million-dollar homes, or a program about millionaire housewives visiting spas or sitting around talking about their new jewelry, homes, cars, vacations, etc. I don't recall movies where Wall Street executives became multi-millionaires overnight selling stocks, and spending lavishly on office parties, fast cars and huge homes.

I don't recall watching a show about helping millionaires find a mate through a dating service only serving millionaires, as if non-millionaires were not worthy of finding a mate. There were no reality shows that covered the actual family lives of millionaires as they flew on their private jets, relaxed at the pool or winery, sipped expensive drinks, or had surgical procedures done to improve their appearance.

There was no coverage of teens or young adults making videos that 'went viral', making them stars apparently overnight, at least for a few weeks or months. (of course, this was the 70's when there was no social media!)

I don't remember sports stars signing contracts that overnight made them worth hundreds of millions of dollars. I also don't remember sports fans being too interested in the political views of the highest-paid sports stars or movie stars for that matter.

Growing up, I cannot remember watching movies about grisly murders, or movies about wild bachelor and bachelorette parties where hotel rooms and cars were totally trashed due to alcohol or drugs. I don't remember where sex and violence were glamorized as much as we see today in programs and movies or music.

WHAT IS THE MESSAGE TODAY?

From my view of the world and what I observe, there seems to be many more examples of 'get rich quick' stories in our media today, and far too few examples of someone working hard and taking pride in their work over perhaps a lifetime, and gradually earning a comfortable financial situation via saving, investing in themselves and improving their skills, gaining more responsibility in their careers, etc.

Somehow, some way, over the past several decades, via TV shows, movies, magazines, newspapers, music, and social media, it appears as though our society is sending the message that if you <u>cannot see your way to becoming extremely wealthy, that your life is not interesting or worthwhile</u>. The message seems to be that if you are 'stuck' in a humdrum job, the 'system' is just using you, when you deserve much better. In effect, I get the sense that the message is "Only suckers work menial jobs making average wages." A side message seems to be that what is on the outside that people can see, is more important than what is on the inside.

I find it sad that younger generations grew up without the opportunity to experience what many Boomers take for granted about their youth years. I worry that perhaps some in the younger generations lack hope and a positive outlook about their lives going forward.

WHAT ABOUT BUSINESSES?

Over time, it seems that the businesses that provide solid products, services, jobs, employee healthcare, community investments, etc., are beginning to be seen as the villains. The story goes that these large company executives underpay and overwork employees, steal, cheat, collect excessive paychecks and bonuses, while ruining our environment.

Somehow, we have transitioned from a culture that valued these companies, their products, and the good-paying jobs they provided, to one that seems to report on as many negatives as possible in any business success. I leave that observation for others to help explain, because I cannot explain it nor understand it.

Clearly, some of this sentiment likely derives from real examples of companies which were poorly run or which had questionable ethics. Perhaps the parents or grandparents of the younger generations had negative things happen at the hands of their employers, such as layoffs, downsizing, shutdowns, divestitures, etc., and this generation may remember those events all too well.

However, I would hypothesize that much of this anti-capitalist sentiment comes from the thousands of hours of programming, movies, social media, and publications that are watched or read across our country every day, every hour, every minute. I would challenge the 'media' to consider what they may be doing to the outlooks of so many in our society.

EPILOGUE

I began this journey spurred by reading an article about how Gen Y and Gen Z felt more positive about socialism than capitalism. Although I did explore this issue with the Boomers in the book, the entire effort exposed me to so many more worthwhile issues and worthwhile lives.

I learned in doing my research that there was a growing conflict between generations, one of which I was not fully aware. I am very aware now!

I learned so much about my fellow Boomers and their unique experiences and varied paths. The effort forced me to reconsider my own beliefs and opinions, given the diversity of views I encountered. Never in my wildest imagination would I have thought that 14 Boomer lives would be so different from one another, and so different from my life!

Perhaps there would be similar value in writing the same style of book about one of the younger generations, to explore their individual lives to see what sort of contrasts or similarities there may be vs. Boomers, or even versus other younger generations, such as Gen X vs. Gen Z.

Or, maybe choosing another set of Boomer lives would be even more interesting. I could determine if these 14 Boomers were similar to a completely different group of Boomers. (Sex, Drugs, Rock and War II?)

My ultimate hope is that for the Boomers who read this, they can 'wax nostalgic', and also reflect on these lives relative to their own, and to examine their own beliefs and values with a new perspective of how their early lives likely contributed to their beliefs in a more significant way than they ever believed. I also hope they will reach out to those within Generations X, Y and Z in the future to get to know them better and to engage in some discussion of these issues of generational conflict.

For the younger generations who read this, I hope that they can better understand the world of Boomers, and perhaps see that the Boomer generation might not be entirely to blame for many of the problems in our country or world. Clearly, the impact of technology changes has been significant in creating an entirely different world today relative to the one in which Boomers developed. I hope you reach out to Boomers now and then to get to know them better.

Daniel Muller

A little listening, discussion, understanding and compassion goes a long way to bridge divides!

ACKNOWLEDGEMENTS

I want to thank the fourteen Boomers, plus their families, who invested significant time working with me on this book. Their time investment in thoughtfully completing the questionnaire, reviewing text, and participating in one or more interviews was greatly appreciated. I want to also thank other Boomers that completed the questionnaire later in the schedule, but who I could not include in this book due to deadlines and space. I hope to include their stories in a later effort.

To these fourteen Boomers, please stay in touch, and I hope your families and friends enjoy reading about your life. You are forever friends, and the greatest value to me in this whole effort was making fourteen new friends that I respect so much.

ABOUT THE AUTHOR

(www.danielmullerauthor.com)

Daniel Muller grew up in a blue-collar small town in Ohio. Athletic and academic success in high school paved the way for a small scholarship to a state university, where he became the first in his family to attend college. He lettered four years on the varsity golf team, and succeeded academically as well, as he graduated Summa Cum Laude in his undergraduate and graduate programs.

He spent most of his career in the business world, with various responsibilities taken on during a thirty-five-year career. He ended his career as a Senior Vice-President / Chief Information Officer of a Fortune 500 company, and also held other senior roles such as leading corporate strategic planning as a senior vice-president, and becoming president of a major division. He retired from his fulltime executive role in 2014.

Muller is now an author, and president of his own consulting company, DEM Consulting, LLC. He wrote and published his first book in 2019, entitled "CHANGING COLLARS: Lessons in Transitioning from Blue-Collar Roots to White-Collar Success". His second book, entitled "SEX, DRUGS, ROCK and WAR: The Boomer Generation" was written in an attempt to capture the life stories of various Baby Boomers, and to explore the sources of friction between Baby Boomers and Generations X, Y, and Z.

He currently lives near his early hometown in Northeast Ohio. He has been recognized via various state and local awards, including being named CIO of the Year in Northeast Ohio, as well as being inducted into his high school Hall of Honor in 2017. He continues to serve as a guest speaker for various organizations, sharing insights extracted from his two books, as well as his business career. He is an avid golfer, winning 10 club championships over his career. He is married and has two children and five grandchildren.

Daniel Muller